THOUGHT SUPPRESSION

THOUGHT SUPPRESSION

ERIC RASSIN

Psychology Institute, Erasmus University Rotterdam, The Netherlands

ELSEVIER

Amsterdam – Boston – Heidelberg – London – New York – Oxford
Paris – San Diego – San Francisco – Singapore – Sydney – Tokyo

ELSEVIER B.V.
Radarweg 29
P.O. Box 211,
1000 AE Amsterdam
The Netherlands

ELSEVIER Inc.
525 B Street, Suite 1900
San Diego, CA 92101-4495
USA

ELSEVIER Ltd
The Boulevard, Langford Lane
Kidlington, Oxford OX5 1GB
UK

ELSEVIER Ltd
84 Theobalds Road
London WC1X 8RR
UK

First edition 2005

Library of Congress Cataloging in Publication Data
A catalog record is available from the Library of Congress.

British Library Cataloguing in Publication Data
A catalogue record is available from the British Library.

ISBN: 0-08-044714-7

∞ The paper used in this publication meets the requirements of ANSI/NISO Z39.48-1992 (Permanence of Paper).
Printed in The Netherlands.

Contents

Preface

Since the original white bear study by Wegner, Schneider, Carter, and White in 1987, dozens of thought suppression experiments have been published, in addition to several reviews, and books. I have been trying to follow the developments in the suppression literature since 1997, when I started my PhD research project. In 2000, I wrote my PhD thesis titled "Limitations of the thought suppression paradigm as a model of obsessive intrusions and memory loss." That thesis book focused on the relation between thought suppression and a cognitive bias called thought-action fusion, and on the effect of suppression on memory. When I started working on this book, soon after finishing my PhD, I thought that I might adapt my thesis book and transform it into this monograph. However, it soon became clear that the structure of the two books was too divergent for the thesis to serve as a mall for this monograph. This meant that I had to work harder and longer than anticipated. It also gave me a chance to learn more than had been necessary to complete my PhD. Not only did I learn about the thought suppression literature, but also about surrounding fields of scientific research. I have learned that while writing a review, it is nearly impossible to keep up with the latest developments. It seems that thought suppression is still a topic on which scientific reports are published quite regularly. Hence, at the same time that a draft is completed, it is already dated. Nonetheless, to provide a review of thought suppression studies is the main goal of this volume.

The review is structured in a way that deserves some comment. In the first two chapters, the issue of defining thought suppression is addressed. Specifically, the differences between suppression, repression, and dissociation are highlighted. Chapters 3, 4, and 5 focus on methodological aspects, such as measurements, possible artefacts, and individual differences. Chapters 6, 7, and 8 target the applications of the thought suppression literature. Obsession is discussed separately in Chapter 6, because the suppression paradigm has been primarily applied to obsession. In addition, Chapter 6 focuses on the idea that thought suppression is not the only contributing factor in the development of obsession. I find this idea appealing because it taps on the inevitable explanatory limitations of any single theoretical account. Like suppression and obsession, a complete chapter is devoted to the relation between suppression and (traumatic) memory. This was done, because in daily life, suppression and the repression of traumatic memories are often mentioned in one breath. In that sense, Chapter 7 leans back on Chapter 2. Chapter 8 addresses a variety of applications other than obsession and memory. To me, this is one of the most interesting chapters, because it makes clear how broadly the phenomenon of thought suppression has been applied.

The idea that thought suppression can be placed in the broader framework of ego depletion is also very appealing, in my opinion. In the final chapter, I tried to summarize the literature, to discuss some recent developments, and to seek future challenges in the area of thought suppression research.

I owe gratitude to various people who have facilitated the work on this book. For one thing, the people at NWO who financed my current research project on thought suppression. Ernst Koster gave me valuable comments on an earlier draft of the manuscript. So did Jack Rachman, who also encouraged me to complete the book.

Introduction

Most people experience thoughts that seem to come out of the blue, from time to time. These thoughts invade consciousness and can therefore be referred to as intrusions. Some intrusions are quite harmless because their content is neutral or pleasant. Examples of such intrusions are mentally rehearsing catchy melodies, and spontaneous memories of pleasant events. However, other intrusive thoughts can be upsetting because of their unpleasant content, for example, involuntary aggressive or sexual fantasies, and worries about all sorts of things. This kind of unpleasant intrusive thoughts is probably unwanted. One way to deal with unwanted intrusive thoughts is to try to suppress them. However, suppression of intrusive thoughts, sometimes, seems hard, or even impossible. Consider, for example, how hard it is to not think of ongoing problems, how difficult it is to banish an upsetting sexual thought, and how paradoxical attempts to suppress a burst of laughter can be.

In 1987, Wegner, Schneider, Carter, and White reported the results of their experimental study of the human capacity to suppress a specific thought. Participants had to try to not think of a white bear for 5 minutes. In spite of their suppression attempts, participants thought of white bears on average seven times. Furthermore, suppression resulted in a relative increase of white bear thoughts after the 5-minute period. Apparently, suppression is an ineffective and even paradoxically counterproductive control strategy. This finding is striking, but also somewhat disturbing if one considers how often people are inclined not to think of certain things, how often we try to concentrate and thus suppress irrelevant thoughts, and how often we are told not to think, say, or do certain things. The finding by Wegner and colleagues (1987) provides scientific evidence for the idea that controlling one's thoughts is extremely difficult, and may even be a senseless endeavor.

The study by Wegner and colleagues (1987) has been replicated numerous times. The replications have answered questions that were raised by the original study (e.g., does the paradoxical effect of suppression also occur in case of upsetting intrusions, instead of neutral ones like white bear?). At the same time, the replications have given rise to new questions. Hence, a complete thought suppression literature has evolved containing dozens of studies, and it is justifiable to speak of a thought suppression paradigm. The purpose of this book is to summarize the literature, and to describe the background from which the thought suppression paradigm has risen, thus hopefully providing an overview of the importance of the paradigm. The book is structured in a way that it consists of three major sections. The first two chapters deal with the definition of thought suppression. Chapters 3 through 5 address what might be called methodological issues (e.g., alternative explanations of the findings of Wegner and colleagues, 1987; and individual differences). Finally, in Chapters 6 through 8, the applications of the thought suppression paradigm are discussed.

In Chapter 1, the experiment by Wegner and colleagues (1987) is discussed in detail. Replications by other researchers are reviewed. Some replications used other target thoughts, and relied on slightly different experimental setups. As might be expected, the different setups have yielded different results, which make it hard to draw general conclusions. This chapter also addresses theoretical mechanisms responsible for the inefficiency of suppression attempts. Chapter 2 seeks to distinguish between the related concepts of suppression, repression, and dissociation. For the lay person, it may be tempting to treat these concepts interchangeably, because they all contain an element of blocking information, or forgetting. However, there are marked differences. To illustrate these differences, Chapter 2 commences with a short expose of Freud's ideas about repression, followed by a scientific scrutinization of these ideas. Next, contemporary operationalizations of repression are discussed. Finally, dissociation and its clinical manifestations are considered. Interestingly, the term dissociation simultaneously refers to a coping strategy as well as to a psychiatric syndrome. The concepts of repression and dissociation are discussed in some depth to demarcate thought suppression.

Chapter 3 deals with a possible methodological concern regarding the validity of results obtained in thought suppression experiments. Because the number of intrusive thoughts is the main dependent variable in such studies, all of the dangers of self-reports lie in wait. For example, how can we be sure that participants are able and willing to accurately report the number of white bear thoughts? Does the manner of reporting affect the results, such that retrospective estimation may yield less accurate results than does prospective counting? Although these critical questions are in line, and the threats surrounding self-reports should not be underestimated, Chapter 3 also addresses the positive sides of self-reports, and their inevitability. In Chapter 4, two additional methodological concerns are raised. First, the precise content of the suppression and control instructions is argued to potentially influence the study outcome. For example, in some studies, control instructions dictate that the participant has to think as much as possible of white bears, while in other studies, participants are free to think of anything, including white bears. These differential instructions may well produce divergent intrusion frequencies. Another methodological comment is fuelled by the fact that other paradigms concerned with the blocking or forgetting of specific information (e.g., directed forgetting) have delivered results that are more favorable of the human capacity to "suppress" unwanted thoughts. Therefore, the thought suppression paradigm is compared to these paradigms in terms of set-up specifics. Chapter 5 addresses individual differences with regard to thought suppression. It has been argued that individuals differ in their tendency to react with suppression to the occurrence of unwanted thoughts. There is a measure to tap this suppression proneness. Another important individual difference is the extent to which people are able to successfully suppress thoughts at will. This aspect has not been studied extensively, but it is important in that it may help to explain why some studies failed to produce the paradoxical effect of thought suppression introduced by Wegner and colleagues (1987). Suppression efficacy may be determined by a variety of factors such as intelligence, practice, self-efficacy, and the precise suppression technique.

The striking findings of Wegner and colleagues (1987) were originally applied to the phenomenon of obsession, because obsessions are textbook examples of intrusive and unwanted thoughts. Roughly summarized, the thought suppression theory states that people who suppress an intrusive thought will paradoxically experience even more intrusions, thus inflating their intrusion to the extent that it becomes a clinical obsession. Chapter 6 deals with obsession, and with the alleged role of thought suppression in the development thereof. It must be acknowledged that there are surprisingly few studies in which actual patients suffering from obsessions have been submitted to a thought suppression procedure. In addition to the relative lack of applied suppression experiments, there is a psychological theory that constitutes a strong alternative explanation of obsessions. In this cognitive theory of obsession, it is not the coping strategies (cf. suppression), but the original interpretation of intrusions that determines the clinical significance. The cognitive theory, and an attempt to reconcile this theory with the thought suppression paradigm, are discussed. In Chapter 7, another application of the thought suppression research is discussed, namely traumatic intrusions. Just as obsessions, traumatic memories can be quite intrusive, and can thus become the target of suppression attempts. However, whereas obsessions are probably rather concrete, traumatic recollections are far more elaborated. Hence, the question arises whether suppression may not only affect thought frequency, but also the content of the suppressed information. Chapter 8 provides a compilation of suppression applications other than obsession and traumatic memory. It seems that suppression bears relevance to a variety of anxiety disorders, and also to nonanxiety syndromes. Next, it is argued that the application of thought suppression research is not limited to the clinical domain. Suppression attempts abound in everyday life, and their paradoxical effects can be observed in numerous situations. Interestingly, there is reason to argue that thought suppression fits into the broader theory of self-regulation. This theory implies that individuals only have a very limited amount of mental energy that is consumed by every action aimed at self-regulation. Depletion of this energy source results in a lack of control over thoughts, impulses, and overt behaviors. In extreme, this means that suppressing thoughts about a specific overt behavior (e.g., swearing in church) may result in actually carrying out precisely that behavior. This sheds new light on the idea that engaging in unwanted behavior (e.g., criminality) generally is the result of lack of inhibition.

The concluding ninth chapter summarizes the main findings, and discusses the clinical implications of the thought suppression research. Finally, possible future research lines are described.

Chapter 1

The Thought Suppression Paradigm

White Bears

Although the topic of controlling unwanted thoughts has been of interest to psychologists for at least more than one century (Erdelyi, 1993), there is good reason to argue that the thought suppression paradigm originates from 1987. In that year, Wegner and colleagues (1987) published their white bear experiment. These authors were struck by the apparent human incapacity to wish away unwanted thoughts. From personal experience, they knew that it is hard or even impossible to banish thoughts about traumatic events, or thoughts about food when dieting. They were also inspired by Russian literature in which trying not to think about polar bears seemed to be made into a sport (Wegner et al., 1987, mention Tolstoy as one of the examples of white bear anecdotes).

Against this background, Wegner and colleagues (1987) came up with the idea to test the human capacity to banish thoughts from consciousness in a laboratory experiment. They developed the following design. Seventeen undergraduate students were invited to the laboratory and were instructed to "try not to think of a white bear" (p. 6) for 5 minutes. If white bear thoughts were to occur, in spite of suppression attempts, participants had to ring a bell and/or verbally report this cognitive intrusion. After this initial suppression period, participants were invited to "try to think of a white bear" (p. 7) for 5 minutes. In this way, Wegner and colleagues were able to compare the number of white bear thoughts during suppression attempts with target thought frequency during expression attempts. In addition, they included a second condition ($n = 17$), in which the order of instructions was reversed, that is, first thinking, followed by suppressing.

The number of reported white bear thoughts as a function of experimental instruction is displayed in Figure 1.1. As can be seen in this figure, suppression was never completely successful, in that participants reported on average approximately seven white bear thoughts during the suppression period. Target thought frequency during the expression period was approximately 19 when averaged between the two groups of participants. Interestingly, when comparing the number of white bear thoughts during expression between groups, it became clear that participants in the initial suppression condition expressed more thoughts (i.e., 22) than those in the initial expression condition (i.e., 16).

These findings gave rise to two conclusions. First, suppression of a specific thought is very hard, if not impossible. Second, participants who engage in suppression

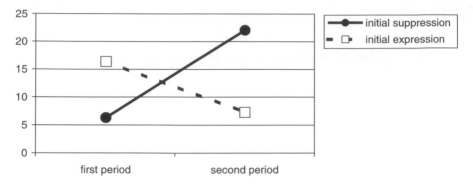

Figure 1.1: White bear thought frequency during suppression and expression attempts. (From Wegner, D.M., Schneider, D.J., Carter, S.R., & White, T.L. (1987). Paradoxical effects of thought suppression. *Journal of Personality and Social Psychology, 53*, 5–13.)

attempts will experience an increase of target thoughts later on, when suppression instructions no longer apply. The latter phenomenon has become known as the rebound effect of thought suppression. Given the object of suppression attempts in this study, both the immediate failure and the delayed paradoxical effect are sometimes referred to as the white bear effect. Wegner and colleagues (1987) argued that this white bear effect "though fairly tame in the laboratory, might conceivably create powerful mental preoccupations in natural settings" (p. 12). Hence, they believed that suppression may be dangerous, in that it could seriously backfire unwanted cognitions. They also stated that their findings may mirror "and perhaps underlie, a wide array of psychological phenomena: emotional, cognitive, and behavioral as well" (1987, p. 12). Soon afterward, the findings of this study were interpreted as a laboratory model of counterproductive avoidance, fostering the occurrence and increase of obsessions as prevalent in obsessive-compulsive disorder (OCD; American Psychiatric Association, 2000). In Wegner's words: "An obsession can grow from nothing but the desire to suppress a thought" (1989, p. 167).

The Mechanism Behind the Paradoxical Effect

How can the paradoxical increase of intrusions due to suppression be explained? According to Wegner (1994; Wegner et al., 1987), people who want to suppress a specific thought will try to achieve this by distracting themselves. For example, a person who does not want to think of a white bear might concentrate on an environmental cue, such as a painting on the wall. However, during such a distraction attempt, the target thought may come to mind nonetheless. If the distraction is not really interesting, the person may return to the target thought by having thoughts like "What am I doing? Oh yeah, I am trying to not think of a white bear." In this example, the painting on the wall is no longer a fruitful distracter, but has turned into a retrieval cue. Therefore, a new distraction is needed. However, chances are that the new distraction will also become associated with the target thought. If this process continues, the person will soon find himself surrounded by cues that remind him of white bears. Hence, he is more likely to think of white bears than someone who has not tried to suppress white bear thoughts. By this view, failing distraction attempts are the vehicle behind the paradoxical effect of thought suppression. Although distraction can also take place by focusing on other thoughts (i.e., internal stimuli), this hypothesis is known as the "environmental cueing" hypothesis.

Wegner and colleagues (1987) themselves offered support for this hypothesis in a second experiment, in which distraction (as a means to suppress white bear thoughts) was manipulated. In this experiment, three conditions were included: an "initial suppression" condition (first 5 minutes of suppressing followed by 5 minutes of expressing white bear thoughts), an "initial expression" condition (first expression, then suppression), and a "focused distraction" condition, which was identical to the initial suppression condition, but with the addition that participants were instructed that "if you happen to think of a white bear, please try to think of a red Volkswagen instead" (p. 10). The authors hypothesized that participants in the third condition would be prevented from getting caught in a vicious circle of failing distraction and seeking new distractions. Participants in the initial suppression condition were given no further instruction as to how they should prevent white bear thoughts from entering consciousness, and they would therefore rely on as many distractions as they saw fit. In other words, the initial suppression condition allowed for "free distraction." This nuance was thought to render participants in the initial suppression condition vulnerable to a rebound effect, unlike those in the focused distraction condition. The hypothesis seemed to be true. The mean number of white bear thoughts during expression was approximately 16 in the initial expression group, 34 in the initial suppression group, and "only" 21 in the focused distraction group. Although the 21 white bear thoughts in the focused distraction group clearly exceeded the 16 in the initial expression group, this difference failed to reach significance. Note that in the first Wegner and colleagues (1987) experiment, initial suppression participants reported on average 22 target thoughts during subsequent expression.

Further evidence for the environmental cueing account was delivered by Wegner, Schneider, Knutson, and McMahon (1991). Compared to the original experiment by Wegner and colleagues (1987), series of slides, projected on the wall facing the participant were added. Depending on the condition, participants saw the same slides during suppression and subsequent expression, or were shown a different series of slides during expression. It seemed that participants who saw the same slides experienced a thought rebound, while those who saw a new series did not. Apparently, the original slides had indeed turned into retrieval cues for white bear thoughts. Alternatively, it can be argued that the new series of slides served as fresh distractions. In that case, the difference in intrusion frequency should not merely be attributed to increased intrusion frequency caused by environmental cueing in the same-slides condition, but to the absence of such an increase due to the temporary efficacy of fresh distractions in the new-slides condition. Muris, Merckelbach, and De Jong (1993) sought to find further evidence for the environmental cueing hypothesis. In their study, 27 participants were first instructed to suppress white bear thoughts, and subsequently to think of anything including white bears. The laboratory in which this study was conducted was purposely untidy. There were eight salient objects present (e.g., a ping-pong ball, a newspaper, and a package of chewing gum). After the second period, participants were given a recognition test in another room, which included 16 items that had actually been present during the experiment (the eight salient objects and eight laboratory furniture items), as well as 16 items that had not been present. During the analyses, Muris and colleagues compared the number of reported white bear thoughts among the 13 participants who scored best on the recognition task, and the 14 lower scoring participants. The first group of participants seemed to have suffered more white bear thoughts during and after suppression (i.e., 7.4 and 6.8, respectively) than did the group of low scoring participants (mean numbers of target thoughts during suppression and expression being 4.0 and 3.6). This finding supports the environmental cueing hypothesis because participants who paid closer attention to environmental stimuli (as a means to distract themselves from the target thought?) were less effective in their suppression attempts, compared to those who made themselves less familiar with the environment during the experiment.

In his 1994 review, Wegner offered a more elaborate explanation for the rebound phenomenon. To understand this "two opponent processes" theory, a closer look at distraction seeking is helpful. People who do not want to think of a white bear, and choose to achieve this by distracting themselves, engage in a conscious and effortful endeavor. Trying to concentrate on something else than what is currently on one's mind is an active and demanding thought control strategy. Therefore, Wegner (1994) refers to distraction seeking as an "operating process." Because of its expended effort, this process suffers from concurrent cognitive operations. This implies that if one's cognitive capacity is invoked by multiple attention-demanding tasks, suppression attempts will be less successful. Wegner and Erber (1992) demonstrated that suppression is less successful if participants have to simultaneously carry out dull word association tasks under time pressure (i.e., high cognitive load), compared to when such concurrent tasks are carried out without time pressure (i.e., low cognitive load).

During suppression attempts, a second process is activated. This "monitoring process" is so evident, automatic, and almost trivial, that it may easily be overlooked. If one tries to not think of a white bear by distracting oneself from that thought, one automatically creates a state of sensitivity for the target thought. Before one can engage in distraction seeking, one has to be alerted that the unwanted thought has occurred in consciousness and that distraction is indicated. Attempted suppression has to be preceded by monitoring consciousness for the unwanted thought. This monitoring process is, compared to the operating process, less effort demanding, and suffers less from concurrent cognitive actions. Moreover, Wegner (1994) argues that the monitoring process lingers even after the operating process has stopped. The ongoing monitoring results in a state of hypersensitivity for the to-be-suppressed thought. In turn, this hypersensitivity translates into an increase of the detected number of unwanted thoughts (i.e., a paradoxical effect).

To sum up, according to Wegner and coworkers (Wegner, 1994; Wegner et al., 1987) the paradoxical effect of thought suppression should be attributed to failing distraction attempts. Distraction can be counterproductive for two reasons. First, if distracters fail to keep one's attention, they are likely to transform into retrieval cues for the to-be-suppressed thought. Second, distraction is accompanied by a monitoring process that readily results in a hypersensitivity for the to-be-suppressed thought.

Replications: Green Rabbits and Red Volkswagens

The lesson to be learned from the Wegner and colleagues (1987) experiment is that one should not try to suppress unwanted thoughts because suppression is at best ineffective, or paradoxically even leads to more intrusions. Over the past one-and-a-half decade, many researchers have replicated their thought suppression study. Compared to the original white bear experiment, most of these replications were slightly adapted. One of the adaptations pertains to the nature of the suppressed thought. One example is a study by Clark, Ball, and Pape (1991), who did not use white bear thoughts as suppression target, but thoughts of a short story about a green rabbit. Not only did these authors vary the suppression target, they also developed a differential procedure. Whereas Wegner and colleagues (1987) used suppression-expression and expression-suppression conditions, Clark and colleagues relied on three conditions ($n = 16$ each). Participants in all three conditions underwent two subsequent 2-minute periods. One condition entailed a suppression and a subsequent "think-of-anything" period. The second condition consisted of two subsequent think-of-anything periods. In the third condition, the instruction for the first period was that participants were allowed to think of anything including the story about the green rabbit, while the second period was, like in the other two conditions, a think-of-anything period. During both periods, participants had to verbalize their every thought into a tape recorder. Afterward, these tapes were analyzed and the percentage of green rabbit thoughts was calculated. Results suggested that during the first period, suppression participants spent approximately 15% of the time thinking about the green rabbit story, while those in the other conditions reached percentages of about 53%. However, during the second period, participants who had previously suppressed green rabbit thoughts, now thought 24% of the time about it, while those who had not engaged in suppression only were absorbed 9% of the time by the green rabbit. This implies that suppression indeed resulted in a thought rebound.

The targets used by Wegner and colleagues (1987) and by Clark and colleagues (1991) are rather neutral or even meaningless to most people. An attractive theoretical feature of the thought suppression paradigm is that the content of the thought is irrelevant. It makes no difference whether the target thought concerns obsessive fears about contamination, violence, or sex. It can be hypothesized that the paradoxical increase of unwanted thoughts occurs regardless of the target thought's content. Notably, paradoxical increases in thought frequency even seemed to occur with a thought as trivial as that of white bears or green rabbits (Lavy & Van den Hout, 1990, instructed their participants to suppress thoughts about vehicles, and also found paradoxical effects). It is the position of Wegner and colleagues (1987) that the real-life paradoxical effects of suppressing truly unwanted thoughts are likely to be even stronger than those observed in their experiment which relied on a, by and large, trivial target thought.

Other authors have argued that the ecological validity of the thought suppression paradigm would increase if more serious thoughts were used in the experiments. These authors discard the inductive line of reasoning that the paradoxical effect will definitely occur with suppression of real-life obsessive thoughts, merely because such an effect was observed with a nonrealistic thought like white bear. Against this line of reasoning, they pose the argument that experimental proof of a paradoxical effect of suppression in case of a neutral thought (white bear) does not necessarily justify the conclusion that such an effect is also likely to occur with unpleasant and/or personally relevant thoughts. Indeed, by now, many researchers have conducted thought suppression experiments in which participants were instructed to suppress unpleasant and/ or personally relevant thoughts, rather than irrelevant thoughts like white bear. For example, Salkovskis and Campbell (1994) asked 75 participants to identify one or more unpleasant thoughts that they had experienced regularly during the previous month. Subsequently, they were instructed to suppress (or not) that personally relevant and unpleasant thought for 5 minutes. Interestingly, the authors gave different suppression instructions to the various groups of participants. In one condition, suppression instructions per se were given. In another condition, participants were instructed to achieve suppression by distracting themselves. In the third suppression condition, the instructions included the assignment that participants should use whatever strategy they wanted to suppress the target thought except distraction. In the last condition, suppression was accompanied by the instruction to simultaneously carry out a pencil and paper test (i.e., an attention demanding and focused distraction task). After this first 5-minute period, a second 5-minute followed for which all participants were instructed to think of anything they wanted. During both periods, participants had to press a button whenever the target thought intruded consciousness. The number of target thoughts were analyzed with analyses of variance (ANOVAs). By and large, the five groups of participants could be divided into two camps for both experimental periods. The control group, suppression-without-distraction group, and suppression-with-additional-test group reported approximately two target thoughts during both the first and second experimental period. The suppression-per-se and the suppression-with-distraction groups, on the other hand, reported significantly more targets during both periods (i.e., approximately 3.7 per period). These findings have several implications. First, they delivered support for the paradoxical effect of suppression. Second, they imply that this paradoxical effect also occurs with personally relevant and unpleasant thoughts. Third, the findings underline that free distraction may be the mechanism underlying the paradoxical effect of thought suppression. Lastly, the findings suggest that suppression may not only result in immediate failure, and thought rebound, but furthermore in an *immediate enhancement* of target thoughts. Note that even during the first period, suppression and suppression-with-distraction participants suffered more intrusions than participants in the other three conditions.

Muris and colleagues (1992) made their participants listen to one of two versions of an audio taped story. In the emotional version (derived from Wenzlaff, Wegner, & Roper, 1988), a baby died in a car crash, while in the neutral version of the story, emotional elements like the death of the baby were replaced by more neutral ones. Some participants were instructed to suppress story-related thoughts, while others did not receive suppression instructions. Hence, four conditions were formed: suppressing emotional material, non-suppressing emotional material, suppressing neutral material, and non-suppressing neutral material. All participants were left in the laboratory for 5 minutes. During this period, they had to ring a bell whenever thoughts of the story came to mind. Following this 5-minute period, all participants were instructed to remain in the laboratory for another 5 minutes. Again, they had to monitor story-related thoughts, if any. This way, Muris and colleagues examined differential effects of suppression in case of emotional and neutral material. It seemed that suppression had a paradoxical effect with the neutral story, but not with the emotional story.

Kelly and Kahn (1994) were interested in the influence of the emotional valence of the to-be-suppressed thought on the eventual efficacy of suppression attempts. They invited 104 participants to visualize their most frequently occurring intrusive thought. Participants were also instructed to make a drawing that symbolized the intrusions. Half of the participants were told to come up with a pleasant intrusive thought, while the other half was instructed to generate an unpleasant intrusion. Participants were then exposed to an experimental procedure similar to that introduced by Wegner and colleagues (1987). Some participants were placed into an initial suppression condition, while others were placed in an initial expression condition. The two experimental periods lasted 9 minutes each. Participants were given stream-of-consciousness-verbalization instructions for both periods, which means that they had to write down every thought that came to mind. Afterward, the researchers studied the verbal reports and counted the number of thoughts that were related to the self-reported target intrusion. When looking at the number of target thoughts, participants in the initial suppression condition experienced 2.3 targets during suppression and 4.9 during subsequent expression. Those in the initial expression condition experienced 7.1 targets during expression and 2.3 during subsequent suppression. These results imply an "anti-rebound" effect: Expression after suppression resulted in fewer intrusions than expression before suppression. Furthermore, the pattern of results for unpleasant intrusions did not diverge from that of pleasant intrusions. Hence, Kelly and Kahn concluded that their data did "not support the idea that the valence of the thought plays a role in whether the rebound occurs" (1994, p. 1001).

Because of the disappointing results (i.e., suppression of a personally relevant intrusion resulted in an anti-rebound), Kelly and Kahn (1994) conducted a second experiment to compare the effects of suppression in case of an emotional target (whether pleasant or unpleasant) with that in case of a neutral target (i.e., the original white bear thought). The experimental setup was virtually the same as that in their first study. Four conditions were included: initial suppression and initial expression groups with white bear thoughts as target, and two corresponding groups with participants' "most frequently occurring intrusive thought" (p. 1002) as target. The reported number of target thoughts are displayed in Table 1.1. As can be seen, the crucial finding was that suppression of white bear thoughts resulted in a thought rebound, while suppression of personally relevant thoughts did not.

Roemer and Borkovec (1994) included six conditions in their suppression experiment ($n = 92$). These conditions were formed by two variables. First, participants were assigned to a suppression-expression condition, or to an expression-expression

Table 1.1   Target Thought Frequency as a Function of Thought Content and Experimental Instruction.

		Suppression period	Expression period
White bear thoughts	Initial suppression	7.1	16.0
	Initial expression	4.8	9.4
Personally relevant	Initial suppression	3.5	7.9
thoughts	Initial expression	3.6	8.1

From Kelly, A.E. & Kahn, J.H. (1994). Effects of suppression of personal intrusive thoughts. *Journal of Personality and Social Psychology*, 66, 998–1006.

condition. Second, participants were instructed to suppress and/or express one of three possible targets: a neutral thought (e.g., an overheard conversation), depressing thoughts about a past loss, or frightening thoughts about future rejection or criticism. Participants had to verbally mention every occurrence of the target during both 5-minute periods. Overall, regardless of thought content, participants in the suppression-expression condition displayed an increase in target thoughts during the second period. Those in the double expression condition experienced fewer target thoughts during the second period, compared to the first. The authors speak of a habituation effect. When looking at the thought content, the increase of targets during expression-after-suppression was strongest for depressing thoughts about losses. Anxious thoughts about future rejections caused the second large increase, and neutral thoughts displayed the smallest increase. Hence, Roemer and Borkovec found evidence to suggest that suppressing emotional thoughts is more difficult than suppressing neutral ones.

In part inspired by the contradicting findings of Kelly and Kahn (1994) and Muris and colleagues (1992) on the one hand, and Roemer and Borkovec (1994) on the other, Harvey and Bryant (1998a) conducted a further investigation into the role of target-valence in attempted thought suppression. Seventy-two participants were enrolled in either a suppression-expression procedure or an expression-expression procedure. Both experimental periods lasted 3 minutes. Depending on condition, the suppression target was either a 3-minute neutral, humoristic, or distressing film fragment. The pertaining film clip was shown to the participants before the experiment. Of course, participants were again instructed to monitor every thought about the film during both 3-minute periods. Table 1.2 presents the reported number of film-related thoughts by instruction and stimulus valence.

Several conclusions can be drawn from these findings. First, during period 1, suppression instructions (regardless of film valence) resulted in fewer intrusions compared to expression instructions. Since there was no immediate enhancement effect, the opposite seemed more likely. Second, during period 2, more target thoughts were reported by participants who had engaged in suppression during the first period, than by those who had not previously suppressed. Again, this pattern was the same for all three film fragments. Thus, these findings indicate that suppression has a paradoxical effect regardless of stimulus content. Interestingly, the findings diverge from those reported by the previously discussed authors. That is, suppression is harder

Table 1.2   Target Thought Frequency as a Function of Thought Content and Experimental Instruction.

Stimulus valence	Condition	First period	Second period
Neutral film	Suppression-expression	3.5	6.3
	Expression-expression	5.7	4.1
Humoristic film	Suppression-expression	4.7	7.7
	Expression-expression	8.3	5.5
Distressing film	Suppression-expression	8.0	10.9
	Expression-expression	11.8	7.1

From Harvey, A.G. & Bryant, R.A. (1998a). The role of valence in attempted thought suppression. *Behaviour Research and Therapy*, *36*, 757–763.

in cases of nonrelevant thoughts (white bears) than with personally relevant thoughts (Kelly & Kahn, 1994), harder in cases of emotional thoughts than with neutral thoughts (Roemer & Borkovec, 1994), and equally hard with neutral, aversive, and pleasant thoughts (Harvey & Bryant, 1998a).

Trinder and Salkovskis (1994) not only used personally relevant thoughts in their experiment, but also extended the relevance of their study by prolonging the suppression period over 4 days, instead of the usual 5 or even fewer minutes. These authors invited 48 participants to identify a recent negative intrusive thought. They were then allocated to one of three conditions: a record only, a suppression, or an expression condition. All participants were given a diary in which they had to put a tick every time that the pertinent intrusion occurred, for 4 days. Participants in the suppression condition were additionally instructed that is was "very important, whenever the thought comes into your mind, I'd like you to suppress it, to get rid of it as quickly as possible, and try to make sure it does not return" (Trinder & Salkovskis, 1994, p. 836). Those in the expression condition were instructed as follows: "It is very important that whenever the thought comes into your mind, I'd like you to think about it for as long as possible without changing it, just stay with it" (p. 836). When the participants came back to the laboratory, 4 days later, they were asked several questions (e.g., concerning the unpleasantness of their intrusion). The data indicated that participants who had received suppression instructions had suffered more intrusive thoughts than those in the other two conditions. Interestingly, they also reported more discomfort from their intrusions than did the other participants. These findings suggest that the paradoxical effect of suppressing a personally relevant thought was maintained during all 4 days of the study. However, it is important to recognize that the current design does not allow for a differentiation between the immediate and delayed effects of suppression. Admittedly, it appears to be unlikely that suppression participants flawlessly complied with the instructions for all 4 days, and hence, it is possible that suppression-free periods did occur, but it is impossible to determine whether the reported intrusions occurred during or after suppression attempts. In addition, the researchers did not intend to include a rebound period, because participants were instructed to suppress their intrusions for the complete 4-day period.

Therefore, it seems justified to interpret the findings of Trinder and Salkovskis (1994) as supportive of an immediate enhancement effect, rather than a rebound effect. Another interesting aspect of this study is that it suggests that suppression may lead to, or at least is associated with, increased discomfort. This implies that suppression may not only inflate the number of target thoughts, but indirectly make them more aversive as well.

Reviews and Books

Since the original white bear study in 1987, dozens of thought suppression studies have been published, in various international journals. In addition, several thesis books have been devoted to this topic (e.g., Purdon, 1998; Rassin, 2000). Although the paradoxical effect of suppression has not always been observed, most researchers did find some indications that suppression generally is a counterproductive or at least an ineffective control strategy. Furthermore, the replications have addressed questions that were not answered by the experiment of Wegner and colleagues (1987). As discussed in the previous paragraph, the nature of the to-be-suppressed target is one of the studied mediators in the relation between suppression and intrusions frequency. Another topic that has emerged in the suppression literature is the influence of the precise instructions on the eventual findings. For example, do the findings vary depending on whether control participants are instructed to express the target thought, or merely to think of whatever they want? Likewise, does one obtain different results when using a within-subject design versus a between-subject design? And what is the best way to record the occurrence of intrusions: retrospective estimation, bell-pressing, or stream of consciousness verbalization? Another issue is whether individuals differ in their tendency to experience intrusive thoughts, and more importantly in their capacity to successfully suppress such intrusions. Some of these issues will be discussed in the chapters to come.

Meanwhile, the still growing number of thought suppression studies has inspired several authors to publish reviews of this research field. One of the first thought suppression reviews was actually a book written by Daniel Wegner (1989) with the meaningful title "White bears and other unwanted thoughts." In this book, he argues that the paradoxical effect of suppression may indeed play a role in the development obsessive intrusions. This can be illustrated by quotations like "... when no obvious trauma is present, there is the good possibility that the obsession has crept up on us slowly, synthesized over time by a series of our own acts of suppression," and: "What this means is that the development of a synthetic obsession is totally dependent on suppression as the first step" (1989, p. 173).

Review articles addressing the thought suppression paradigm have been published in various outlets (e.g., Purdon, 1999; Purdon & Clark, 2000; Rassin, Merckelbach, & Muris, 2000; Wegner, 1994; Wenzlaff & Wegner, 2000). A review that deserves special attention is that written by Abramowitz, Tolin, and Street (2001). These authors conducted a meta-analysis of thought suppression experiments. They limited their analysis to studies that comprised at least one no-suppression control condition.

Despite this and other inclusion criteria, their eventual analysis pertained to no less than 28 suppression experiments, indicating that the original study by Wegner and colleagues (1987) has had quite a spin-off, and that one can indeed speak of a paradigm. The first question that Abramowitz and colleagues (2001) tried to answer is whether suppression does lead to an increase of target thoughts. The initial analysis did not yield evidence to support this ($d = .07$). However, next they differentiated between the initial effect and the delayed effect. From these analyses it became clear that, when looking at the whole of the suppression studies, there was an negative effect size for the immediate effect ($d = -.35$), suggesting the opposite of an immediate enhancement effect. In other words, suppression may be somewhat effective in the short run. As to the delayed effect, a positive effect size ($d = .30$) indicated that in general, suppression is counterproductive in the longer run. Other important findings were that the precise instruction (i.e., expression vs. think of anything) is of no influence to the eventual effects of suppression, and that the valence of the target thought (neutral, positive, or negative) has little influence either.

Although the meta-analysis of Abramowitz and colleagues (2001) is of great value, it should be noted that meta-analyses, by definition summarize large data sets. In the process of summarizing, possibly important interactions can become overshadowed or completely lost. For example, even if the content of control instructions and the emotional valence of the target are irrelevant in general, it cannot be excluded that expression instructions result in larger rebound effects in combination with, say, positive target thoughts alone.

Chapter 2

Suppression, Repression, and Dissociation

Freudian Repression

In their original article, Wegner and colleagues (1987) refer to the work of Sigmund Freud. They interpret his writings as suggesting that suppression was primarily an unconscious process. In their words: "...that the unconscious was capable of performing the thought suppression for consciousness. So, although the unconscious could not remove the thought from itself, and consciousness also could not remove the thought from itself, the unconscious could perform this housecleaning for the separate, conscious part of the mind" (p. 5). This interpretation leaves little doubt about the nature of Freudian suppression (which is commonly referred to as "repression"). That is, in this view, repression is by definition unconscious. In contrast, suppression as studied by Wegner and colleagues, is defined as a conscious attempt to ban a specific thought from consciousness.

In the literature, there is some discussion about what Freud precisely meant with his concept of repression. Before discussing Freud's theory of repression, a few general remarks about his work are necessary. For one thing, it is important to recognize that Freud was not a psychologist, but a psychiatrist. He lived and worked in a time when psychology was hardly a full-grown discipline. Furthermore, his work stems from before-contemporary philosophies of scientific progress (see subsequent discussion). Last, Freud's work is very sizable, and for the most part written in German. Moreover, Freud adapted his views from time to time. All these circumstances make his work poorly organized. Also, some parts of his work are susceptible to multiple interpretations.

In his work as a psychiatrist, Freud encountered many patients who seemed to have found ways to convert or distort certain realities in their mind. He believed that such distortions serve as means to protect the psyche from unpleasant insights that may threaten normal functioning. For example, someone who was fired may conclude that he did not like his job anyway (rationalization). A married man who is sexually attracted to someone other than his spouse, may believe that the object of his affection is actually attracted to him, instead of vice versa (projection). As another example, most of us, sometimes, react disproportionately agitated to little misbehaviors by people close to us, if we have been annoyed by someone with whom we are not familiar enough to speak up to (displacement). All these different defense mechanisms share the element that some type of information is repressed from consciousness, and replaced by another, less-threatening alternative. In rationalization, the true reason for our current situation is repressed. In projection, it is the knowledge of the agent of the intolerable impulse that is repressed. Displacement entails repression of the original target of the impulse. Given that most of the defense mechanisms lean on the principle of repression, Freud (1955) concluded that repression must be the most important mechanism of defense. If Freud confronted his patients with the notion that they might have distorted reality by some kind of mental defense mechanism, they often seemed to be unaware of this. Therefore, Freud concluded that defense mechanisms, including the fundamental mechanism of repression, can be used unconsciously.

At this point, readers of Freud's opus differ in their interpretation. In one of Freud's rare definitions, he described repression merely as follows: "the essence of repression lies simply in the function of rejecting and keeping something out of consciousness" (1963, p. 105). This definition is silent about the individual's awareness of repression. Nevertheless, many people believe that Freud intended that repression is an unconscious mechanism, while he would have reserved the term suppression for the conscious counterpart (Cramer, 2000; Kihlstrom, 2002; Blackman, 2004). Brewin and Andrews (2000) stipulate that Freud used the term repression in various ways, one of which "referred to a process whereby unwanted material is turned away before it reaches awareness" (p. 15). However, others do not believe that Freudian repression is exclusively unconscious (Anderson & Levy, 2002). Erdelyi (2001) fiercely resists that idea. In his words: "Sigmund Freud's position – that defense, including repression, could be conscious or unconscious – is the viable position. Whether or not one likes him, whether or not one agrees or disagrees with him on a variety of issues, the scientific community owes Freud his scholarly due: Freud's ideas should be presented rather than misrepresented, and his long-derided ideas, now increasingly mainstream in cognitive psychology, should not be repackaged or rediscovered without attribution" (Erdelyi, 2001, p. 762). This author also disbelieves that Freud distinguished between repression and suppression: "Thus, contrary to the widespread view in both psychology and psychoanalysis, Freud did not hew to a distinction between repression and suppression, which he instead treated interchangeably, from his earliest to his last writings" (Erdelyi, 2001, p. 761).

Regardless of how one interprets Sigmund Freud's idea of repression, that of his daughter Anna leaves less room for discussion. Anna Freud elaborated certain aspects of her father's theories. She came up with inflated postulates such as "Repression is the most dangerous defence mechanism," and "Repression is the basis for the formation of neurosis" (Freud, 1946, p. 44). In her view, which is held by many psychoanalytic therapists today, repression refers to the removal of complete autobiographical memories from consciousness. In the words of Loftus: "According to the theory, something happens that is so shocking that the mind grabs hold of the memory and pushes it underground, into some inaccessible corner of the unconsciousness. There it sleeps for years, or even decades, or even forever – isolated from the rest of mental life. Then, one day, it may rise up and emerge into consciousness" (1993, p. 518). Recently, Karon and Widener (1997) claimed to have found solid evidence for this far-fetched concept of repression. These authors described a World War II veteran who suffered from paralysis. Although he had absolutely no recollection of a particular traumatic event involving the crash of a bomber plane, his paralysis disappeared as soon as the therapist succeeded in recovering this traumatic memory. Clearly, Karon and Widener's interpretation of the concept of repression involves the removal of complete recollections from consciousness.

Scientific Pitfalls of Repression

The definition of repression as the removal of complete recollections is, from a scientific stance, a problem. For one thing, this concept is nearly impossible to investigate. Freud based his theories on his experiences with patients who consulted him for psychiatric interventions. Thus, Freud observed certain phenomena in his patients, formulated a theory, and subsequently verified this theory by looking at more patients. This approach can be called inductivistic (Chalmers, 1976). Inductivism refers to the endeavor of seeking confirmation of formulated hypotheses. This approach is somewhat weak, because, generally, if one really wants to find evidence for one's hypothesis, one will succeed eventually. In other words, the inducting researcher is not very self-critical. With this in mind, Popper (1968) introduced the idea that scientific progress should be achieved by formulating hypotheses, followed by a critical search to reject those hypotheses. Only if a hypothesis survives this critical analysis, may it be accepted as true. Popper's approach (referred to as falsificationism) is, from a scientific viewpoint, better than the inductivistic approach. But to subject a hypothesis to a critical analysis, it must, in theory, be possible to reject that hypothesis. A statement that is formulated in such a way that it can never be rejected, cannot be the subject of a scientific search for falsification. Unfortunately, many statements do not comply with the criterion of falsifiability. Table 2.1 presents a few statements that can never be rejected, and are therefore unscientific. It is important to acknowledge that scientific is not a synonym of true. For example, statements 2 and 3 may not be scientific (because there is no way of rejecting them), but are nonetheless true. The statement "under rising temperature, all materials tend to expand" is scientific, but false, because the volume of melting ice decreases.

Some of the psychoanalytic principles suffer from a lack of falsifiability. Especially the idea that the human mind is for the bigger part unconscious can never be subjected to a scientific test. No matter what is said, one can always uphold the idea that a lot of information is processed unconsciously. This notion is a problem because it decreases the role of our conscious actions relative to our unconscious activity. A study by

Table 2.1   Examples of Unscientific Statements

1. There are creatures on earth that have never been detected by mankind
2. Either it rains, or it does not
3. One may be lucky
4. War is inevitable
5. We are surrounded by aliens that we are unable to detect
6. If no one is watching, toys come to life

Crombag and Van Koppen (1994) may help to elucidate the problematic nature of the assumption of a big unconsciousness. These authors, first, asked a sample of 268 healthy volunteers whether they believed in the idea that people are capable of repressing unpleasant memories. Sixty-eight percent of the respondents answered this question affirmatively. But then, Crombag and Van Koppen sought to tease their participants by confronting them with the ultimate consequence of that belief. They asked whether the respondents believed that it was possible that they themselves had experienced traumatic events (e.g., being the victim of abuse or war), even though they, at present, had no recollection of such events, due to repression. Much to the surprise of the authors (who assumed that respondents would draw the line at this proposal), no less than 38% of the participants endorsed this question. Evidently, once we believe in successful repression of complete recollections, we are open to the idea that anything may have happened to us. Hence, we do not rely on our memory to decide which events we experienced. In that case, we would become extremely susceptible to other people's suggestions.

The fact that it is nearly impossible to study repression experimentally, is not invalidated by the many case reports (Karon & Widener, 1997), in which authors claim to have seen patients who had repressed and recovered traumatic memories. Evidently, such case reports merely add to the bulk of inductivistic evidence already conjured up by Freud. One of the limited number of experimental studies of repression, defined as the unconsciously banning of threatening information, was conducted by Silverman, Ross, Adler, and Lustig (1978). Using their subliminal psychodynamic activation paradigm, they claimed to have found evidence for the psychodynamic notion that the ego can process information while keeping that information hidden from conscious awareness. This unconscious processing of information can be construed as a manifestation of repression, because, apparently, external information enters the cognitive circuit, without intruding the stream of consciousness. In a crucial experiment by Silverman and colleagues (1978), 30 undergraduate students engaged in a dart-throwing contest. They were given eight darts per turn, with which they had to earn as many points as possible. First, a few practice sessions were run, to familiarize participants with the dart-throwing. Next, before each turn, participants underwent a subliminal exposure to slides with different sentences. During these exposures, the stimuli were projected on a white board for such a short time (e.g., 4 milliseconds) that conscious perception is impossible. The different sentences included: "people are walking," "beating dad is wrong," and "beating dad is OK." Before every dart-throw session, an exposure session took place. Within every exposure session, only one sentence was presented. The order of sentences was counterbalanced between participants. In this way, Silverman and colleagues were able to study the effects of the subliminal messages on the dart-throwing performance. It was hypothesized that the stimulus "beating dad is wrong" would impair the dart-throwing performance, because this message would activate unconscious internal conflicts (cf. Oedipus complex). That is, this message would make the participant feel guilty, because his impulse to stand up to his father was condemned. On the contrary, "beating dad is OK" would improve performance, because this message was expected to make the participant (unconsciously) feel relieved. The stimulus "people are walking" was used as control induction. The dart-throw achievements after each stimulus are presented in

Figure 2.1. As can be seen, while the "people are walking" sentence did not affect performance, compared to baseline, participants performed significantly worse after having "seen" (i.e., subconsciously perceived) the sentence "beating dad is wrong." The sentence "beating dad is OK" significantly improved task performance.

Although the findings obtained by Silverman and colleagues (1978) appear to provide evidence for the psychoanalytic conception of repression, their publication was followed by many failures to replicate (Malik, Apel, Nelham, Rutkowski, & Ladd, 1997). Indeed, Silverman and colleagues (1978) themselves argue that obtaining significant results with this paradigm depends on trivial factors such as the lighting in the laboratory. The observed effects would disappear if the lighting was too bright.

A stronger argument against the interpretation of the data from Silverman and colleagues as supportive of Freudian repression is that this paradigm, simply, does not address repression. In more recent psychological theories, the existence of a subcortical information processing route, that enables us to unconsciously process threat-relevant information in a quick and dirty manner, is no longer seen as support-ive of unconscious repression, but rather as an evolutionary determined adaptive mechanism (Mayer & Merckelbach, 1999). Also, it seems that people, generally, are not prone to unconsciously ignore threatening information. By contrast, there seems to be an attentional bias toward emotionally laden stimuli (Mayer & Merckelbach, 1999). Notwithstanding these limitations, Weinberger and Hardaway (1990) conducted a literature review of studies on subliminal psychodynamic activation, and concluded that the findings cannot be completed attributed to artefacts and alternative explan-ations. These authors argue that many of the comments on this type of study are not

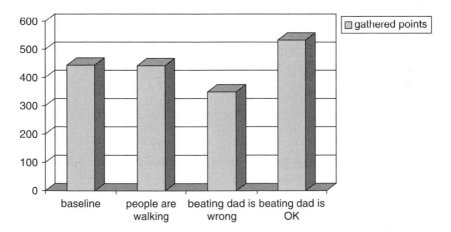

Figure 2.1: Mean scores during dart-throwing as a function of stimulus. (From Silverman, L.H., Ross, D.L., Adler, J.M., & Lustig, D.A. (1978). Simple research paradigm for demonstrating subliminal psychodynamic activation: Effects of oedipal stimuli on dart-throwing accuracy in college males. *Journal of Abnormal Psychology, 87,* 341–357.)

necessarily rooted in scientific critique, but rather in a plain human reluctance to accept results that are counterintuitive and appear incredible, because "science rarely welcomes ideas that run counter to prevailing wisdom" (Weinberger & Hardaway, 1990, p. 753).

In short, it can be concluded that the scientific status of repression, defined as the unconscious neglecting of threatening information, is insufficient. The concept is hardly falsifiable and therefore unscientific. The one experimental paradigm that attempted to deliver experimental evidence has received many criticisms. In addition to this lack of evidence, there are several alternative explanations for the concept of repression. One alternative explanation involves the confusion between repression and normal forgetting due to natural decay (Schacter, 1999). We simply tend to forget with the passing of time. Research indicates that we not only forget trivial details, but also very important pieces of information. For example, Wagenaar and Groeneweg (1990) found that people who were imprisoned in concentration camps during World War II forgot a number of murders they had witnessed. In such cases, it might be tempting to conclude that they had repressed the memories of those murders because they were too painful. However, the findings by Wagenaar and Groeneweg (1990) do not suggest that these concentration camp victims had repressed (i.e., consciously or unconsciously tried to forget) their recollection. Furthermore, if the psychoanalytic notion of repression is correct, one would expect that the concentration camp victims in the Wagenaar and Groeneweg study had no recollections of having been in a concentration camp at all.

As to forgetting due to natural decay, Walker, Vogl, and Thompson (1997) found that people tend to forget unpleasantness slightly faster than pleasantness. These authors instructed 43 undergraduates to enter unique events into a diary for 3 months. In addition to this entry, the pleasantness of every event was rated on a 7-point scale (anchors: $-3 = very\ unpleasant$; $3 = very\ pleasant$). After this diary was completed, participants were invited to the laboratory, where they had to indicate how well they now remembered each of the entered events ($1 = not\ at\ all$; $7 = perfectly$), and how pleasant the events were now in their recollection. Walker and colleagues found that there was a shift in pleasantness ratings, in the sense that the scores displayed regression to the mean. This decrease in intensity was stronger for the unpleasant events than for the pleasant ones ($t[2249] = 22.4$, $P < .001$). When comparing the vividness of participants' current recollection, pleasant events were judged to be slightly better remembered ($mean = 4.43$) than unpleasant events ($M = 4.38$; $t[2118] = 2$, $P < .05$). Hence, these data suggest that the tenacity of emotional intensity of recollections is mediated by the valence of the emotion: unpleasantness fades faster than pleasantness. Furthermore, unpleasant events seem to be forgotten slightly faster than pleasant events, although this postulation rests on self-perceived accuracy of participants' recollections rather than on actual memory tests. The findings of Walker and colleagues are silent about the mechanism underlying the process of forgetting. If anything, the authors think of their results as indicating natural decay, and definitely not repression. In their words: "These data suggest that event memory is largely driven by emotional intensity, such that more emotionally intense events are remembered better than less emotionally intense events. Freud argued just the opposite. According to psychoanalytic theory, emotionally intense unpleasant events would be repressed rather than remembered. In sum, these data suggest that unpleasant memories are not repressed. Instead, people minimize the emotional aspect of unpleasant memories while maintaining their overall memory of the events" (Walker et al., 1997, p. 412).

Winkielman, Schwarz, and Belli (1998) presented a nice illustration of how metacognition may foster the misinterpretation of normal forgetting. They asked 142 undergraduate students the following question: "Regarding childhood memory, are there large parts of your childhood after age 5 which you can't remember?" Answer options were *yes, unsure,* or *no*. However, before this question, some participants were instructed to report four childhood events, while others were asked to report 12 childhood events. Of the participants who had recalled four childhood events, 19% said they had memory lapses, while 52% denied having such lapses. Interestingly, of those who had recalled 12 events, 46% answered the amnesia question positively, while 25% of them denied having amnesia. Hence, participants who had recalled more childhood events reported poorer memory. According to the authors, this finding was caused by the fact that recollection of 12 events was difficult, while this difficulty in turn made participants believe that their memory must therefore be bad. Participants who had to recall no more than four events did not have to think so hard, and therefore had no reason to assume that their memory was flawed. In short, priming of availability may affect individuals' perception of the quality of their memory (Tversky & Kahneman, 1973). By analogy, a similar effect can be assumed to occur with the belief in repression of recollections.

Another strongly advocated alternative explanation for the concept of repressed and later-recovered memories is that memories recovered during therapy are actually pseudo-memories idiosyncratically created by therapeutic interventions such as "guided imagery," a procedure in which the patient is instructed to imagine unpleasant events to make it easier to talk about events that really happened to that patient (Loftus, 1993; Loftus, Joslyn, & Polage, 1998). From literature it has become clear that it is sometimes difficult to distinguish between memories of real events and memories of imagined or dreamed events (Johnson, Foley, Suengas, & Raye, 1988). For example, Rassin, Merckelbach, and Spaan (2001) found that approximately 10% of their 255 normal participants regularly had difficulties distinguishing between dreams and real events. Some participants reported to have acted against others based on what later turned out to be a dream. In short, repeated conversations, including suggestive techniques during psychotherapy, may lead people to believe that they had been victims of abuse, even though they did not remember this at all prior to therapy.

It would be a mistake to think that Freud was insensitive to the possibility of suggested memories. Bowers and Farvolden (1996) presented a catching narrative on how political motivations may have influenced the development of a part of Freud's theory. According to these authors, Freud started off with his "discovery" that 18 hysteric female patients must have been abused in their childhood. This observation led him to conclude that repression of abuse stands at the basis of psychopathology (Freud, 1959a). By the way, Bowers and Farvolden wonder what this implies with respect to the psychopathogenic power of abuse that is not repressed. Freud's observation of these 18 women resulted in his "The Aetiology of Hysteria" in 1896. Ten years later, in 1905, he published an essay titled "My views on the part of sexuality in the aetiology of the neurosis" (Freud, 1959b). In that article, he says to have overestimated the occurrence of actual abuse in his sample of patients. Some of the reported abuse would not reflect actual maltreatment, but the patients' fantasies that are the result of internal conflicts. Hence, with this essay, he changed his trauma theory into a conflict theory. Some authors see this shift as a way for Freud to remain on friendly terms with the parents and caretakers of his patients, most of whom were leading figures in society (Masson, 1985). Thus, this shift from trauma to conflict is considered by some to be a scientific mistake. Even if the patients' claims of being abused are not thought to reflect historical truth in his later work, Freud did not imply that the abuse fantasies of his patients were the result of his suggestions. These fantasies were caused by conflicts between id, ego, and superego. Given that these conflicts and the resulting fantasies were largely unconscious, Freud argued that suggestion was a legitimate intervention to make them conscious. While Bowers and Farvolden argue "that therapeutic efforts to recall repressed memories is a risk factor for suggesting them" (1996, p. 362), Freud believed that his patients would only indulge his suggestions if they were in line with the patient's history or fantasies. The notion that patients might also accept suggestions that did not resemble their fantasies or actual experiences was fiercely rejected by Freud. Bowers and Farvolden argue that there is no way of knowing whether Freud actually believed that such suggestion is impossible, or that he merely stated so to save his own theory. In their words: "...Doing so was critical. For if patients merely internalize therapists' suggestions, then their memories or fantasies regarding childhood sexuality are not an independent confirmation of Freud's theories but are simply a perverse echo of them" (1996, p. 365).

Ironically, the lack of experimental evidence for repression, and the strong alternative explanations for repressed and recovered memories have not prevented many alleged abuse victims from making large financial claims for abuse that took place decades earlier. The reason for this delay was that the memory of the abuse had been too painful and had therefore been completely repressed. Only thanks to recent therapeutic interventions, the memories were recovered. Given the substantial legal and financial consequences of such recovered memories, in addition to the scientific critiques discussed above, several authors have opposed to the acknowledgment of these memories (Gudjonsson, 1997a; Van Koppen & Merckelbach, 1999). Whereas scientists may be sceptical about the accuracy of recovered memories, the general public is much less so. Golding, Sego, Sanchez, and Hasemann (1995) presented one of three fictive case vignettes to 123 undergraduate students. All three vignettes dealt with a civil lawsuit against a Mr. McGuire. This man was said to have sexually assaulted the 6-year-old Miss Williams. In one version, the civil lawsuit had been initiated soon after the alleged assault would have taken place. In the second condition, the suit was filed no sooner than 20 years afterward. This delay was due to the fact that "she had not remembered the assault during he past 20 years; the memory of the assault came back to her recently in the course of psychotherapy" (1995, p. 589). In the third condition, the suit was filed 20 years after the alleged assault, although this time, there was no reason provided for this delay, and it was mentioned that the victim had always remained aware of the abuse. Participants were asked to rate the credibility of

Table 2.2   Mean Values on the Believability and Decision Scales

	Immediate trial	Delayed trial due to repression	Delayed trial not due to repression
Victim's believability	7.3	6.2	6.2
Decision rating	6.2	5.0	5.2

From Golding, J.M., Sego, S.A., Sanchez, R.P., & Hasemann, D. (1995). The believability of repressed memories. *Law and Human Behavior*, *19*, 569–592.

the alleged victim's complaint on a 10-point scale (1 = *not at all*; 10 = *completely*). They were also asked to indicate whether they would rule a decision in favor of the defendant or in favor of the plaintiff, using a similar scale (1 = *completely in favor of the defendant*; 10 = *completely in favor of the plaintiff*). The results are displayed in Table 2.2. ANOVAs and planned post hoc comparisons indicated that immediate action on the part of the victim resulted in increased believability and increased favorable rulings, compared to both delayed conditions. Interestingly, the two delayed conditions did not differ from each other on either variable. Hence, it can be concluded that people find repression as good a reason as any other for a delayed course of action following abuse.

Trait-Repression

Some academics have proposed to define repression not so much as a specific reaction to a single traumatic event, but rather as a general broad coping style. By this view, individuals differ in their tendency to rely on repression in various threatening situations. Furthermore, it is hypothesized that the use of repression is not only stable over various situations, but also stable in time. Hence, this form of repression should be open to measurement. Gleser and Ihilevich (1969) developed a questionnaire that aims to measure various defense mechanisms including repression. This instrument, the Defense Mechanism Inventory (DMI), consists of 10 case vignettes that describe frustrating situations (e.g., being cheated on by one's partner and one's best friend). Every vignette is followed by four questions addressing the respondent's actual and fantasized reactions, thoughts, and feelings. For every question, five answers are presented. The respondent is instructed to choose which answer would be the most typical of him/her, and which answer is the least typical. The DMI measures five broad defenses: turning-against-object (TAO), projection (PRO), principalization (PRN), turning-against-self (TAS), and reversal (REV). The latter defense style taps denial, reaction formation, and repression. This reversal subscale consists of items in the vain of "I would be happy that my partner and best friend get along so well," and "I would not mind that I was cheated on." Respondents who consistently choose this kind of answer options (rather than "I would like to kill them both") are said to engage in repression because they react in a neutral or even positive manner in a situation that is very likely to evoke a negative reaction. Other researchers have argued that the DMI also allows for the computation of one composite measure (Juni, 1982). The formula for this computation is PRN + REV − TAO − PRO. Individuals who obtain a positive score rely more on avoidant defense mechanisms (principalization and reversal) than on active acting-out defenses (reacting in an aggressive manner toward the threatening object or toward a third object).

The DMI has received some attention in the medico-psychological literature. For example, Anderson and Leitner (1991) had 173 undergraduates complete the DMI and the Symptoms Checklist (SCL-90; Derogatis, 1977), a list that measures general psychopathology. They found that higher scores on the PRN and REV subscales correlated negatively with self-reported psychopathological complaints (SCL-90). PRO and TAO, on the other hand, were positively correlated with the SCL-90. These findings suggest that repression has beneficial effects on mental health. However, some caution is warranted in the interpretation of these data. The manifestation of repression measured by the DMI is that of a (conscious or unconscious) denial, neglect of threatening information. Individuals who score high on the REV subscale and/or on the composite measure appear to be uninterruptedly happy. They always look at the bright side of things. Feelings of regret, vengeance, and even plain sadness are strange to them. Given this definition, it is possible that such individuals under-report psychopathological complaints. Hence, a negative correlation between repression and SCL-90 may not only reflect positive effects of repression on mental health, but also a neglect of existing psychopathological complaints.

Waldinger and Van Strien (1995) were interested in whether repression as measured by the DMI can be located specifically in one of the brain hemispheres. Twenty-four participants underwent a computer task in which they were expected to recognize series of letters that were presented on screen for 100 milliseconds, either in their left or right visual field. The presented letters (e.g., C, F, or H) were preceded by a word presented in the middle of the computer screen for 2 seconds. This word could be either neutral (e.g., "design"), positive (e.g., "lovely"), or negative (e.g., "sinister"). The dependent variable was the number of correctly recognized letters. Independent variables were the visual field in which the letter was presented (left vs. right), the valence of the preceding word (neutral, positive, or negative), and the score on the composite measure of the DMI (the sample was divided into a low and high scoring group). Results indicated that low-scorers recognized more letters if they were presented in the right visual field, and when they were preceded by a neutral or positive word. Letters that were preceded by a negative word were recognized equally often whether presented left or right. High-scorers displayed a divergent pattern of recognition. They seemed to have a right-sided preference in case of both positive and negative precursors, but a left-sided preference in case of neutral words. The fact that high scoring participants recognized more words in the right visual field if preceded by an emotional word indicates that their left hemisphere was hyperactivated by that emotional word. Based on this idea, Waldinger and Van Strien (1995) concluded that repression is associated with a left hemispheric activation and/or a right hemispheric inhibition.

Weinberger, Schwartz, and Davidson (1979) introduced a different strategy to identify individuals who habitually repress threatening information. Their method requires a trait anxiety measure (e.g., the State/Trait Anxiety Inventory; STAI; Spielberger, 1983) and a scale measuring social defensiveness (e.g., the Marlowe-Crowne Social Desirability Scale; SDS; Crowne & Marlowe, 1964). With these questionnaires, four different response patterns can be distinguished: 1) low-anxious and low-defensiveness, 2) high-anxious and low-defensiveness, 3) low-anxious and high-defensiveness, and 4) high-anxious and high-defensiveness. The third response pattern is considered to reflect repressive coping. People displaying this kind of response are referred to as "repressors." This operationalization of repressive coping entails a combination of being very eager to behave in a correct manner, and presenting oneself in a positive (and thus non-anxious) fashion. Interestingly, despite their low self-reported anxiety, repressors do have normal or even elevated physiological response patterns when confronted with stressful stimuli (Weinberger, 1990). The combination of low self-reported anxiety and high defensiveness may be interpreted in different ways. One obvious explanation of this response pattern would be that repressors deliberately underreport their feelings of anxiety to maintain a positive self-image. Another possibility is that repressors truly believe that they are low-anxious, in spite of their normal or even elevated physiological reactions. To test which of these mutually exclusive explanations is most likely, Derakshan and Eysenck (1999) conducted the following experiment. They selected 79 participants out of a larger sample ($n = 220$) based on their scores on the STAI and SDS. Of these 79 participants, 19 were classified as repressors. All participants were attached to a polygraph that measured, among other things, skin conduction. While connected to the polygraph, participants could view their physiological responses on line. To increase respect for the polygraph, the experimenter said "I am going to ask you a very personal question, it could be quite embarrassing for you and you might find it very difficult to answer" (1999, p. 7). Immediately after this announcement, the skin conductance of all participants increased dramatically. Next, the participant was asked to complete the STAI and SDS, while still connected to the polygraph. This procedure is sometimes referred to as a "bogus pipeline" condition. Derakshan and Eysenck compared participants' scores on the STAI and SDS completed before the experiment, with those obtained while attached to the polygraph. Repressors' scores on the STAI did not seem to have increased due to the bogus pipeline condition as compared to standard conditions of questionnaire completion. Their scores on the SDS decreased under bogus pipeline condition, but this was also true for the remainder of the 79 participants. As to the polygraph data, repressors did not differ in their Galvanic skin conductance responses from the non-repressors. Based on these findings, Derakshan and Eysenck concluded that repressors genuinely believe to be low on anxiety. In their words: "repressors are self-deceivers rather than other-deceivers" (1999, p. 15), which means that repressors do not underreport their self-perceived anxiety, but actually under-perceive their feelings of anxiety.

Numerous studies have been devoted to the exploration of differences between repressors and non-repressors. Baumeister and Cairns (1992) invited 104 undergraduates to complete several computerized personality inventories. The participants were told that the computer would analyze their answers and would generate a personality profile consisting of 30 adjectives. Half of them were told that this profile was to be shown to them only. The other half was told that their profile would also be shown to peer participants. Next, participants were exposed to their personality profile. The 30 adjectives appeared on screen one by one, and the participant could retrieve the following adjective by pressing the space bar. In fact, the computer registered how long every participant studied his or her profile. In reality, the so-called personality profiles were fake. Half of the participants were shown a bogus favorable profile, while the other half were shown a bogus unfavorable set of adjectives. It was hypothesized that the repressors among the participants would spend a differential time looking at their profile, depending on whether the profile was favorable or not, and depending on whether they thought that this profile would be shown to others or not. Such a differential pattern of attention was not expected for the non-repressors. The amount of time spent looking at the personality profile is displayed in Table 2.3.

As can be seen in this table, non-repressors spent approximately 1 minute looking at their profile, regardless of its content, and regardless of whether they had been told that it was for their eyes only or public. The repressors, however, displayed quite a different interactional pattern. Those who had been told that their profile would be public studied it more thoroughly if it was unfavorable compared to if it was favorable. On the other hand, repressors who thought that their profile would not be displayed to others, spent more time looking at it if it was positive than if it was negative in content. The authors concluded from this that repressors were bothered by the notion that their unfavorable profile would become known to peers because that might threaten their positive self-image. Hence, they looked for a relatively long time at this negative profile. If they were not bothered by future public knowledge of their unfavorable personality profile, they used their favorite defense mechanism: to pay little attention to ego-threatening information.

Next, Baumeister and Cairns (1992) asked all participants to reproduce as many of the 30 adjectives from the personality profile as possible. Non-repressors remembered, on average, 10.3 favorable and 11.3 unfavorable words. Repressors recalled 13.5 favorable and only 9.3 unfavorable words. This latter finding suggests that repressors somehow managed to "forget" unwanted information. Although it is tempting to

Table 2.3 Number of Seconds Spent Looking at the Personality Profile

	Repressors		Non-repressors	
	Public	Private	Public	Private
Favorable profile	49.6	83.9	63.4	61.1
Unfavorable profile	100.5	63.0	56.1	58.0

From Baumeister, R.F. & Cairns, K.J. (1992). Repression and self-presentation: When audiences interfere with self-deceptive strategies. *Journal of Personality and Social Psychology, 62*, 851–862.

argue that repressors in this study may actually have repressed the unfavorable adjectives, they might as well merely have been reluctant to reproduce these words.

Boden and Baumeister (1997) reported three interesting studies on the avoidant coping style of repression. In their first study, 30 repressors and 30 non-repressors were shown either a 5-minute aversive film clip or a neutral fragment of the same length. After having viewed this film clip, participants were instructed to recall "a time in life you felt particularly happy" (1997, p. 49). The dependent variable in this study was the time needed to conjure up such a pleasant memory. It was hypothesized that non-repressors would take longer if they had been exposed to an aversive film clip compared to a neutral fragment (cf. mood congruency). Repressors, on the other hand, were hypothesized to have a decreased response latency in case of an aversive film clip, because it would be in their nature to cope with aversive stimulation by means of generating pleasant thoughts. These hypotheses were confirmed: non-repressors took on average 29.8 seconds to generate a happy memory after having seen an unpleasant film clip, and 13.7 seconds after being shown a neutral film. The corresponding latencies of repressors were 15.5 for the aversive condition and 25.9 for the neutral condition, respectively.

Boden and Baumeister's (1997) second study included 17 repressors who were all shown an aversive film fragment. Some were instructed to produce a happy memory, while others had to generate an unhappy memory. In contradiction with mood congruency, yet in line with the hypothesized seemingly happiness-orientation of repressors, they needed less time to come up with a happy memory (9.8 seconds) than to produce a sad memory (17.6 seconds).

In their third study, 129 students underwent the following procedure. First, they had to write down every thought that came to mind during a 5-minute period. Next, they were shown either a positive or neutral 5-minute film clip. After this, they again had to write down their thoughts for 5 minutes. The valence of the reported thoughts was labelled by a researcher who was blind to the status of the participant and the film clip. On average, non-repressors reported 0.77 pleasant thoughts after having seen the neutral film clip, and 0.19 subsequent to the aversive clip. By contrast, repressors wrote down 0.07 pleasant thoughts after the neutral film clip, and 0.88 after the aversive fragment. This interaction was statistically significant ($P < .001$) even if the number of pleasant thoughts written down before the film fragments were shown was included in the analysis as a covariate. These three studies indicate that repressors are characterized by a tendency to generate positive thoughts in reaction to unpleasant and threatening stimuli.

Newman and Hedberg (1999) sought to investigate whether repressors have fewer unhappy memories than happy memories. Seventy-three participants (25 of whom were categorized as repressors) were given a list with 20 items prompting a positive recollection (e.g., "learned very much in school,") and 20 items prompting a negative memory (e.g., "performed poorly in a sports event"). They were instructed to report whether they had personally experienced each of the 40 events. Of the possible 20, non-repressors endorsed 11.2 negative items and 13.8 positive items. Repressors endorsed 9.8 negative and 14.6 positive items. Hence, while all participants reported more positive than negative items to apply to them, this difference was more pronounced for the repressors than for the non-repressors. Thus, it seems that repressors indeed put aside negative information, and that they have fewer unpleasant memories than do non-repressors. But again, these findings may also merely reflect a reluctance to report negative self-image threatening information.

Up to now, there has been little attention for the commonalties and differences between repression (as measured by the DMI, or by the STAI and SDS) and suppression as defined by Wegner and colleagues (1987). One effort to compare both defenses is reported by Myers, Vetere, and Derakshan (2004). These authors asked 80 participants, preselected based on anxiety and social desirability, to complete the Courtauld Emotional Control Scale (CECS; Watson & Greer, 1983). The CECS is a 21-item self-report addressing self-control (i.e., behavioral inhibition) in three different areas, namely anger, anxiety, and depression. When comparing the three CECS subscale scores for repressors and non-repressors, Watson and Greer found that the only group difference pertained to the CECS anxiety subscale. Repressors did not report to hide their depressive and anger feelings more than did non-repressors. The group difference on the CECS anxiety subscale is likely to be an artefact, because repressors score low on anxiety scales by definition. Hence, the authors conclude that suppression and repression are different constructs.

In conclusion, whereas Wegner and colleagues (1987) define thought suppression quite clearly as a conscious mechanism, the definition of repression is more problematic. Freud's work has given rise to various interpretations. Thus, repression can be considered to be the same as suppression, to refer to unconscious banishing of information, to include both conscious and unconscious mechanisms, to be a specific reaction to traumatic events, or to be a broader defense mechanism. If repression is defined in terms of an unconscious defense mechanism resulting in complete forgetting of traumatic events, this concept becomes problematic from a scientific stance, and is to be distinguished from the thought suppression paradigm as introduced by Wegner and colleagues (1987). Freud formulated his ideas about repression long before present-day scientific standards (e.g., falsifiability) were applied to psychological knowledge. Unlike the unconscious banning of complete memories, the operationalization of repression as a broad tendency to pay as little attention as possible to threatening (i.e., self-esteem endangering) information is susceptible to scientific study. Indeed, several studies have delivered results suggesting that some individuals habitually and apparently successfully repress unpleasant information by shifting their attention to pleasant thoughts. One study published to date, addressing the overlap between this kind of repression and suppression, seems to indicate that these concepts are quite different from each other.

Dissociation

Repression is often mentioned in one breath with dissociation (Singer, 1990). Like repression, dissociation is a concept that can be defined in various ways. In its broadest meaning, dissociation refers to the disconnection of processes that are usually associated. For example, smiling when one is actually furious represents a dissociation between affect and behavior. This everyday manifestation of dissociation enables us to function in a socially acceptable fashion. Indeed, on many occasions it may be quite desirable to inhibit one's true emotions temporarily. Gershuny and Thayer define dissociation as "some kind of divided or parallel access to awareness in which two or more mental processes or contents are not associated or integrated, and awareness of one's emotions or thoughts are diminished and avoided" (1999, p. 637). Dissociative phenomena can become inflated to the extent that clinical borders are passed. The DSM-IV-TR contains a complete chapter devoted to dissociative disorders. In that chapter, four dissociative syndromes are described. First and foremost, dissociative amnesia is defined as a loss of autobiographical memory that is too substantial to reflect ordinary forgetfulness. Second, dissociative fugue refers to finding oneself in an unfamiliar place, far away from home, without recalling how one got there. Third, dissociative identity disorder, formerly known as multiple personality disorder, is a syndrome in which the patient believes that other people live inside his or her body. Consequently, the patient has to share his body with these alter egos. Lastly, the depersonalization disorder is characterized by feelings of being detached from one's own body or mind. Structurally, DSM-IV-TR also includes a category of dissociative disorders not otherwise specified. Dissociation can also be found elsewhere in the DSM. For example, the description of posttraumatic stress disorder (PTSD) contains symptoms like "inability to recall an important aspect of the trauma," and "feelings of detachment or estrangement" (APA, 2000, p. 468).

Generally, the DSM is strictly descriptive; that is, it contains global diagnostic criteria but is reluctant to refer to possible etiologies of the described syndromes. PTSD is an exception to this rule because people suffering from this anxiety disorder were by definition exposed to a traumatic event "that involved actual or threatened death or serious injury, or a threat to the physical integrity of self or others" (APA, 2000, p. 467). As to the dissociative disorders, the DSM also hints that trauma may cause, or at least inflate, symptoms of dissociative identity disorder. Such symptoms are said to "reemerge during episodes of stress or trauma" (APA, 2000, p. 528). Even if the references to trauma as a cause of dissociation are scarce in the DSM, the clinical literature is soaked with the idea that trauma causes dissociation (Joseph, 1999; Gershuny & Thayer, 1999). The coming paragraphs will focus on some of the problems of the assumption that trauma causes dissociation. First, dissociative identity disorder will be discussed, followed by dissociative amnesia. Next, the role of trauma in the development of dissociation in general (i.e., without reference to any specific dissociative syndrome) will be targeted.

Dissociative Identity Disorder

Some clinicians claim that dissociative identity disorder (DID) is actually the result of inflated avoidance coping (Ross, 1997). By this view, a child who is exposed to a traumatic event (e.g., abuse) may react with an attempt to block this experience. He or she may pretend that someone other than him- or herself experienced the event. In this way, the child develops an additional personality, an alter ego. This alter ego may be invoked again if new traumatic experiences occur. Alternatively, the child may develop new alter egos. The DSM-IV-TR informs us that one patient may host many alter egos: "The number of identities reported ranges from 2 to more than 100. Half of reported cases include individuals with 10 or fewer identities" (APA, 2000, p. 527). Some alter-egos are well aware of each other's existence, while others are completely ignorant of each other. In such cases, the alter egos are said to be symmetrical. Asymmetrical relations are also possible: alter ego A may be aware of the existence of alter ego B, while B is unaware of A. Alter egos may even have different names and different gender.

The general assumption is that the alter egos live through traumatic experiences to protect the mental health of the original individual. Although this may seem a fruitful defense, it has more than one flipside. For example, to ensure the mental health of the primary ego, that ego must be kept unknowing of what the additional alter egos experience. In other words, there must be at least some form of inter-identity amnesia. This unknowingness, although apparently beneficial in the short run, prevents the traumatic experience from being processed and integrated in memory and cognition. Furthermore, while this inter-identity amnesia may protect the main ego from being confronted with traumatic events, it certainly also implies that the main ego is non-active some of the time. In other words, the original ego suffers from blackouts, lost time, or if one will, dissociative amnesia. This dissociative amnesia can represent a problem. Indeed, dissociative amnesia is in itself, like DID, a reason to seek psychiatric help, according to the DSM-IV-TR. Anyway, people who believe that DID is an inflated reaction to trauma, take the concept of dissociated identity quite literally. The alter egos are construed as independent personalities, and there is at least some inter-identity amnesia. This interpretation elucidates why DID was formerly referred to as multiple personality disorder (MPD): It is believed that more than one person lives inside one body. In the latest versions of the DSM, the name MPD was replaced by DID, because, if for no other reason, MPD may cause confusion, in that it is not a personality disorder, although its name unjustly suggests so.

There are many case-reports of DID (Merckelbach, Devilly, & Rassin, 2002). Apart from clinical pictures, some recent reports included advanced imaging techniques. For example, Tsai, Condie, Wu, and Cheng (1999) discovered that a DID patient produced differential functional magnetic resonance image (fMRI) patterns depending on which alter ego was currently dominant. In a similar vein, Reinders, Nijenhuis, Paans, Korf, Willemsen, and Den Boer (2003) discovered that DID patients display differential patterns of cerebral blood flow depending on which identity is dominant. These authors did not use fMRI, but relied on positron emission tomography scans.

The diagnosis of DID is a problem. Given the inter-identity amnesia, the patient is unlikely to be aware of his alter egos and more importantly of the underlying traumatic event(s). To break this barrier, the therapist has to suggest certain symptoms, by asking questions like "Have you ever felt as if there were large gaps in your memory?," "Do people sometimes say to you that they have the impression that your personality differs with time?," "Has it ever happened to you that a stranger started talking to you, and called you by another name?," and "Is it possible that there is another side to you, that I have not yet talked to?" (Huntjens, 2003; Lilienfeld, Lynn, Kirsch, Chaves, Sarbin, Ganaway, & Powell, 1999). Once it has become clear that the patient suffers from DID, it is important to create an overview of the various alter egos. To that end, the therapist can simply call the alleged alter egos during therapy sessions. Hypnosis is thought to help all alter egos to surface. The therapy is primarily aimed at integrating the alter egos. To achieve this, the patient can be instructed to keep a diary in which different alter egos can write communications to each other. In addition, the patient may want to organize "inner board meetings," that is, mental discussions between different alter egos (Ross, 1997). Controlled studies of the efficacy of such treatments are lacking (Lilienfeld et al., 1999).

Many researchers oppose to the operationalization of DID as described previously (Merckelbach et al., 2002). They question whether DID is rooted in trauma, as well as the idea that DID is really characterized by the presence of distinct multiple personalities. Instead, they propose a sociocognitive model of DID (Lilienfeld et al., 1999). According to that model, DID is the result of an inflated difficulty to cope with daily ambiguity. We all feel somewhat ambiguous from time to time. For example, we may love and hate our work at the same time. Therapists who suspect DID, unknowingly cultivate such ambiguity by asking questions such as "Do you sometimes feel as if you were two different persons in one?" They further inflate the concept of multiple personalities by instructing the patient to give names to the alter egos, and to map the personality-structure. Whereas the efficacy of such therapies is merely supported by uncontrolled studies, methodologically similar studies also favor the exact opposite treatment. Extinction (i.e., systematic ignoring of the patient's expression of multiplicity) has been reported to be effective in reducing DID symptoms (Kohlenberg, 1973). Some authors go so far as to claim that DID is an iatrogenic disorder. This would be supported by the fact that the incidence of DID tends to increase after DID has been in the media, for example in films such as The Exorcist (Friedkin & Blatty, 1973) and Fight Club (Fincher, Palahniuk, & Uhls, 1999). In addition, whereas most psychiatric disorders are diagnosed equally often in various settings, the diagnosis and treatment of DID seems to be a prerogative of a small group of specialists (Lilienfeld et al., 1999).

The sociocognitive model emphasizes that the alter egos should not be construed as distinguishable identities, but as metaphors of the patient's ambiguities. Hence, this model predicts that inter-identity amnesia does not really exist at a level of objective measurement. The fact that DID has been documented in many case studies is not considered to be a threat by those who defend the sociocognitive model. This is also true for the seemingly convincing fMRI studies (Tsai et al., 1999). Although the differential cerebral blood flows of different alter egos may appear to prove that these alter egos are indeed distinguishable personalities, the absence of control participants prohibits that conclusion. That cannot be washed away by catchy titles such as "One brain, two selves" (Reinders et al., 2003) or one-liners such as "Now we can watch multiple personalities emerge in the brain" (Adler, 1999, p. 26). Indeed, it seems that actors who are instructed to identify with different roles also display different brain activity depending on the imagined character. Coons, Milstein, and Marley (1982) concluded over 20 years ago: "It is not as if each personality is a different individual with a different brain. Instead, to put it simply, the EEG changes reflect changes in emotional state" (p. 825).

Huntjens (2003) conducted an experiment to determine whether DID is character-ized by inter-identity amnesia. She invited 19 female patients with DID to participate in a memory experiment. The participants were instructed to memorize a list of 24 words (wordlist A). Next, an alter ego was asked to take over consciousness. This alter (B) was first asked whether she was indeed amnestic for what alter A had just experienced. If so, alter B was instructed to memorize a different list of 24 words (list B). Two hours later, alter ego B was given a recognition test. She had to recognize words from list B out of a list of 96 words. This list contained all words of list B and the words of list A (for which alter ego B claimed to be amnestic). In addition, the recognition list contained 48 new filler words. It was hypothesized that if the alter egos suffered inter-identity amnesia, alter ego B would recognize none of the list A words. The author also invited 25 healthy controls who were submitted to the same procedure, and who were instructed to simulate amnesia for list A during the recognition test. Furthermore, 25 healthy controls were instructed to recognize all words from both lists. The percentages of recognized words as a function of list are presented in Figure 2.2. First of all, as can be seen in this figure, the controls recognized virtually the same number of words from both lists. This is good, because these participants had no reason to recognize fewer words from list A than from list B. Simulants did recognize fewer words from list A than from list B, although they failed to feign complete amnesia. That is, they could not help to report recognizing 40% of the words presented in list A. A similar pattern of results was seen with the DID patients. They recognized fewer words from list A than from list B, but still recognized no less than 33% of the list A words. These findings suggest that there was no inter-identity amnesia, even though the patients felt as if their alter egos were amnestic for each other. The findings can be taken as support for the sociocognitive model of DID.

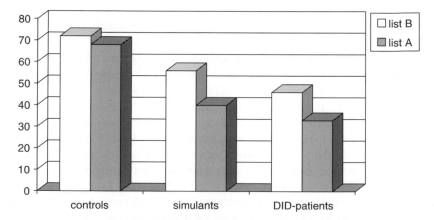

Figure 2.2: Percentages of recognized words per list. (From Huntjens, R. (2003). *Apparent amnesia: Interidentity memory functioning in dissociative identity disorder.* Academic thesis, Utrecht University.)

In sum, the original trauma theory of DID recently suffers serious competition from the sociocognitive model. The original trauma theory rests on many case reports but on virtually no controlled studies. Furthermore, there are various alternative explanations that are more parsimonious than the trauma account. Lastly, recent controlled studies are supportive of the sociocognitive model of DID, and thus in contradiction with the trauma theory, in that inter-identity amnesia (a necessary feature of the trauma theory) fails to be proven experimentally.

Dissociative Amnesia

Like DID, dissociative amnesia is claimed to emerge from trauma (Joseph, 1999). For some people, some traumatic events are just too painful to deal with. Hence, these experiences are blocked from consciousness resulting in an "inability to recall important personal information" (APA, 2000, p. 523). As mentioned previously, the DSM is reluctant to refer to possible causes of the described diagnoses. In the literature, however, various explanations of dissociative amnesia can be found. One obvious cause is suppression, or repression. If one succeeds is removing a painful recollection from memory (whether consciously or unconsciously), dissociative amnesia is the result. Another cause of dissociative amnesia is dissociation. Although this may appear to be a word game, it is not. Some authors distinguish dissociative complaints from the defense mechanism of dissociation. Unlike suppression (or repression), dissociation takes place during the traumatic experience. Whereas suppression refers to the process of trying to ban existing cognitions from consciousness, dissociation aims at preventing the experience from penetrating the psyche in the first place (Huntjens, 2003; Singer, 1990). To stipulate this, some authors speak of "peritraumatic" dissociation (Gershuny & Thayer, 1999), while suppression would be categorized as a posttraumatic cognitive operation. Thus, it is important to discriminate between suppression, repression, and dissociation. Admittedly though, while their underlying mechanisms may differ, the theoretical result (say, dissociative amnesia) is the same. Indeed, Van den Hout, Merckelbach, and Pool (1996) found that suppression as measured by the White Bear Suppression Inventory (Wegner & Zanakos, 1994) is correlated with scores on the Dissociative Experiences Scale (Bernstein & Putnam, 1986), a scale tapping various dissociative complaints.

Researchers claiming that dissociative amnesia is caused by peritraumatic dissociation generally invoke biological mechanisms to explain how this happens. Joseph (1999) argues that prolonged or repetitive trauma results in an overdose of stress hormones such as norepinephrine and, more crucially, cortisol. These hormones damage a certain brain structure called the hippocampus. More specifically, they may lead to shrinkage of dendrites and nerve cell atrophy in that brain area. The hippocampus plays a major role in consolidating new information and storing it in long-term memory. Therefore, trauma may ultimately result in an impaired ability to process ongoing traumatic events (cf. dissociation). This explanation, which is largely based on animal studies, primarily addresses amnesia after prolonged or repeated traumatization, but fails to address the occurrence of dissociative amnesia in the case of a single trauma. An alternative explanation of dissociative amnesia for repeated events can be found in a study by Van den Hout and Kindt (2003a). These authors were not at all interested in dissociation, but in compulsive checking (e.g., of gas stoves or door locks). They conducted an experiment in which participants were instructed to repeatedly check a gas stove. This task was carried out in virtual reality. It seemed that participants who checked the virtual stove more frequently had a less clear mental image of doing so. This finding illustrates that repeated actions may paradoxically fail to result in increased certainty that the action was actually carried out. Hence, while unique experiences are likely to result in specific recollections, repetition may result in a loss of such detailed memories. Something similar might apply to traumatic experiences. For example, a child who has been molested once will be able to recall the exact day and time of this incident, as well as the clothing of the perpetrator. On the other hand, if a child is molested more than 100 times, it becomes nearly impossible to maintain detailed recollections of all these molestations. One or two molestations may be completely forgotten. However, this explanation does not account for a complete dissociative amnesia for all traumatic experiences.

Brewin, Dalgleish, and Joseph (1996) propose a dual representation theory of dissociation. By this view, traumatic events are stored in a different memory system compared to everyday experiences. The latter experiences are stored in the verbally accessible memory system (VAM). Recollections that are stored here are fully integrated and accessible at will. The VAM is, so to say, the normal memory system. Traumatic experiences, on the other hand, are stored in the situationally accessible memory system (SAM). The SAM contains recollections of situations that are so threatening that the body can automatically initiate flight-or-fight responses should a similar situation occur in the future. Flipside of this automaticity is that the memories stored in the SAM are not under conscious control. Therefore, traumatic memories can intrude consciousness quite unexpectedly (cf. flashbacks). At other times, we can be completely ignorant of the content of SAM recollections (cf. dissociative amnesia).

While some authors search for possible causes of dissociative amnesia (see above), others argue that dissociative amnesia does not exist in the first place. Pope, Hudson, Bodkin, and Oliva (1998) boldly conclude that "dissociative amnesia remains unproven" (p. 214). These authors reviewed the literature on dissociative amnesia, and came to the conclusion that most studies do not live up to necessary methodological standards and thus fail to exclude all possible alternative explanations. Those studies that were of sufficient quality did not deliver support for the concept of dissociative amnesia. Some of the methodological comments of Pope and colleagues deserve attention. The authors stipulate several pitfalls of dissociation research. For one thing, it is extremely important that the researcher obtains certainty that the alleged traumatic event actually occurred. Furthermore, alternative explanations must be excluded. For example, childhood amnesia, and amnesia caused by biological factors (e.g., injury or drug intake) should not be mistaken for dissociative amnesia. In addition, as mentioned previously, ordinary forgetfulness is easily confused with dissociative amnesia. Lastly, the fact that respondents fail to report certain information should not be automatically interpreted as evidence for amnesia. Pope and colleagues cite a study in which respondents failed to report a recent visit to the doctor when asked about their medical history. This failure to report was not due to amnesia, but to the fact that the respondents did not think that the visit to the doctor was important enough to be mentioned. Another reason for non-reporting may be the respondent's reluctance to talk about sensitive personal topics. Again, this does not mean that the respondent has lost recollection of those topics.

In summary, when using strict scientific standards, some authors (Pope et al., 1998) argue that there is not enough evidence to conclude that dissociative amnesia actually exists. Interestingly, a study by Kindt and Van den Hout (2003) seems to reconcile the lack of scientific evidence for dissociative amnesia with the intuitive plausibility of this concept. The authors invited 40 undergraduates to watch a 29-minute aversive film fragment. Immediately after this film clip, participants completed several items pertaining to peritraumatic dissociation (e.g., "What was happening seemed unreal to me, like I was in a dream"). Four hours later, participants' memories of the film clip were tested, by means of cued recall and recognition tests. In addition, several meta-memory questions had to be answered (e.g., "How fluent/smooth is your recollection of the film clip?"). Interestingly, scores on the peritraumatic dissociation items did not correlate with actual memory performance. However, they did correlate with meta memory, in that stronger peritraumatic dissociation was associated with decreased perceived accuracy of memory. Thus, dissociation led to a perception of fragmentary and incomplete recollection, while in fact, the recollection was unaffected.

Trait-Dissociation

Whereas the previous paragraphs dealt with the role of trauma in the development of DID and dissociative amnesia specifically, some authors have elucidated the problematic nature of the assumption that trauma results in dissociative complaints, without specifying precisely which kinds of complaints. This line of reasoning is nicely summarized by Merckelbach and Muris (2001). First, these authors conclude that much of the research on the trauma-dissociation link rests on cross-sectional designs. Therefore, in theory, it cannot be excluded that trauma does not only lead to dissociation, but that the causation goes the other way around as well. Indeed, there is some reason to believe that certain rudimentary dissociative complaints are so common that they are unlikely to all be rooted in trauma. For example, Gershuny and Thayer (1999) conclude that approximately 80% to 90% of the people in the general population experience "some type of dissociative experience at least some of the time" (p. 637). At the same time, these authors conclude that the prevalence of traumatic experiences in the general population is quite high (estimates range from 40% to 72%), but not as high as that of dissociation. Apparently, certain dissociative experiences may not be trauma-related, but rather "a component of an individual's character" (Gershuny & Thayer, 1999, p. 639). This type of trait-dissociation is reflected in a mean score of 10 (rather than 0) on the Dissociative Experiences Scale (DES; Bernstein & Putman, 1986) in the general population (Kihlstrom, Glisky, & Angiulo, 1994). The DES consists of 28 items of which the respondent has to indicate how often they apply to him or her

(0 = *never*; 100 = *always*). The DES taps three dissociative phenomena: absorption (e.g., "Missing part of a conversation"), depersonalization (e.g., "Feeling as though one's body is not one's own"), and dissociative amnesia (e.g., "Finding unfamiliar things among one's belongings"). It has been argued that the absorption subscale addresses the more common and benign dissociative symptoms (e.g., involvement in daydreaming), while the other subscales (depersonalization and dissociative states) pertain to the clinically relevant facets of dissociation (Ross & Currie, 1991). Although in nonclinical samples the distribution of scores on the DES is strongly skewed to the right, most respondents indicate that they experience certain dissociative complaints regularly. In traumatized individuals, DES scores are strongly elevated (Gershuny & Thayer, 1999; Kihlstrom et al., 1994). Whereas such findings are commonly interpreted as supportive of the notion that trauma results in dissociation, Merckelbach and Muris (2001) argue that it may well be the other way around. By this line of reasoning, an individual who is diagnosed as suffering from dissociation often turns out to have been traumatized. However, according to these authors, it may as well be the case that an individual who is high on trait-dissociation has an inherent tendency to overendorse trauma items. In the words of Merckelbach and Muris: "One distinct possibility that should be considered is that high DES individuals display a positive response bias on retrospective self-report indices of trauma" (2001, p. 248). These authors came up with the phenomenon of "fantasy proneness" as the major reason for such overreporting of trauma. Fantasy proneness refers to the tendency to deeply involve in fantasy and imagination (Lynn & Rhue, 1988), and correlates with dissociation as measured by the DES (Kihlstrom et al., 1994). Hence, fantasy proneness, as reflected in high DES scores, may contribute to the overreporting of trauma, for example by confusing fantasies with real memories, or by tending to label ambiguous events as "traumatic." Hence, against the original trauma-dissociation model, Merckelbach and Muris (2001) place their alternative dissociation-trauma model.

Merckelbach, Horselenberg, and Schmidt (2002) stipulate the difficulty of studying the relation between trauma and dissociation longitudinally. They then argue that "in the absence of longitudinal research, the second best alternative to shed some light on the causality issue is provided by structural equation modeling performed on cross-sectional data" (Merckelbach et al., 2002, p. 697). Using this technique in a sample of 109 undergraduates, these authors compared the computational "fit" of the traditional model in which self-reported trauma (measured by the Childhood Trauma Questionnaire; CTQ; Bernstein & Fink, 1998) leads to dissociation (DES), with that of their alternative model in which dissociation leads, via fantasy proneness (measured with the Creative Experiences Questionnaire, CEQ; Merckelbach, Horselenberg, & Muris, 2001), to self-reported trauma. Their findings suggested that the data accorded equally well with the alternative dissociation-trauma model as with the traditional trauma-dissociation model. When looking at specific fit indices (e.g., the root mean square error of approximation, and the Bentler-Bonett non-normed fit index), the analyses even delivered results in favor of the alternative model.

To further explore the possible effect of existing dissociation on trauma reports, Rassin and Van Rootselaar (in press) conducted a study based on the following idea. If dissociation does (via fantasy proneness or otherwise) result in overreporting of past traumas, dissociation is also likely to have the same effect with ongoing "traumatic" or ambiguous events. Hence, individuals who score high on the DES can be expected to evaluate an ambiguous stimulus as more traumatic than do individuals with low DES scores. To test this hypothesis, 41 undergraduates completed among others the DES and the CEQ, and were subsequently shown an 8-minute fragment of the motion picture "Snatch" (Ritchie, 2000). This fragment contained several car accidents that appear realistic, but are also somewhat humorous. This fragment was chosen because of its ambiguous nature, that is, it can be perceived as traumatic, but also as comical. Lastly, the participants were asked how many traumatic scenes the film clip contained, in their opinion. It was hypothesized that individuals with higher DES and CEQ scores would report to have seen more traumatic scenes than those with lower scores on these scales. The questionnaire scores were entered as predictors in a regression analysis in which the number of perceived traumatic scenes was the predicted variable. Interestingly, DES-amnesia was indeed positively correlated with traumatic scenes frequency ($\beta = .46$, $P < .01$). However, DES-absorption ($\beta = -.45$, $P < .01$), DES-depersonalization ($\beta = -.35$, $P < .05$), and CEQ ($\beta = -.44$, $P < .01$) were negatively correlated with the number of perceived traumatic scenes. In short, these findings support the notion that some manifestations of dissociation (i.e., dissociative amnesia) foster overreporting of trauma, but fantasy proneness was not found to be the vehicle behind this overreporting. In addition, other dissociative phenomena (absorption and depersonalization) seemed to serve as protectors against overreporting of trauma.

To summarize, there is some reason to argue that not all dissociative phenomena are rooted in trauma, and more importantly, that trauma reports in turn may be affected by dissociative experiences. The most important clinical implication of this is that it may not be that wise to search for traumatic events in the past of dissociation patients. Whereas a discovered trauma may well serve as a reassuring reason for ongoing complaints, it is important to recognize the risk of implanting pseudo-memories of traumas, with all its adverse consequences. Furthermore, there is growing evidence for the notion that dissociation may not necessarily be caused by trauma.

Conclusion

Suppression is associated with repression and dissociation. Like suppression, repression and dissociation aim at banning information from consciousness. However, there are also fundamental differences between these three phenomena. Whereas suppression is quite clearly defined as a conscious attempt not to think of a specific target, repression is less clearly defined. In the literature, it has been defined rather diversely. Repression can refer to suppression, but also to the successful voluntary "forgetting" of complete autobiographical recollections, whether conscious or unconscious. It has also been defined as a habitual ignoring of ego-threatening information. Apart from the differential definitions, suppression and repression seem to differ in their efficacy. Ultimately, both defences turn out to be ineffective: Suppression results in a thought rebound, and repression leads to neurotic complaints. In the shorter run however, suppression is again ineffective, but repression is fruitful. For example, in Freud's vision, traumatic memories can be repressed for some time. Likewise, contemporary research on the repressive coping style has delivered findings suggesting that repressors are indeed able to ignore threatening information.

As to dissociation, this term can refer to both a defense mechanism and a psychiatric complaint. The defense mechanism consists of a shutting out of traumatic information during the traumatic event. Whereas suppression and repression are post hoc defenses, dissociation is a peritraumatic reaction. The psychiatric complaint dissociation has several manifestations that all share some form of amnesia. Confusion may occur at this point because the psychiatric complaint dissociation can be caused by the defense mechanism dissociation, but also by posttraumatic reactions such as repression.

Chapter 3

Measuring Intrusions and Suppression

Boundaries of the Original White Bear Study

As mentioned previously, the original thought suppression study of Wegner and colleagues (1987) has been replicated many times. Indeed, it has initiated a complete literature, and can thus be termed a classic study. Recently, Wegner and Schneider (2003) were invited by the journal *Psychological Inquiry* to write an article about their 1987 article. In that "meta article," they modestly and humorously describe some characteristics of classic psychological articles. Although these characteristics are said to pertain to classics in general, it is quite clear that they also characterize the study by Wegner and colleagues (1987) in particular. According to Wegner and Schneider, a classic study first of all needs to be somewhat counterintuitive or even uncomforting. In this case, the idea that people are not even able to suppress a futile white bear thought for a few minutes served that requirement. In addition, simplicity is a requisite. The rationale and method of a classic study can be explained in no more than a few sentences. More importantly, the authors acknowledge that most classic studies lack characteristics that should be part of good research. The original white bear study, for example, lacked theoretical underpinning. Wegner introduced the theory not before 1994. Another omission is that an adequate control condition is not prioritized in classics. The point can also be made without control groups.

Wegner and Schneider (2003) fail to give a critique that touches the validity of the whole thought suppression paradigm. That is, thought suppression studies typically rely on self-reports, and self-reports are susceptible to numerous biases. For example, participants' incapacity to monitor and simultaneously report target thoughts may result in an underestimation of intrusion frequency. Likewise, a tendency to respond in a socially desirable manner may contaminate self-report data (Schwarz, 1999). The fact that target thought frequency is a self-report variable is an important topic in the discussion about the validity of the thought suppression paradigm.

Measurement of Target Thought Frequency

Given the hypothesis that suppression paradoxically leads to more intrusive thoughts, these thoughts construe the main dependent variable in suppression research. The occurrence of intrusive thoughts has been measured in different ways, across suppression studies. Wegner and colleagues (1987) described three possible measures. First, participants can be instructed to speak out every thought they have. The verbalized thought stream is audio taped, so that the tape can be scanned for the target word afterward. A possible disadvantage of this technique is that our thoughts may sometimes run too fast to keep up the verbalization, especially if we think non-verbally (e.g., in visual images). Also, the experience of highly personal thoughts might hinder a complete stream of thoughts verbalization. Wegner and colleagues' (1987) second technique is the verbalization of target thoughts alone. Third, instead of verbally mentioning every target thought, participants can be instructed to ring a bell upon every occurrence. Alternatively, participants might press a button, or put tally marks. Trinder and Salkovskis (1994) sent their participants home with pencil and paper to tally target thoughts for 4 days (cf. a diary method). These methods share the notion that the target thought is monitored prospectively, generally using an external device (a bell, button, or pencil and paper) to count its occurrence. It can be argued that such a device might serve as a retrieval cue for the target thought. By this line of reasoning, seeing the bell, button, or pencil will remind the participant of the target thought, and thus, artificially increases its frequency (Merckelbach, Muris, Van den Hout, & De Jong, 1991). However, this effect can also be expected in the control condition, and thus it does not necessarily inflate the paradoxical effect of thought suppression.

In an attempt to avoid hypervigilance for the target thought, prior monitoring instructions can be omitted in favor of retrospective frequency estimations. It seems plausible though, that these estimates are less accurate than actual counting. It may be more difficult to reconstruct the precise number of target thoughts in hindsight, than it is to count the target thought. Furthermore, it may be hard to distinguish discrete target thoughts from each other. For example, a participant who is instructed to think of a white bear for 5 minutes may mentally rehearse the words white bear for 300 times. Alternatively, he may fantasize about a polar bear continually. In the first scenario, he will report 300 thoughts, while in the second, he will only have had one white bear thought. However, in both cases, he thinks of a white bear during the full 5 minutes. Distinguishing thoughts is sometimes difficult, not only when retrospectively estimating thought frequency, but also during actual counting (Purdon & Clark, 2000). Therefore, it has been advocated to ask participants to indicate the amount of time that was consumed by target thoughts during the pertaining experimental period (Clark, Winton, & Thynn, 1993). When framed as "time spent thinking about the target" (possible answer format: 0 = *none at all*; 100 = *all the time*), the dependent variable appears more robust, and thus better protected against unreliability, compared to target thought frequency.

Unreliability of Self-Reports

Whether counted or retrospectively estimated, thought frequency remains by definition a self-reported variable, as does time spent thinking about the target thought.

Therefore, it can be argued that the validity of this variable is questionable. That is to say that participants may not report the actual number of target thoughts accurately, because they are unable to do so, or unwilling (cf. experimental demand or social desirability effects). Indeed, there are many examples of unreliabilities of self-reports. Schwarz (1999) composed a nice review of such unreliabilities. In one of his typical studies, respondents were asked to indicate on a 11-point scale how successful they were in life (Schwarz, Knäuper, Hippler, Noelle-Neuman, & Clark, 1991). Some of the respondents were given an 11-point scale ranging from 0 (*not at all successful*) to 10 (*extremely successful*), while others were presented with anchors −5 (*not at all successful*) and 5 (*extremely successful*). Among other things, the authors found that when given the 0 through 10 scale, 13% of the respondents scored below 5, and thus indicated that they were not very successful. Interestingly, this percentage was significantly higher in the condition with the anchors −5 and 5, that is 34%. Apparently, people are more reluctant to evaluate themselves with a lower score when using a unilateral scale (0 to 10), than when using a bilateral scale (i.e., −5 to 5).

In another study, Schwarz, Strack, and Mai (1991) examined the effect of question order on the derived answers. Respondents were asked how satisfied they were with their lives in general and with their marriage in particular. The correlation between the two satisfaction judgments was .32. However, in another condition, in which the order of questions was reversed (i.e., first satisfaction with marriage and subsequently with life in general), the correlation increased to .67. According to the authors, this finding might be explained with an assimilation effect. That is, when judging their life satisfaction, respondents who had already judged their marital satisfaction incorporated that judgment into their life satisfaction judgment. In a third condition, participants were prompted that they would be asked two questions about satisfaction, one about general life satisfaction and one about marital satisfaction. This prior information decreased the correlation between the items to .18. Apparently, the warning in advance made respondents reluctant to carry over their judgments to one another.

As a last example, Strack, Schwarz, and Gschneidinger (1985) asked their participants how happy they were, on a scale from 1 to 11. Before answering this question, participants were instructed, depending on which condition they were in, to recall three past positive life events, three recent positive life events, three past negative life events, or three recent negative life events. Happiness scores were 7.5, 8.9, 8.5, and 7.1, respectively. Hence, activation of recent positive as well as past negative events increased happiness scores. The recent positive events might have had such an effect because of mood congruency (cf. assimilation effect), while past negative events may have produced higher happiness ratings through a contrast effect: Recalling unhappy past events may lead one to conclude that at present things are better than before.

In conclusion, there is ample evidence to suggest that self-reports may be flawed due to framing, order, or congruency effects. Possible causes of unreliability discussed here can easily be expanded with for example, social desirability tendencies, unwillingness to reply truthfully, or deficient recollections. Hence, the threat of unreliability is far from imaginary when working with self-report data.

Flipsides of Non–Self-Reports

Just because self-reports are susceptible to unreliability does not mean that researchers should continually strive to collect non–self-report data. One important reason to work with self-reports is that they are in some cases the only possible variables. It could be argued that this is true for thought suppression studies, in which the ultimate variable is the number of experienced intrusions. Intrusions cannot be made visible other than by means of self-reports, although some researchers have come close to non–self-report alternatives, as will be discussed later. McNally (2001) points out a division in contemporary cognitive psychology between researches who rely on self-reports and those who do not. This author breaks a lance for self-report variables. First, he concludes that it is easy for researchers who use variables that are not completely under conscious control (e.g., reaction time in Stroop, 1935, tasks), to criticize self-reports. But then, McNally argues that self-reports are sometimes the only way of gathering information about a psychological phenomenon. For example, if one is interested in the level of depression in a patient, the only way to find out is by asking. Non–self-report measures (e.g., cortisol or serotonin levels) are, in this case, at best no more than indirect. McNally goes even further and argues that self-reports are inevitable in any psychological study, even in experiments conducted by researchers who claim to solely rely on non–self-report measurements. Consider that the validity of an experiment in which reaction time during a computerized test is compared between anxiety patients and normal controls completely depends on self-reports, because the formation of samples is based on self-reported anxiety levels. In McNally's words: "Likewise, certain phenomena, such as obsessions, have no outward manifestations other than that revealed in language. Even PET studies of OCD patients require one to confirm that the person is, indeed, obsessing in the scanner" (2001, p. 520). Hence, a first flipside of non–self-report measures is that their applicability is somewhat restricted, compared to self-reports. For many psychologically relevant phenomena, self-reports are simply the only outward manifestation. As Schwarz puts it: "Self-reports are a primary source of data in psychology and the social sciences" (1999, p. 93). In those instances in which self-reports are the sole possible variables, the discussion about their validity is less fruitful.

A second flipside of non–self-reports is that the attractiveness of hard data can be blinding to researchers. Benschop and Draaisma (2000) provide an example of this with their analysis of scientific progress made by Wundt in the late nineteenth century. Wundt and his coworkers sought to find objective quantifications of the concept of mind. To that end, they developed stopwatches with which they could measure reaction times in normal participants. Although they proceeded very successfully, it can be argued that the Wundtian laboratory got out of hand for at least two reasons. First, after a while, the participants had to be trained to such an extent that they no longer could be seen as "normal" participants. Second, the precision of the stopwatches created by Wundt and coworkers was so great that the scale of these stopwatches became too fine to measure reaction times. That is, the stopwatches reached a precision of tenths of milliseconds, a finesse that was even not custom in beta sciences, by which Wundt was inspired. Given this extreme precision, reaction times by

Wundt's participants (which ranged at the level of milliseconds) went off scale. This illustrates that it is possible to become too focused on hard data, and thus to lose perspective of the relevant research questions. By this line of reasoning, it might be argued that the contemporary search for neurological correlates of behavior lacks theoretical underpinning and practical relevance. For example, one may wonder what the previously mentioned uncontrolled studies by Tsai and colleagues (1999) and Reinders and colleagues (2003) on neural correlates of DID really add.

Reliability of Self-Reports in Thought Suppression Research

Discussing the inadequacy of self-reports is a grateful exercise. Analyses of false memories, lack of insight, and lies are generally received with much interest. However, it is important to acknowledge that most human communications travel by means of self-reports, and there is reason to argue that in the majority of cases, self-reports are reliable. Indeed, there are also some experimental data to suggest that self-reports are sometimes more reliable that might be expected. For example, Wright, Gaskell, and O'Muircheartaigh (1997) conducted a study on the claimed confounding effect of item order in memory research. These authors were interested in flashbulb memories, that is, the phenomenon that people maintain detailed recollections of the time and place that they learned about an event of major societal impact. For example, relatively many people still remember where they were when they first heard about the 9–11 twin tower plane crashes. Flashbulb memories are somewhat extraordinary, because in general, recollection of the source of information is not prioritized. In flashbulb memory research, respondents are asked how well they remember the context of the information acquisition, how important they felt that the event was, and how emotional they were when hearing the news. In theory, the order of these questions may be of influence to the given answers. For example, if a respondent remembers the context quite well, he may be tempted to conclude that, at that time, he must have felt that the news was very important and emotion eliciting. To test whether item order affects the answers, Wright and colleagues (1997) asked 4289 British respondents about how they first heard that Margaret Thatcher (a former prime minister) had announced her resignation. Different respondents were asked the three crucial questions (pertaining to clarity of recollection, perceived importance of event, and emotional reaction) in different orders. Contrary to what might be expected, the item order did not influence the mean scores on the questions. Hence, these findings indicate that in some cases, self-reports seem to be resistant to feared confounders.

Studies pertaining to the validity of self-reports relevant to thought suppression research are scarce. Nelson-Gray, Herbert, Herbert, Farmer, Badawi, and Lin (1990) compared the accuracy of counting and retrospectively estimating frequency of target words in a word list. These authors found that counting leads to more accurate frequency reports than estimating, although both methods yielded fairly accurate results. Similar findings were reported by Frederiksen, Epstein, and Kosevski (1975), and Hasher and Zacks (1984). Clearly, these findings do not pertain to thought frequency, because there is no way of establishing the actual frequency of a target thought.

However, some indirect empirical evidence for the validity of self-reported thought frequency comes from a study by Rassin, Merckelbach, Muris, and Spaan (1999). These authors were interested in the possibility of inducing a negative evaluation of a neutral thought in healthy participants, by fooling them into believing that that thought might have external and negative consequences. To achieve this, participants (45 high school students) were connected to a bogus electroencephalography (EEG) apparatus that was introduced as a measurement of specific thoughts. Participants in the control condition were given the following written instructions: "During the next 15 minutes you should try to relax and sit quietly. As you may know, the process of thinking is accompanied by electrical activity in the brain. Therefore, it is possible to read thoughts by monitoring the electrical activity in the brain and we have an EEG apparatus, which is very good in this respect. In this study, we want to document that our equipment is sensitive enough to 'read' simple thoughts. Two electrodes will be placed on your head. You may think of anything, for example the word 'apple.' " Participants in the experimental condition were instructed as follows: "During the next 15 minutes you should try to relax and sit quietly. As you may know, the process of thinking is accompanied by electrical activity in the brain. Therefore, it is possible to read thoughts by monitoring the electrical activity in the brain and we have an EEG apparatus, which is very good in this respect. In this study, we want to document that our equipment is sensitive enough to 'read' simple thoughts like 'apple.' Two electrodes will be placed on your head. This study is combined with another one. You should know that each time you think of 'apple,' the apparatus will pick up the thought and send a signal to the adjacent room where it is transformed into an electrical shock applied to the other participant you just met. He is participating in an experiment in which he is exposed to unpredictable shocks. The shocks do not cause any damage, of course, but are unpleasant. Note that the system does not function perfectly. That is, on some occasions, it may be that your thought of 'apple' is not followed by an electrical shock. Finally, if you feel uncomfortable because the other participant receives a shock, you may interrupt the signal by pressing the button in front of you within 2 seconds after the word 'apple' has surfaced in your stream of consciousness. Note that you are not obligated to do so. Also, you are not obligated to think of 'apple.' "

Before experimental participants received these instructions, they had met the second participant, who was in fact a coworker. After they had read the instructions, two bogus electrodes were attached to the participants' forehead. During the 15 minutes that followed, the number of times that the "signal-interrupting" button was pressed was monitored. Of course, no EEG activity was recorded and no shocks were administered. After these 15 minutes, participants had to answer several questions, one of which was how many thoughts of apple had occurred. Participants in the control group reported three thoughts, while those in the experimental group reported 12 apple thoughts ($P < .01$). The number of "signal-interrupting" button presses was five, suggesting that participants had pressed this button less than half the time. Given that there seems to be no plausible reason for participants to overreport the number of target thoughts, in this setup, it can be concluded that the number of button presses (a behavioral measure modeling a compulsion aimed at preventing unwanted negative outcomes) validates the occurrence of at least half of the reported thoughts. Notably, the correlation between button presses and thoughts was .94 ($P < .01$).

In a more direct test of the validity of self-reported thought frequency in suppression studies, Rassin (2004) adapted the design of Nelson-Gray and colleagues (1990). Participants were shown two film fragments containing conversations. It was decided to use word "fuck" as target, because this word is commonly used, but at the same time considered by most people to be somewhat inappropriate, making it suitable as a model of an unwanted thought. After having seen the first fragment, participants had to estimate the number of times that the target word had occurred. Before seeing the second fragment, participants were instructed to count the target word. Hence, accuracy of retrospective estimation, and counting could be compared. However, half of the participants were given suppression instructions, before both fragments. To illustrate, part of these instructions before the second fragment was: "...You must try to ignore, suppress that word. However, if you do happen to notice that word, in spite of your suppression attempts, you must use the pencil and paper to tally every time you hear the word fuck." Analysis of the manipulation check indicated that suppression participants had, indeed, attempted to not pay attention to the target word. The estimated and counted target word frequencies are displayed in Figure 3.1. As can be seen in this figure, counting resulted in accurate frequencies (8), while estimation led to an overreporting (240% in the control group, and 129% in the suppression group). These results suggest that counting yields more accurate frequencies than does estimating. Furthermore, there seems to be no reason to assume that suppression instructions compromise the accuracy of self-reports. If anything, the opposite seems more likely.

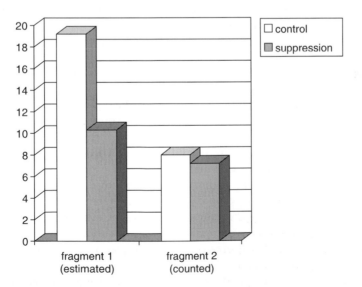

Figure 3.1: Reported frequencies of the target word (actual frequency = 8). (From Rassin, E. (2004). Snatching thoughts: The validity of self-reported thought frequency in thought suppression experiments. Unpublished manuscript.)

A few final words regarding the idea that self-report measures are possibly contaminated by unwillingness to report accurately about certain topics are in line. The argument of biased self-reports is easy for researchers who have an overview of the data. However, the viewpoint of the individual participant is far narrower. Imagine a participant who is susceptible to experimental demand, and, thus, tends to answer questions in a way that he thinks the experimenter wants him to do. Such a participant, first of all, has to see through the experimental design, and has to understand the underlying hypothesis. This may be quite hard for undergraduate students who have no specific expertise in the phenomena at hand. Next, the willing participant needs to have a reasonable idea about which answer is desired. For example, if one wants to please the experimenter, by reporting to have experienced only a few target thoughts, how much is a few (e.g., zero, two, or ten)? Lastly, the fact that the bulk of suppression studies have delivered data suggesting that suppression increases thought frequency contradicts the experimental demand idea, because that idea should predict that suppression instructions dictate susceptible participants to report fewer instead of more intrusive thoughts.

To summarize, there is little reason to doubt the validity of self-reported thought frequency. First, only a few studies have addressed the accuracy of estimated and counted target frequencies. Results from those studies suggest that counting yields most accurate results, although estimations are, generally, also fairly accurate. Second, the sole study pertaining to accuracy in a suppression setup indicated that suppression instructions do not compromise self-report accuracy. Third, the hypothesis of invalid self-reports intuitively predicts effects that are opposite to those generally obtained in suppression studies. Lastly, even if self-reports were inaccurate, it has to be acknowledged that certain phenomena inevitably depend on self-reports, regardless of the possible psychometric deficiencies.

Non–Self-Report Measurements in Thought Suppression Research

In the previous paragraph, several arguments have been postulated to defend the use and validity of self-reported thought frequency in suppression studies. One major point is that intrusion frequency (i.e., the most important dependent variable in thought suppression research) is by definition a self-report variable. However, the strength of the thought suppression paradigm would benefit further if suppression were found to have effects other than that on self-reported thought frequency. Such effects would indicate that suppression also influences variables that are not susceptible to the flaws that threaten the validity of self-reports. Indeed, several researchers have succeeded in this area. This paragraph will discuss some of the studies suggesting that the paradoxical effect of suppression can be proven to exist other than by means of self-reported thought frequency.

As a first example, Wegner and Erber (1992) invited participants to engage in a word association task. Some participants were instructed to suppress certain words (e.g., house) before and during the association task Other participants were instructed to concentrate on these target words. Of course, some of the words in the association assignment were related to the target (e.g., home). Word associations had to be made either within 10 (i.e., low cognitive load) or 3 (high cognitive load) seconds. When comparing suppression and concentration data for the low load stimuli, concentration seemed to result in more target word responses to target-related prompts than did suppression. However, under high cognitive load, suppression participants responded more often with the target than did concentration participants. This suggests that suppression was somewhat successful under low cognitive load, but failed completely under high load. Hence, these findings indicate that the paradoxical effect of suppression actually manifests as a cognitive hyperaccessibility, not just as a self-reported target thought increase.

Lane and Wegner (1995) applied the suppression paradigm to the domain of secrecy. Participants in this study (95 undergraduates) had to complete a Stroop (1935) task. In this task, the participant is presented with a list of words, printed in different colors. The task entails that the participant has to name the color of the ink as fast as possible. It seems that the word content tends to interfere with this task. For example, if the word "red" is printed in yellow, people find it harder to respond with "yellow," compared to when the word content is, for example, "Monday." Interfering word content results in increased response times. The interference of word content has been used as a measure of attention capacity in neuropsychological studies. However, the word content can also relate to personally relevant issues. Lane and Wegner (1995) instructed participants to keep some words (e.g., mountain) secret from the experimenter. In a subsequent Stroop test, as expected, reaction time increased with these target words relative to nontargets. According to the authors, these findings indicate that suppression of a target word increases the significance, hyperaccessibility, and interference of that word. Using a modified Stroop test, Wegner and Erber (1992) obtained similar findings in their second experiment. In this experiment, participants had to press one of two keys on a keyboard depending on whether the stimulus word presented to them was printed in blue or red. Before this test, some participants had been instructed to suppress certain words (e.g., house), while others were instructed to remain concentrated on them during the Stroop test. Cognitive load was manipulated by instructing participants to continually rehearse a one-digit number (low cognitive load) or a nine-digit number (high load). Participants were subsequently shown 64 words, some of which were the target words or related to these targets (e.g., home). Under low load, suppression participants were faster in their naming of the colors in which the words were presented than were the concentration participants. However, in the high load condition, suppression participants were significantly slower than concentration participants. Again, this suggests that under high load, suppression of certain words, paradoxically made these words more accessible resulting in increased interference with the related naming task.

Wegner, Shortt, Blake, and Page (1990) asked participants to suppress and express four different thoughts, namely one exciting thought (sex) and three less exciting ones

Table 3.1   Target Thought Frequencies

	Sex	Dancing	Mother	Dean
Suppression	3.2	3.9	3.5	2.6
Expression	5.6	9.0	6.2	3.9

From Wegner, D.M., Shortt, J.W., Blake, A.W., & Page, M.S. (1990). The suppression of exciting thoughts. *Journal of Personality and Social Psychology, 58*, 409–418.

(dancing, participants' mother, and the faculty dean). Suppression and expression periods lasted 3 minutes each (the order was counterbalanced). The self-reported (i.e., counted) target thought frequencies are shown in Table 3.1.

The data presented in Table 3.1 suggest that suppression was, once again, incomplete, although significant paradoxical effects were absent. Furthermore, the pattern of exciting thoughts (sex) did not deviate from the other three thoughts. However, Wegner and colleagues (1990) also measured skin conductance levels during the experimental periods. Data from these measurements suggested that sex thoughts (whether suppressed or expressed) made participants sweat more, compared to baseline, than the other thoughts. The skin conductance level data are displayed in Figure 3.2. The results obtained in this study suggest that either participants underreported the number of sex thoughts, which made them sweat more, or, assuming that the thought occurrences were reported accurately, suppression of exciting thoughts had more physiological flipsides than did the suppression of the less laden thoughts. Either way, suppression of exciting thoughts seemed to be associated with increased levels of skin conductance.

Skin conductance was also used as a dependent variable in two studies by Wegner, Broome, and Blumberg (1997). In their first study, participants were either instructed to relax (i.e., suppress all tension and anxiety) or received no such instruction. Participants were briefly instructed how they could relax by using progressive relaxation (i.e., the subsequent relaxation of different muscle groups). As in previous studies, cognitive load was manipulated by rehearsing one- (low load) versus nine-digit numbers (high load). Under low load, relaxation actually resulted in decreased skin conductance compared to the no instruction control condition. Under high load, relaxation yielded higher skin conductance levels than no instruction control. However, this difference was not significant ($P = .25$). In their second experiment, Wegner and colleagues made two alterations. That is, first, cognitive load was no longer manipulated by means of number rehearsing, but by means of answering several questions. In the high load condition, these items were introduced as an IQ test. In the low load condition, they were presented as some irrelevant items to kill time with. The second adjustment was that participants were no longer trained in progressive relaxation, but were merely given relaxation instructions. In this second experiment the increase of skin conductance under high cognitive load and relaxation attempts, compared to no instruction control, did reach significance ($P < .05$).

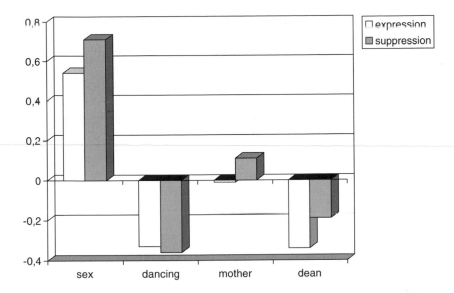

Figure 3.2: Changes in skin conductance levels (μ mhos) compared to baseline. (From Wegner, D.M., Shortt, J.W., Blake, A.W., & Page, M.S. (1990). The suppression of exciting thoughts. *Journal of Personality and Social Psychology, 58,* 409-418. American Psychological Association. Reprinted with permission.)

Ansfield, Wegner, and Bowser (1996) took relaxation one step further in that they were interested in the efficacy of attempts to fall asleep. Eighty-three participants were asked to monitor their sleep onset latency at a specific night. Some of these participants were instructed to fall asleep as quickly as possible, while others were given no such instruction. In addition, some participants were given recordings of sleep-inhibiting marching music, while others received a tape with sleep-conducive music. It was hypothesized that participants who were trying to fall asleep while listening to the arousing music would take longest to actually fall asleep. As predicted, the authors found that efforts to fall asleep paradoxically resulted in a delayed sleep onset, compared to not trying to fall asleep – especially under conditions of high load (i.e., marching music). Apparently, the paradoxical effect of suppression can also be translated into a trying-to-sleep-is-counterproductive effect. However, in the study by Ansfield and colleagues (1996), participants themselves had to report at what time they had fallen asleep the previous night. A self-reporting variable, after all.

A further example of paradoxical suppression effects other than increases in self-reported thought frequency can be found in an article by Cioffi and Holloway (1993), who exposed their participants to a pain tolerance procedure. Participants had to keep their nondominant hand in a container with ice-water for as long as possible, while either distracting themselves from the pain by thinking of their home, while paying close attention to any pain sensation in their hand, or while suppressing pain-related thoughts and sensations. Meanwhile, participants were repeatedly asked to indicate the amount of experienced pain. Also, skin conductance levels and heart rate were measured. Participants who suppressed pain reported more pain in the 2 minutes after the cold pressor task than did participants in the other groups. Furthermore, during the cold pressor task, suppression participants had higher levels of skin conductance than other participants. After the task, participants were told that they were to engage in a second pain tolerance procedure (which was, in fact, not true). Upon this communication, heart rate acceleration was stronger in the suppression group than in the other groups. In short, suppression seemed to have some paradoxical effects when it comes to pain perception, not only as indexed by self-reports, but also at a physiological level.

Petrie, Booth, and Pennebaker (1998) obtained results suggesting that suppression might even affect the immune system. Sixty-five undergraduate students were randomly assigned to one of four conditions. All participants had to write about a specific topic for 15 minutes, on 3 consecutive days. Half of the sample was instructed to write about an emotional and personally relevant issue, while the other half had to write about what they had done in the previous 24 hours, in a descriptive, non-emotional way. In addition, half of the participants had to suppress any thoughts about what they had written for 5 minutes immediately after the three writing assignments. Given these two independent variables, four conditions were formed: emotional writing, emotional writing with suppression, neutral writing, and neutral writing with suppression. Analyses of obtained blood samples indicated that the number of T lymphocytes was higher in the emotional writing group than in the other groups. In other words, writing about an emotional topic resulted in an increase of T lymphocytes, unless writing was followed by suppression. It seems that suppression inhibited the beneficial effects of emotional expression.

Macrae, Bodenhausen, Milne, and Jetten (1994) found evidence to suggest that the paradoxical effect of suppression can reflect on overt behavior. Participants in the study of these authors were shown a picture of a male skinhead, and were invited to described what, according to them, a typical day in the life of this skinhead looks like. Half of the participants were instructed to avoid (i.e., suppress) stereotyped ideas about skinheads, while completing this task. The other half received no suppression instructions. After this task, participants were guided into an adjacent room in which eight chairs were positioned. The first seat was evidently taken by the skinhead, because his belongings were in it (i.e., a jacket and bag). Participants were asked to take a seat and wait for the skinhead, who had apparently gone to the bathroom, to return, after which a short social conversation was to take place. Analysis of the transcriptions revealed that suppression participants, indeed, used fewer stereotyped expressions in their narratives than did controls (5.6 vs. 6.8; $P < .05$). Interestingly, however, suppression participants seemed to take more physical distance from the skinhead than did controls, judging from the chair they chose to sit in, after the experimental task. Control participants left, on average, 4.4 chairs between themselves and the skinhead's belongings, while suppression participants left 5.3 chairs in between ($P < .05$).

In summary, although intrusion frequency, the major dependent variable in suppression research is by definition a self-report variable, several researchers have succeeded in detecting paradoxical effects of suppression other than expressed in intrusion frequency. Hence, such research adds to the notion that the paradoxical effect of thought suppression cannot be interpreted as a self-report artefact.

The Measurement of Thought Suppression

Apart from the measurement of target thoughts or other dependent variables, the act of suppression itself has to be quantified as well. In the original study by Wegner and colleagues (1987), such measurement was omitted, but other authors have stressed the importance of measuring actual suppression attempts (Purdon, 1999). For one thing, the respondents have to be asked to what extent they engaged in suppression, as a way to check whether the experimental manipulation (i.e., the suppression instruction) has succeeded. Generally, the extent of actual suppression attempts is indicated on a visual analogue scale (VAS), ranging from 0 (*not at all*) to 100 (*to a very large extent*). If suppression participants fail to comply with the suppression instruction, non-significant differences in intrusion frequency are possibly caused by this noncompliance. Not only is it possible that suppression instructions are not carried out, but in some cases it may also be the case that participants in the control condition spontaneously engage in suppression attempts. This may be especially so if the target thought is of adverse nature (e.g., a personally relevant distressing thought). For example, Rassin (2001a) sought to induce stress in participants by instructing them to fill in the name of a person close to them in the sentence "I hope... will soon be in a car accident." Next, half of the participants were instructed to suppress any thoughts about this sentence, while the other half were forbidden to suppress thoughts related to this sentence. Participants in the suppression condition scored on average 48.0 on the suppression effort VAS, while those in the non-suppression condition scored 27.7. Although the difference was statistically significant, it is noteworthy that participants who had been forbidden to suppress, engaged in suppression to some extent nonetheless. Apparently, the stress-inducing manipulation had resulted in a natural suppression tendency. In extreme cases, high levels of suppression in the control condition can result in failure of the experimental manipulation, in that the extent of suppression attempts is no longer significantly different between the suppression and control condition.

Although suppression attempts are generally measured by means of self-reports, two recent studies took quite a different angle to quantify thought suppression attempts. Wyland, Kelly, Macrae, Gordon, and Heatherton (2003) asked 12 healthy volunteers to suppress a personally relevant thought (e.g., thoughts about an examination), to suppress all of their thoughts (i.e., to think of nothing), or to think of whatever they wanted, in different orders. While carrying out these instructions, fMRIs of the participants' brains were obtained. As it turned out, suppression was associated with activation of the anterior cingulate. Although the authors stipulate the importance of their findings, because "understanding the brain mechanisms that support the capacity to control mental contents may provide insights into the nature of various psychological disorders that are characterized by the recurrence of unwanted and intrusive thoughts" (Wyland et al., 2003, p. 1866), some comments are in line. For one thing, the authors start their article with the assumption that "a fundamental human capacity is the ability to regulate and control our thoughts and behaviors" (2003, p. 1863). Given the numerous studies indicating that thought suppression is far from perfect, this assumption can be questioned. More importantly, Wyland and colleagues failed to collect self-reports about the actual suppression efforts of their participants. Thus, there is no guarantee that the observed cerebral activation actually reflects suppression attempts. For all we know, it might as well indicate the occurrence of intrusive thoughts. Apparently, neither the authors nor the editors of the high impact journal in which this study was published thought much of these comments. Anderson, Ochsner, Kuhl, Copper, Robertson, Gabrieli, Glover, and Gabrieli (2004) used a different experimental setup. These authors first instructed their participants to memorize a number of word pairs. Next, they instructed them to mention the paired word when prompted with the other word. For other word pairs however, the instruction was that they should suppress the recollection of the associated word when confronted with the first word. Hence, some word pairs were strengthened while others were suppressed. During these cognitive operations, fMRI was performed. It seemed that the act of suppressing had various effects on the recollection of the word pairs. In some cases, suppression of the previously learned association resulted in a paradoxical subsequent better recollection (up to 8% increase compared with control items). In other cases, suppression indeed weakened the learned association (up to 32% inhibition of the association). More importantly, analyses of the brain images suggested that the act of suppression was associated with an increased activation of the anterior cingulate, and parts of the prefrontal cortex. In addition, suppression was associated with a decrease in hippocampus activity. The authors are not modest when it comes to the interpretation of their findings. They believe that their "findings provide the first neurobiological model of the voluntary form of repression proposed by Freud, a model that integrates this otherwise controversial proposal with widely accepted and fundamental mechanisms for controlling behavior" (Anderson et al., 2004, p. 235).

Conclusion

The central topic in this chapter is the validity of the variables generally used in thought suppression studies. Given that the most frequently used variables are self-reports (i.e., the number of experienced intrusions), it must be acknowledged that these variables are susceptible to self-report biases. By this line of reasoning, the results of thought suppression studies might be accounted for by self-report artefacts. The following can be concluded with respect to this concern. Regarding the measurement of target thought frequency, the few studies conducted in this area have yielded results suggesting that counting instructions before the experimental period deliver the most accurate reports, although retrospective estimation seems to yield fairly accurate results as well. The mere fact that this measure is a self-report does not invalidate the obtained results, for several reasons. First, considering that some phenomena are not measurable by other means than self-report, it is unfruitful to discard self-report measures. Second, it is unlikely that the paradoxical effect of thought suppression is the result of a self-report bias, because it can be expected that such a bias would render results in the opposite direction (i.e., suppression participants would be likely to report fewer target thoughts). Third, as mentioned previously, research has indicated that self-reports can be accurate, and that suppression instructions do not compromise accuracy. Fourth, several suppression studies have used non–self-report variables, and succeeded in finding paradoxical effects, so there is reason to believe that the effects that spring from thought suppression studies are not limited to (and therefore not caused by) self-report measurements. In short, there are strong indications to suggest that the paradoxical effect is not a self-report artefact, but a real and robust phenomenon.

In addition to the number of intrusions, the independent variable (i.e., the actual suppression efforts) has to measured as well. Although Wegner and colleagues (1987) omitted this manipulation check, others have emphasized the importance thereof. Not only has to be verified that suppression instructions were carried out sufficiently, it also has to be excluded that control participants engaged in spontaneous or natural suppression. Although some recent studies have shown that the act of suppression can actually be detected with fMRI, suppression efforts are generally measured with self-report scales.

Chapter 4

Possible Research Artefacts

Introduction

In the previous chapters, several methodological comments on thought suppression research have been discussed. In this chapter, the importance of the precise wording of the control instructions will be discussed. In addition, the thought suppression paradigm will be compared with other paradigms. Interestingly, while the general message of the thought suppression paradigm is that people are unable to block target thoughts from consciousness at will, other paradigms have delivered results suggesting that blocking or forgetting specific information is achievable after all.

Wording of the Control Instructions

The design of the original study by Wegner and colleagues (1987) included two groups of participants. The first group was instructed to suppress white bear thoughts for 5 minutes, first, and to think about white bears afterward. In the other group, these instructions were reversed (i.e., first thinking of white bears, and subsequently suppressing white bear thoughts). This design, together with the reported frequency of white bear thoughts is displayed in Table 4.1. From this table, it can be concluded that suppression attempts were not very successful, because, during the suppression period, participants could not prevent themselves from thinking approximately seven times of white bears. Furthermore, the number of white bear thoughts during the thinking period, was higher when participants had previously suppressed (22.1), than without previous suppression (16.4). Hence, the term rebound effect.

Table 4.1 Self-Reported Target Thought Frequency

	Period 1	Period 2
Initial suppression group	6.3 (during suppression)	22.1 (during thinking)
Initial thinking group	16.4 (during thinking)	7.3 (during suppression)

From Wegner, D.M., Schneider, D.J., Carter, S.R., & White, T.L. (1987). Paradoxical effects of thought suppression. *Journal of Personality and Social Psychology*, *53*, 5–13.

A close look at the study by Wegner and colleagues (1987) reveals a remarkable aspect. That is, the exact wording of the instructions for the control period was "try to think of a white bear for 5 minutes" (Wegner et al., 1987, p. 7). This instruction invites participants to think of white bears, and hence this control procedure has been referred to as a thinking or expression condition. However, the reason for this framing of the control instruction is not completely clear. The precise content of the instruction in the control condition or control period is an important topic in the discussion about the validity of the thought suppression paradigm.

By using expression instructions in their control condition, Wegner and colleagues (1987) limited the external validity of their findings in three ways. First, on face validity, it seems unlikely that people who are plagued by unwanted thoughts interchange suppression periods with periods of purposely having unwanted thoughts. More likely, a period of experiencing and suppressing unwanted thoughts is followed by a calmer period in which few unwanted thoughts come to mind, and hence, there is little reason for suppression (Purdon & Clark, 2000). In fact, Wegner (1989) himself seems to argue that suppression periods are followed not by expression periods, but by periods during which the thought is not actively suppressed (in these periods, thought rebounds occur). He refers to this combination of suppression and suppression-free periods as indulgence cycles. Hence, it could be argued that in suppression experiments a more liberal instruction (e.g., "you can think of white bears or anything else") is more ecologically valid. Strictly speaking, white bear thoughts that pop into consciousness during an expression period should not be referred to as intrusions, because they are not unwanted, but, contrarily, deliberately produced.

Second, from a research stance, the design by Wegner and colleagues (1987) does not permit conclusions about the immediate effect of suppression. Admittedly, the fact that participants reported to have thought seven times of white bears in spite of suppression attempts, suggests that suppression is ineffective. However, the lack of a neutral control period prohibits more quantitative conclusions. Such conclusions would require a design in which intrusion frequency during suppression is compared with frequency during a suppression-free period. A possible instruction for such a suppression-free period could be "you might think of a white bear, but you don't have to" (see Merckelbach et al., 1991). In a number of later studies, a liberal suppression-free control period was included. This inclusion yields the opportunity to compare intrusion frequency between suppression and liberal periods in a between-subjects design. It is sometimes argued that, compared to baseline (i.e., thought frequency during a liberal period, without prior suppression attempts), suppression leads to an immediate enhancement of target thought frequency (Salkovskis & Campbell, 1994). However, in their meta-analysis, Abramowitz and colleagues (2001) found no evidence for such an initial enhancement effect. In summary, it is safe to conclude that suppression is ineffective in the short run, and even has a paradoxical rebound effect in the longer run, but there is only limited evidence to conclude that suppression instructions immediately increase the intrusion frequency.

A third flipside of expression instructions is the theoretical possibility that these instructions, when following suppression instructions, might inflate the rebound effect compared to liberal instructions. Merckelbach and colleagues (1991) copied the experimental design from Wegner and colleagues (1987), with the exception that the expression instruction was replaced by a liberal instruction ("you might think of a white bear, but you don't have to", p. 229). Table 4.2 shows the number of white bear thoughts in the study by Merckelbach and colleagues (1991). As can be seen in this table, there was no rebound effect. The number of white bear thoughts during the liberal period was not significantly higher when following suppression (10.1), compared to without prior suppression (7.4). Therefore, Merckelbach and colleagues (1991) concluded that the rebound effect of suppression might be an artefact of the expression instruction (Liberman & Förster, 2000).

In a more direct test of the influence of the wording of control instructions, Rassin, Muris, Jong, and De Bruin (2005) compared the effects of expression versus liberal control instructions in a between and a within subjects design. In a first experiment, participants ($N = 60$) were asked to suppress the thought of a white bear for 5 minutes, to think as much as possible about white bears, or to think of anything they wanted. On average, participants in the suppression condition reported to have thought of white bears 6.7 times, those in the expression condition had 20.3 target thoughts, and those in the liberal condition reported 8.8 white bear thoughts. Analysis of variance indicated that expression participants reported more target thoughts than those in the other two groups, while suppression and liberal participants did not differ from each other in the number of white bear thoughts. In a second experiment, four conditions were included. In the suppression-expression condition, participants were first instructed not to think of white bears for 5 minutes, and subsequently to think as much as possible about white bears for 5 minutes. In the expression-suppression condition, these instructions were reversed. In the suppression-liberal condition, the first period was spent suppressing white bear thoughts, but during the second period, participants were free to think of anything they wanted. Finally, in the liberal-suppression condition, these instructions were given in reversed order. Figure 4.1 presents the mean intrusion frequencies for conditions in which expression instructions were given (either during the first or second period). Figure 4.2 presents the numbers for the liberal conditions. From these figures it can be concluded that expression instructions produced much more pronounced results that did liberal instructions. Thus, these findings support the notion that expression following suppression tends to increase (or even to cause) the rebound effect. Notwithstanding these findings, Abramowitz and colleagues (2001) argue that, when looking at the suppression literature as a whole, the

Table 4.2   Self-Reported Target Thought Frequency

	Period 1	Period 2
Initial suppression group	9.9 (during suppression)	10.1 (liberal period)
Initial liberal period group	7.4 (liberal period)	6.7 (during suppression)

From Merckelbach, H., Muris, P., Van den Hout, M., & De Jong, P. (1991). Rebound effects of thought suppression: Instruction dependent? *Behavioural Psychotherapy*, *19*, 225–238.

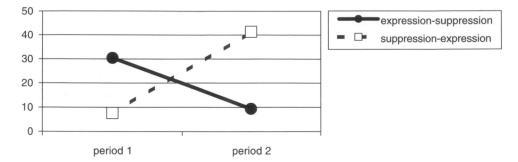

Figure 4.1: White bear thought frequency in the expression conditions. (From Rassin, E., Muris, P., Jong, J., & De Bruin, G. (2005) Summoning white bears or letting them free: The influence of the content of control instructions on target thought frequency. *Journal of Psychopathology and Behavioral Assessment*, *27*, 253–258. With kind permission of Springer Science and Business Media.)

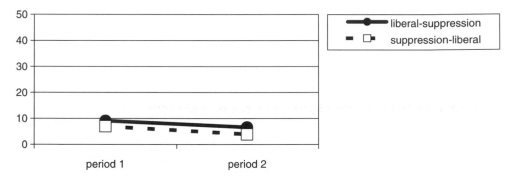

Figure 4.2: White bear thought frequency in the liberal conditions. (From Rassin, E., Muris, P., Jong, J., & De Bruin, G. (2005) Summoning white bears or letting them free: The influence of the content of control instructions on target thought frequency. *Journal of Psychopathology and Behavioral Assessment*, *27*, 253–258. With kind permission of Springer Science and Business Media.)

occurrence of a rebound effect is not limited to studies in which expression instructions are used. Several researchers did succeed in observing a rebound effect, while using liberal instructions (Clark et al., 1991; Clark, Winton, & Thynn , 1993).

While the expression instruction has raised the concern of rebound inflation, one might also worry about finding no results in an experiment because participants not only complied with suppression instructions, but also engaged in suppression spontaneously during the control period. As mentioned previously, this might be the case when the target is an aversive stimulus, promoting natural suppression tendencies in participants (Purdon, 1999). For example, if participants are to suppress a personally relevant unwanted thought, during period 1, they might also suppress that thought during period 2 (the control period), thereby hindering the rebound effect. To prevent this from happening, instructions during the control period should contain an "anti-suppression" statement. Such an instruction was used by Rassin (2001a), who wanted to study the effect of suppressing an obsessive fantasy about a dear person being in a car accident. The control instruction in that study was: "During the next 5 minutes you should sit quietly. You are allowed to think of anything. If any thoughts of the accident come to mind, you might be tempted to try to suppress them (for example by shifting your attention to another subject). However, you should try not to do that. It is important that you do not suppress thoughts about the accident, if any. If thoughts about the accident do come to mind, you should just let them run free." Interestingly, in spite of this suppression prohibition, participants reported to have engaged in suppression to a considerable extent (i.e., 27 on a scale from 0 [*not at all*] to 100 [*very strongly*]).

In short, the content of the control instructions is important in suppression studies, because participants' mental activity during control periods affect the eventual outcome. For example, expression following suppression has been argued to inflate the rebound effect, while suppression during control periods might decrease the rebound effect. Liberal instructions, possibly including a suppression prohibition, seem to be most preferable, because they enable the researcher to compare suppression effects with baseline measurements, and because they are ecologically most valid.

Competing Paradigms

Apart from the fact that critical comments can be made with regard to the methodology of thought suppression studies (e.g., pertaining to instruction content), it has to be recognized that there are a few competing paradigms that address the banishing of specific thoughts from consciousness. It is important to compare the thought suppression paradigm with these competing paradigms with respect to methodology. This is especially so, because these competing paradigms have delivered more optimistic results when it comes to the question whether people are able to ban thoughts at will.

Directed Forgetting

The directed forgetting paradigm seems to be in competition with the thought suppression paradigm, because, in directed forgetting, conscious attempts to forget target words are at stake. However, in contrast with the results of suppression studies, directed forgetting researchers regularly claim to have found results suggesting that people are able to forget target thoughts at will. In a typical directed forgetting experiment, the participant is shown a list of, say, 20 words under the instruction to memorize them. After exposure to this list, the experimenter declares that all this was just practice, and that the participant no longer has to remember the words presented during this test trial. The actual test begins thereafter, with a new list of 20 to-be-remembered words. If participants in this kind of study are asked to recall all presented words, including those in the first list (i.e., the forget list), the forget words are remembered less well than those in the second list (i.e., the remember list). Apart from this within subjects analysis, the percentage of eventually remembered words in the first list can also be compared with the number of remembered first list words by participants who do not receive forget instructions after the first list. Positive results obtained with this paradigm have been interpreted as supportive of the idea that people are able to forget target thoughts at will (Myers, Brewin, & Power, 1998). Hence, the directed forgetting paradigm seems to be in contradiction with the thought suppression paradigm.

The success of directed forgetting depends on several factors. One possible confounding factor is the way in which participants encode the presented words. Words can be encoded thoroughly, in an elaborative manner, or more shallowly, by means of rehearsing, just so that they are remembered for a short while. Encoding style may interact with the type of forget instruction. In the experimental setup described previously, the forget instruction is global. That is, a complete list of words is to be forgotten. Alternatively, an instruction may be distinctive, in the sense that after every individual word, the forget or remember instruction for this particular word is given. The latter method fosters shallow encoding, because the participant will be reluctant to elaborate a target word if there is a 50–50 chance that a few seconds later, a forget instruction will be received. Encoding style may bias the eventual results, because impaired recall of forget-words may not be attributable to forgetting (as it should be), but rather to incomplete encoding in the first place. A third factor determining the efficacy of directed forgetting is the employed dependent variable. It seems that most positive results are obtained when using recall. Recognition tests often fail to produce a directed forgetting effect. Similarly, studies using more implicit measures, such as word completion tasks and association tasks, generally fail to find positive results (for an overview of the factors discussed here, see Johnson, 1994).

As to comparison between directed forgetting and thought suppression, several methodological differences are evident. For example, whereas in thought suppression a single and often discrete thought (e.g., white bear) is the target, in directed forgetting, a complete list of words is targeted. Hence, directed forgetting tends to be a memory paradigm, while thought suppression is more directed at mental control. Indeed, the crucial dependent variable in thought suppression is intrusion frequency, while that in directed forgetting is memory. Another important characteristic of directed forgetting is that recall accuracy of forget-words is compared with that of remember-words. This is reminiscent of a suppression setup in which suppression is compared with expression, but not with liberal instructions. Employing a forget versus remember setup eliminates the possibility of comparing forget instructions with a more liberal instruction such as "you may think of the words in this list, but you don't have to." In other words, the control procedure (i.e., remembering the second word list) may be the opposite of the forget procedure, instead of a neutral control. Hence, the effects observed in directed forgetting experiments may be inflated compared to a setup in which forgetting is compared with "think of whatever you want."

The fact that directed forgetting participants are not only instructed to forget a set of words, but also have to remember another, constitutes a further important difference with suppression studies. In directed forgetting, the participant is given a strong and powerful distracter (i.e., remembering the second word list), while in suppression studies, no such distracter is provided, generally. The consequence of this is that, in suppression setups, individuals attend to a large array of environmental stimuli that become retrieval cues of the to-be-suppressed thought. Interestingly, Wegner and colleagues (1987) noted that the rebound effect of suppression does not occur when participants are given instructions to focus on one single, outstanding distracter (e.g., red Volkswagen) whenever the to-be-suppressed thought comes to mind. This suggests that distracters may, indeed, play a vital role in whether or not suppression produces a preoccupation with the target material. It seems plausible that strong distracters really interfere with the suppressed targets, while weak distracters do not, and may be experienced as retrieval cues, or even as mere cognitive load enhancers, reducing suppression efficacy.

Another methodological difference, possibly accounting for the different findings in suppression and directed forgetting studies, is that in the latter paradigm, the target is trivialized. That is to say that the forget-list is presented as a practice task that precedes the real memory task. For example, Myers and colleagues (1998, p. 143) instructed their participants as follows: "What you have done so far has been practice. You can forget about those words. I will now show you the actual set of test words...". Yet, in a suppression experiment, the instruction might have been more like: "I want you not to think about the words I have just shown you." These instructions communicate quite different actions. In directed forgetting, participants are allowed to ignore the targets, while they should concentrate on words presented in a subsequent remember-list. By contrast, in suppression studies, the target thought is made outstanding by the simple act of presenting it as the to-be-suppressed target, while no distracter is provided.

To date, only one published study has investigated a possible reason for the apparently contradictory findings of the paradigms. Whetstone and Cross (1998) hypothesized that the differential effects may be caused by the fact that suppression participants are instructed to report intrusions of the target thought, while directed forgetting participants are not. Hence, unlike in directed forgetting, in thought suppression procedures, the monitoring process described by Wegner (1994) is activated. This monitoring of target thought intrusions is one of the theoretical causes of the paradoxical effect found in suppression research. To test whether the reporting of intrusions is, indeed, a crucial difference between both paradigms, Whetstone and Cross (1998) came up with the following experiment. Sixty-four participants underwent a directed forgetting procedure, with four conditions. One condition was an original forget-list, remember-list procedure with ten words in each list. The second condition used the same lists, but the forget instruction after the first list was omitted here. Conditions three and four were similar to one and two, respectively, with the addition that participants had to report every thought of the first list during the presentation of the second list. The results of the experiment are displayed in Table 4.3. As can be seen, the recall of words presented in list 2 was slightly better than that of words in list 1, in all conditions. In the standard forgetting condition, list 1 recall was worse than that in the remember condition. Hence, a directed forgetting effect occurred. Interestingly, in the forget with report of intrusions condition, no effect was observed. This suggests that focusing on intrusions is indeed a crucial factor explaining the failure of suppression.

Table 4.3 Percentages Recalled Words

		List 1	List 2
Intrusions not reported	Remember	30.0	39.4
	Forget	17.5	54.4
Intrusions reported	Remember	30.0	38.1
	Forget	31.9	41.8

From Whetstone, T. & Cross, M.D. (1998). Control of conscious content in directed forgetting and thought suppression. Available at: http://psyche.cs.monash.edu.au/v4/psyche-4-16-whetstone.html.

In short, the technical differences between directed forgetting and thought suppression paradigms are likely to account for the conflicting results that these two research lines have generated. Meanwhile, the question arises which paradigm is more ecologically valid as a model for real life obsessive intrusions. It is intuitively plausible to argue that thought suppression has more everyday equivalents than does directed forgetting. It is noteworthy that patients with obsessive-compulsive disorder (OCD) are inadequate directed forgetters. For example, Wilhelm, McNally, Bear, and Florin (1996) found the well-known directed forgetting effect in a standard directed forgetting experiment relying on 24 healthy volunteers. However, the same procedure did not yield such an effect when used with 36 OCD patients. Apparently, OCD patients did not forget the words that they no longer had to remember. Similar findings were reported by Tolin, Hamlin, and Foa (2002). These authors not only recruited OCD patients and non-anxious controls, but also a sample of non-OCD anxiety patients. The results of their experiment suggested that, in all samples, remember-words were remembered better than forget-words, during free recall. However, in a subsequent recognition test, this effect disappeared in the OCD group, but not in the two control groups. Again, it seemed that OCD patients did not forget target words even though they were allowed to do so. This effect seemed to be especially strong with words related to their own obsessions. These findings are reminiscent of those reported by Radomsky and Rachman (1999) who concluded that OCD patients are very alert when it comes to their obsessions, and therefore have a memory bias toward threat-relevant information.

Retrieval-Induced Forgetting

Recently, an article by Anderson and Green (2001) attracted much attention, because it was claimed that it contained, for the first time, solid experimental evidence for the concept of Freudian repression. By and large, the pertinent experiment had the following setup. Undergraduate students ($N = 32$) had to memorize 40 pairs of words that are not intrinsically related (e.g., "ordeal-roach"). Once participants proved to have learned at least 50% of the pairs, in that they were able to recall one word of the pair when prompted with the other, the experiment commenced. The word pairs were divided into "think" and "no-think" pairs. In a large number of trials (approximately 400), one word was presented for 4 seconds on a computer screen. In response to some words, participants had to speak out the associated words. In response to others, participants had to not speak out the associated word, and even had to suppress the thought of that word. Which words had to be responded to, and which had to elicit suppression, was explained beforehand. A further variable was the number of times that words were presented. Presentation frequency varied between 0 and 16 times. After this experimental procedure, participants were asked to recall all words. This was done through presentation of the associated word (e.g., ordeal), but also by using description that had not been used previously in the experiment (e.g., "Do you remember any words referring to insects?"). Overall, the results indicated that words that had been previously suppressed were less often recalled than those in the speak-out condition. This effect occurred not only when prompted with the counter word, but also when prompted with a neutral description. Furthermore, financial reward for every recalled word did not eliminate the effect. The strength of this inhibiting effect was positively correlated with the number of trials.

These findings suggest that, compared to suppressing, active recalling stimulates later memory performance. However, the ultimate recall of suppressed words was not only worse than that of rehearsed words, but also compared to words that had been presented zero times during the procedure. Hence, suppression seemed to decline memory even when compared to control words, rather than remember words. Notwithstanding, in this "think/no-think" paradigm, suppression instructions were combined with remember instructions. Therefore, it cannot be excluded that the suppression attempts were not intrinsically motivated ("I really want to suppress this bothering thought"), but might have been received as a relief ("Thank God, one less instruction to recall a target word"). Furthermore, the remember word pairs likely constituted strong distracters. Indeed, given the limited capacity of human memory, recalling some memories, by definition, interferes with the recollection of others, hence the term "retrieval induced forgetting" (Anderson & Green, 2001). Another difference with the thought suppression paradigm is the duration of suppression. Originally, paradoxical suppression effects are obtained after minutes of suppression. In the Anderson and Green (2001) study, suppression lasted only 4 seconds.

In short, again, the diverging results can be explained by means of differences in the experimental setup. And again, the question arises whether the ecological validity of the think/no-think paradigm matches that of the thought suppression paradigm. Anderson and Green (2001) do not seem to be interested in the technical specifics of their and others' paradigms, and boldly conclude that their "findings thus support a suppression mechanism that pushes unwanted memories out of awareness, as posited by Freud" (p. 368). Likewise, in his comment on the Anderson and Green study, Conway (2001) declares to be convinced that Freud was right after all: "What was needed was a way to investigate memory repression in the laboratory, and Anderson and Green provide just that," and: "This is an important result, which lends support to Freud's original definition of repression: it unambiguously shows the existence of consciously initiated, executive inhibition of memory" (p. 319). These expressions may be somewhat premature, given that the results might also be interpreted, more parsimoniously, as supportive of normal forgetting due to competition.

Conclusion

Like any other paradigm, the thought suppression paradigm is susceptible to methodological critiques. In this chapter, two of such criticisms have been addressed. First, it is important to recognize the power of the instructions given to the control participants. Even though the meta-analysis by Abramowitz and colleagues (2001) yielded results suggesting that the rebound effect of suppression does not depend on the presence of expression instructions, it must be kept in mind that, compared to liberal instructions, such expression instructions may inflate the rebound effect. Hence, there is reason to argue that liberal instructions seem to be preferable, if for no other reason, because they are ecologically most valid.

Second, there are several other paradigms that address the human capacity to ban thoughts from consciousness. Interestingly, whereas the literature on thought suppression suggests that it is nearly impossible to ban thoughts from consciousness, these other paradigms have yielded more positive results. For example, in directed forgetting setups, participants are quite able to forget lists of words on command. However, it must be emphasized that the differences in obtained results between paradigms are most likely due to methodological differences. In effect, directed forgetting is not about banning thoughts from consciousness, but about forgetting while being presented with a strong distracter.

Although between-paradigm differences in methodology may be interesting for academics, they are not quite obvious to lay people. As mentioned previously, many people believe in the possibility of successful suppression, especially suppression of traumatic memories. Crombag and Van Koppen (1994) demonstrated that, in a sample of 268 healthy volunteers, 68% believed in the idea that people are capable of suppressing unpleasant memories. No less than 38% of the participants even believed that they themselves might have been the victim of traumatic events (e.g., abuse or war), even though they had no recollection of such events due to suppression. Apparently, the belief in the human capacity to banish recollections from consciousness, which is based on the old Freudian idea of repression, is strongly rooted. One can speculate about the reasons for this. Perhaps the strength of this idea lies in the face validity of the underlying "common sense" notion that people must be able to forget or at least ignore certain threatening information to function properly. In addition, from time to time, the academic community unleashes "evidence" for processes that are reminiscent of the mechanism of Freudian repression (e.g., Anderson & Green, 2001; Anderson et al., 2004). Unfortunately, lay people are likely to remember the overall conclusion of scientific works (e.g., "This is an important result, which lends support to Freud's original definition of repression," Conway, 2001, p. 319), while they forget, or even disregard, the methodological specifics, that place these conclusions in the right perspective.

Chapter 5

Individual Differences and Successful Suppression

From Experimental Phenomenon to Extra-Laboratory Tendency

In the previous chapters, thought suppression has been discussed as if it were a transient phenomenon, discovered in the laboratory. The obvious clinical implication of the thought suppression paradigm is that it is unwise and even counterproductive to suppress unwanted thoughts. Wegner and Zanakos (1994) argued that the clinical relevance of the paradigm is further reaching, if we consider that some individuals might be prone to habitually engage in suppression attempts if confronted with unwanted thoughts or impulses. Given the experimental findings, such suppression-prone individuals may chronically suffer from the paradoxical effect of suppression. Therefore, chronic suppressors may be at higher risk of developing clinical syndromes in which intrusive thoughts are crucial features (e.g., obsessive-compulsive disorder [OCD]) than are people who rely on thought suppression less often. The idea of chronic suppression adds to the paradigm, because it implies that suppression is not only a strategy that can be induced in experiments, but also a general tendency that can be measured reliably. To test the idea that some people are more likely to engage in suppression than others, Wegner and Zanakos (1994) developed a questionnaire that pretends to measure chronic suppression tendencies. They started with a 72-item self-report that was completed by 735 undergraduate students. After various factor analyses, several factors were discovered (e.g., concentration, negative affectivity), one of which pertained to thought suppression. Ultimately, this thought suppression factor, which contained 15 items, was developed into a thought suppression inventory. Subsequent factor analysis confirmed that this scale had a one-factor structure, explaining 55% of the observed variance. The authors appropriately named this questionnaire the "White Bear Suppression Inventory" (WBSI). The WBSI consists of 15 items that are answered on a 5-point scale (1 = *strongly disagree*; 5 = *strongly agree*). The WBSI items are displayed in Table 5.1.

Wegner and Zanakos (1994) tested the psychometric qualities of the WBSI thoroughly, and concluded that the scale is reliable and valid. Firstly, they asked 162 respondents to complete the WBSI three times. The interval between T1 and T2 varied between 3 weeks and 3 months. The T2-T3 interval was 1 week for all respondents. Test-retest correlations between T1 and T2 were .69, between T2 and T3 .92, and between T1 and T3 .69. These findings led Wegner and Zanakos to speculate about

Table 5.1   The Items of the White Bear Suppression Inventory

1. There are things I prefer not to think about
2. Sometimes I wonder why I have the thoughts I do
3. I have thoughts that I cannot stop
4. There are images that come to mind that I cannot erase
5. My thoughts frequently return to one idea
6. I wish I could stop thinking of certain things
7. Sometimes my mind races so fast I wish I could stop it
8. I always try to put problems out of mind
9. There are thoughts that keep jumping into my head
10. Sometimes I stay busy just to keep thoughts from intruding my mind
11. There are things that I try not to think about
12. Sometimes I really wish I could stop thinking
13. I often do things to distract myself from my thoughts
14. I have thoughts that I try to avoid
15. There are many thoughts that I have that I don't tell anyone

From Wegner, D.M. & Zanakos, S. (1994). Chronic thought suppression. *Journal of Personality, 62*, 615–640.

a trait-like quality. In their words: "These data indicate that self-reports of thought suppression are reliable over time and thus fulfill an important criterion for recognition as a trait" (Wegner & Zanakos, 1994, p. 624). In addition, scores on the WBSI correlated with scores on a scale measuring obsessive complaints (the Maudsley Obsessional-Compulsive Inventory, MOCI; Hodgson & Rachman, 1977). More specifically, thought suppression was found to be associated with obsessive symptoms, but less so with compulsions. These correlations can be interpreted as supportive of the WBSI's validity, because, in theory, individuals who suppress often, will suffer more paradoxical increases of unwanted thoughts, and will, thus, score high on self-reports measuring intrusion-related psychopathological complaints (e.g., obsession). However, the WBSI also correlated with scores on scales measuring depression (Beck Depression Inventory, BDI; Beck, Rush, Shaw, & Emery, 1979), and anxiety (State-Trait Anxiety Inventory, STAI; Spielberger, 1983). It should be noted that these latter correlations are not expected given the theoretical account between suppression and intrusion, because depression and anxiety are not typical intrusion-based symptoms. In fact, the association between the WBSI on the one hand, and the BDI and STAI on the other may even be interpreted as indicative of a lack of specificity of the WBSI. Thus, these correlations may weaken the WBSI's (divergent) validity.

Muris, Merckelbach, and Horselenberg (1996) translated the WBSI into Dutch, and reported positive results regarding the reliability and validity of their version. For instance, in a sample of undergraduate students ($N = 172$), WBSI scores seemed to be stable with time (in this case, a 12-week interval): Test-retest correlation being .80. Again, WBSI scores were found to correlate with scores on scales measuring obsessive problems (e.g., MOCI). However, the WBSI also correlated with scales tapping non intrusion related problems, such as the BDI ($r = .54$) and the STAI ($r = .57$). Thought suppression tendencies were also found to correlate with worrying, as measured by the Student Worry Scale (SWS; Davey, 1993). In a subsequent experimental study, Muris and colleagues investigated whether scores on the WBSI predict the number of intrusions experienced in a thought suppression set-up. Forty undergraduates completed the WBSI, and were subsequently exposed to a thought suppression procedure. Participants first had to suppress a previously identified disturbing personally relevant thought for 5 minutes, and then underwent a suppression-free control period. Participants scoring low on the WBSI reported to experience 2.9 intrusions during suppression attempts, and 1.9 during the subsequent control period. For high WBSI scoring participants, the corresponding numbers of intrusions were 5.1 and 2.7. Thus, it seemed that high scores on the WBSI indeed predict the susceptibility to the paradoxical effect of suppression. After the experiment was concluded, participants were asked to keep a diary for 3 days, in which they were to record intrusions if any. Again, the group of participants was divided over four conditions: low WBSI scoring participants who received suppression instructions, high scoring participants with suppression instructions, and groups of low and high scorers who did not receive suppression instructions. Analysis of the diaries of all participants suggested that for most of them, the number of intrusions decreased over the 3 days, from 7.53 on day 1 to 4.3 on day 3, on average. However, high WBSI scoring participants who engaged in suppression reported an increase of intrusions from 5.7 on day 1 to 6.1 on day 3. This finding is indicative of a rebound effect. In short, the WBSI seemed to possess predictive value with respect to the susceptibility to suffer from paradoxical effects of thought suppression.

To summarize, individual differences in suppression-proneness are clinically relevant, because people who suppress unwanted thoughts on a regular basis may be at increased risk of developing intrusion-related psychiatric complaints. The work of Wegner and Zanakos (1994) indicates that suppression-proneness can be measured reliably by means of the WBSI. The importance of the WBSI lies in the fact that, although it is not the first scale addressing thought suppression, it is the first one to do so in a general manner. For example, the Impact of Event Scale (IES; Horowitz, Wilner, & Alvarez, 1979) contains several items pertaining to cognitive avoidance, but these items specifically address an experienced traumatic event. Likewise, the Defense Style Questionnaire (DSQ; see Andrews, Singh, & Bond, 1993) contains only two suppression items that do not constitute a suppression subscale, but are part of a more broadly defined mature defences subscale (also tapping humor, sublimation, and anticipation).

Doubts about the Validity of the White Bear Suppression Inventory

Although there seems to be some consensus about the validity of the WBSI, the face validity of several items appears to be questionable. Items like "I have thoughts that I cannot stop," and "There are images that come to mind that I cannot erase" seem to address the occurrence of unwanted thoughts rather than suppression attempts. Muris and colleagues (1996) argue that at least five items pertain to unwanted thoughts. Furthermore, these authors reported that their factor analysis initially indicated a four-factor structure. Relying on a fairly large sample of undergraduates ($N = 935$), Blumberg (2000) obtained a three-factor solution, suggesting that eight WBSI items pertain to the experience of intrusive thoughts, four pertain to suppression attempts, and three specifically address distraction (as a mean to suppress unwanted thoughts). Even more recently, Höping and De Jong-Meyer (2003) found that the German version of the WBSI consists of two factors, namely intrusive thoughts (nine items) and thought suppression (six items). Lastly, Rassin (2003) conducted a factor analysis in a non-clinical sample ($N = 674$), and obtained two factors: Intrusions (six items), and suppression (nine items). In addition, two similar factors were obtained in a study with 106 clinical participants (mainly patients with OCD or post-traumatic stress disorder [PTSD]). Table 5.2 summarizes the findings of Blumberg (2000), Höping and De Jong-Meyer (2003), and Rassin (2003). In this table, *I* stands for an intrusive thoughts factor, while *II* refers to a suppression factor. In the Blumberg study, *III* refers to a factor called distraction. From Table 5.2, it can be concluded that in three independent studies, the WBSI was shown to consist of at least two factors, namely a factor addressing the experience of unwanted thoughts (items 2, 3, 4, 5, and 9 loaded on this factor in all three studies), and a factor pertaining to suppression (items 1, 11, and 14 invariably loaded on this factor).

The idea that the WBSI does not only address thought suppression, but also intrusive thoughts has implications for the validity of this scale. Given that several items address the experience of intrusive thoughts, the WBSI is not a pure measure of coping style, but, in part, a measure of psychological complaints. Thus, WBSI scores not only reflect the general tendency to suppress unwanted thoughts, but also the occurrence of such thoughts (i.e., the reason to engage in suppression). This has consequences for the way in which correlations between the WBSI and questionnaires measuring psychological complaints should be interpreted. Such correlations may not necessarily reflect the theoretical path from suppression, via increased thought frequency, to more complaints. Alternatively, it may well be the case that the inclusion of intrusion items in the WBSI artificially inflates the correlation with measures of psychopathological complaints. Indeed, Höping and De Jong-Meyer (2003) found moderate and highly significant correlations between the WBSI on the one hand, and the MOCI, BDI, and STAI on the other. However, after excluding intrusion items from the WBSI, these correlations collapsed, suggesting that, in fact, there is no association between suppression per se and psychopathological complaints. Likewise, Rassin (2003) found that the WBSI intrusion factor correlated with the MOCI, while the suppression factor did not. This pattern of results was obtained in the non-clinical as well as in the clinical sample.

Given the results of these recent studies, it could be argued that the WBSI should be divided into two separate subscales. Unfortunately, some items are difficult to label as either intrusion or suppression items. For example, whereas item 9 ("There are thoughts that keep jumping into my head") is evidently an intrusion item, and item 13 ("I often do things to distract myself from my thoughts") clearly refers to suppression, item 14 ("I have thoughts that I try to avoid") simultaneously seems to refer to

Table 5.2   Results of Factor Analyses Obtained in Various Studies

	Blumberg (2000)	Höping and De Jong-Meyer (2003)	Rassin (2003)
1. There are things I prefer not to think about	II	II	II
2. Sometimes I wonder why I have the thoughts I do	I	I	I
3. I have thoughts that I cannot stop	I	I	I
4. There are images that come to mind that I cannot erase	I	I	I
5. My thoughts frequently return to one idea	I	I	I
6. I wish I could stop thinking of certain things	I	I	II
7. Sometimes my mind races so fast I wish I could stop it	I	I	II
8. I always try to put problems out of mind	II	II	I
9. There are thoughts that keep jumping into my head	I	I	I
10. Sometimes I stay busy just to keep thoughts from intruding my mind	III	II	II
11. There are things that I try not to think about	II	II	II
12. Sometimes I really wish I could stop thinking	III	I	II
13. I often do things to distract myself from my thoughts	III	II	II
14. I have thoughts that I try to avoid	II	II	II
15. There are many thoughts that I have that I don't tell anyone	I	I	II

From Blumberg, S.J. (2000). The white bear suppression inventory: Revisiting its factor structure. *Personality and Individual Differences*, *29*, 943–950; Höping, W. & De Jong-Meyer, R. (2003). Differentiating unwanted intrusive thoughts from thought suppression: What does the White Bear Suppression Inventory measure? *Personality and Individual Differences*, *34*, 1049–1055; and Rassin, E. (2003). The White Bear Suppression Inventory (WBSI) focuses on failing suppression attempts. *European Journal of Personality*, *17*, 285–298.

intrusion and suppression. Consequently, factor analyses run on different data sets yield different allocations of certain items (see Table 5.2). Alternatively, when using WBSI total scores, one must realize that the substantial number of intrusion items may well bias the WBSI toward the measurement of unsuccessful suppression. That is, WBSI scores are likely to reflect both suppression and intrusion (cf. failing suppression). As Blumberg puts it: "Low scores on the full scale have been more difficult to interpret: Are these people suppressing successfully, or are these people simply not experiencing any negative thoughts that they wish to suppress?" (2000, p. 949). Consequently, correlations between the WBSI and measures of intrusion-related complaints (e.g., MOCI) should be interpreted with caution, because they may be artificially high, and thus no true reflection of the theoretical link between suppression and intrusions.

Successful Suppression

The WBSI measures individual differences in suppression-proneness, and likely focuses on unsuccessful suppression attempts. However, there may be more individual differences relevant to the thought suppression domain. One important aspect that has been largely ignored by suppression researchers is the extent to which individuals differ in success with their suppression attempts. Although suppression, generally, seems to have a paradoxical effect, there may be individuals who are capable of suppressing unwanted thoughts. A first indication for individual differences in suppression efficacy comes from the study of Merckelbach and colleagues (1991), in which participants were instructed to suppress (or not) white bear thoughts for two subsequent 5-minute periods. These authors found that the number of target thoughts during the suppression and control period correlated significantly (r [35] $= .59$; $P < .01$). This suggests that people who suffer more intrusions during suppression also suffer a larger rebound effect. This also implies, of course, that some people suffer fewer intrusions during and after suppression. A second argument for the idea that suppression efficacy may differ individually, is that depressive mood has been found to be associated with an increase of unwanted thoughts, as well as a weakened capacity to control such thoughts (Rachman, 1997; Wenzlaff et al., 1988). Apparently, mood state determines suppression efficacy.

Rutledge, Hancock, and Rutledge (1996) exposed 153 undergraduates to a procedure in which the first 9-minute period was spent expressing white bear thoughts (baseline), the second period was filled with suppressing white bear thoughts, while the third 9-minute period was, again, spent expressing white bear thoughts. Thought rebound was defined as a score higher than 0.6 in the computation "thoughts during the final expression period divided by thoughts during both expression periods together." Using this analysis, only one third of the participants displayed a thought rebound. Rutledge and colleagues (1996) tried to identify the variables that predicted the occurrence of a thought rebound. Some of their findings are quite remarkable. First, they found that lower scores on the MOCI predicted a rebound effect. Also, anxiety was negatively correlated with thought rebound. They furthermore found that white participants suffered more from thought rebound than did black participants. These findings are striking because they suggest that obsessionality and anxiety protect against the paradoxical effect of thought suppression, while, based on theory, the precise opposite should be true. The observed racial difference remains unexplained. Nonetheless, these findings suggest that slightly obsessive and anxious

African-American participants are more successful than average at thought suppression. Interestingly, Nestadt, Samuels, Romanoski, Folstein, and McHugh (1994) found that the prevalence of OCD is lower in non-white populations than in the white population.

Rutledge, Hollenberg, and Hancock (1993) used the original design of Wegner and colleagues (1987) and failed to find a paradoxical effect. They argue that the effect observed by Wegner and colleagues may be difficult to extrapolate to the general population, because their participants constituted a highly select sample. That is to say that the Trinity University (from which Wegner and colleagues recruited their participants) demands higher American College Testing (ACT) scores than, for example, Lincoln University (Rutledge and colleagues' employer). To test this hypothesis, Rutledge and colleagues (1993) conducted a second experiment that resembled the later study by Rutledge and colleagues (1996). They classified the 84 participants into rebounders (i.e., participants who reported an increase of at least 50% of target thoughts during expression, compared to baseline) and non-rebounders. Only 19% was classified as rebounders. The two groups of participants' ACT scores were compared. As expected by Rutledge and colleagues (1993), participants who suffered from thought rebound scored higher on the ACT test, especially on the mathematics subtest. This finding is important, because it illustrates that the paradoxical effect of thought suppression is not always obtained in experimental studies. Furthermore, this result offers an explanation for this limitation, namely that the rebound effect is moderated by certain cognitive capacities. In this case, it seems that highly developed mathematic skills stimulate the occurrence of a thought rebound, and thus hinder successful suppression.

Brewin and Beaton (2002) submitted 64 volunteers to the experimental procedure by Wegner and colleagues (1987) and subsequently tested their working memory capacity, fluid intelligence, and crystallized intelligence. The authors, then, correlated the number of intrusions during suppression and expression with performance on the three tests. Interestingly, they found negative correlations between target thought frequency during suppression on the one hand, and working memory and fluid intelligence on the other. Crystallized intelligence was positively related with target thought frequency. These findings suggest that working memory capacity and fluid intelligence promote successful suppression, while crystallized intelligence may hinder it. The fact that target thought frequency during expression correlated with none of the three tests, does not affect these conclusions, because the experience of target thoughts during expression attempts is not a likely measure of unwanted intrusive thinking. It is not completely clear how these findings relate to the findings by Rutledge and colleages (1993). If the ACT mathematic test is to be construed as a measure of crystallized intelligence, both patterns of results accord well. If the mathematic test measures abstract fluid insights, the results are more difficult to reconcile. Unfortunately, Brewin and Beaton (2002) hardly comment on this, because they misinterpret the data of Rutledge and colleagues (1993) as suggesting that lower ACT scores were associated with the occurrence of a rebound effect.

Another possible factor in the discussion about successful suppression is practice. Wegner argues: "It might be that people who practice thought suppression often enough, for example, develop such skilled and automatic operating processes that they become quite capable of effective suppression and suffer few intrusions from the ironic monitoring processes" (1994, p. 48). Being successful, or at least believing to be, may be a reason for people to persevere in their suppression attempts. Unfortunately, the effect of practice on suppression efficacy has never been studied. However, some support for the beneficial effect of practice comes from the study by Petrie et al. (1998), who were interested in the consequences of writing about an emotional or neutral topic, and subsequent suppression of any thoughts about the written topic. Participants underwent three daily sessions of writing and suppression. They had to indicate how difficult they found the suppression task. It seemed that participants who wrote about emotional topics found suppression equally hard on the three consecutive occasions. However, participants who wrote about neutral topics reported to have less difficulty with suppressing target thoughts during session three, compared to the first occasion. This effect of allegedly improved suppression efficacy was, unfortunately, not significant ($P = .08$). Nonetheless, this finding is in line with the notion that suppression – at least of neutral thoughts – can be learned.

Most of the phenomena discussed previously (e.g., mood state, intelligence, practice) may contribute to the explanation of individual differences in suppression efficacy. However, a research line distant from the thought suppression paradigm addresses individual differences in successful forgetting without focusing on possible reasons for these differences. That is to say that research has indicated that some people are, as if by nature, prone to ignore personally threatening information, and seem to be quite successful therein. These so-called repressors are people who score high on scales measuring defensiveness (e.g., the SDS), and at the same time, low on anxiety scales (e.g., STAI), even though they do seem to be very physiologically reactive. Compared to average, repressors seem to be less successful in retrieving unpleasant memories, and more successful at forgetting irrelevant information. However, the latter conclusion is not based on thought suppression experiments, but on directed forgetting studies, in which participants are not just presented with a discrete stimulus (e.g., white bear), but with two lists of words. The first list of words is accompanied by the instruction to no longer think about it, while the second list is to be remembered. Sometimes, the emotional valence of the words is varied. Examples of positive words are "merry," "helpful," and "relaxed," while negative words may be "risky," "worried," and "anxious." After both lists have been presented, participants are instructed to recall as many words as possible from both lists (i.e., also from the list that was to be forgotten). Evidently, this paradigm differs from the thought suppression paradigm. Typically, results from directed forgetting studies suggest that participants remember fewer words from the to-be-forgotten list than from the to-be-remembered list. This differential recall is especially pronounced with negative words, compared to positive ones. Furthermore, the effect is more pronounced with repressors than with non-selected participants (Myers et al., 1998). Therefore, the conclusion that some people (repressors) are capable of successful suppression presents itself, although, to date, there has been no published suppression study in which participants were pre-selected repressors.

Yet another individual difference with impact on suppression efficacy may be the presence of positive cognitions about suppression. Imagine someone who is completely convinced that it is possible to suppress a specific recollection. When looking at the previously discussed study by Crombag and Van Koppen (1994), it becomes clear that many people indeed believe that such suppression is obtainable. Would such an individual be more successful at suppressing than someone who is not convinced about suppression efficacy? In addition, are the possible differences between convinced and unconvinced individuals real, or do they merely exist in the perception of the "successful" suppressors? Rassin, Van Brakel, and Diederen (2003) tried to answer the question whether positive beliefs about suppression may actually affect perceived efficacy of suppression attempts (cf. a self-fulfilling prophecy effect). Participants in their study listened to an audiotaped story, and were subsequently assigned to four conditions: a control condition, a suppression condition, a "suppression-works" condition, and a "suppression-does-not-work" condition. Apart from standard suppression instructions, participants in the suppression-works condition were given the following instruction: "In daily life, people often claim to have suppressed certain memories. Recent studies indicate that it is, indeed, possible to suppress recollections to the point that one cannot remember them. This memory undermining effect has been observed after no more than a few hours. The present study seeks to further investigate the effects of suppression on memory". Participants in the suppression-does-not-work condition received the following additional instruction: "In daily life, people often claim to have suppressed certain memories. Recent studies indicate, however, that it is impossible to suppress recollections. Moreover, if one tries to suppress a certain recollection, that recollection will come to mind more often. In fact, trying to suppress information is a very good way to remember it well. This effect of improved memory due to suppression attempts has been observed after no more than a few hours. The present study seeks to further investigate the effects of suppression on memory". Participants were sent home, and returned after 2 hours. During this second session, participants had to answer several questions pertaining to intrusion frequency, and suppression efficacy. Also, their memory of the story was tested. Analyses suggested that the instructions had not affected free recall accuracy (all groups scored approximately 30 of 79 possible details), but did have an impact on intrusion frequency and perceived efficacy of suppression attempts. That is to say that suppression-does-not-work instructions led participants to report twice as many intrusions (6) than participants in the other groups. As to perceived efficacy, participants in the suppression-works group experienced their attempts as more successful (i.e., 80 on a VAS ranging from 0 to 100), than did suppression-does-not-work participants (mean score: 60). At the end of the experiment, participants were asked, what, in their opinion, the effect of suppression generally is. This question had a multiple-choice answer format with anchors "suppression results in a decline of memory," "suppression results in an improvement of memory," or "do not know." The number of participants endorsing these answers is presented in Figure 5.1. From this figure, it can be derived that participants who had not engaged in suppression (controls) most often believed in the detrimental effects of suppression, while participants who had engaged in suppression were less likely to believe this. Most of the participants in the suppression-does-not-work condition indicated that suppression only has paradoxical effects, in this case, an improvement of recollections. All in all, the findings might best

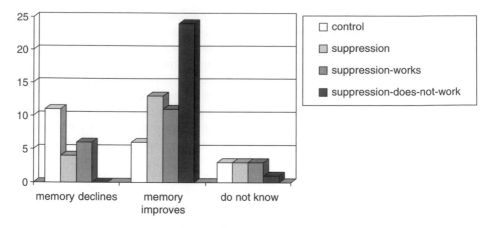

Figure 5.1: Distribution of participants endorsing answers describing expected general consequences of suppression. (From Rassin, E., Van Brakel, A., & Diederen, E. (2003). Suppressing unwanted memories: Where there is will, there is a way? *Behaviour Research and Therapy, 41*, 727–736.)

be summarized as follows. First, it seems relatively easy to make participants believe that suppression is, or is not, a fruitful strategy, that is by means of nothing more than a short written instruction. Second, participants tended to answer questions about suppression efficacy in this experiment and in general, in a manner concordant with the instructions. Third, the induced expectations did not affect memory, but did have an impact on intrusion frequency, which is in itself remarkable.

The findings by Rassin and colleagues (2003) might be considered obvious and even trivial, because it could be argued that participants merely behaved in a way they had been told to do. But if we assume that these results are not the exclusive effect of experimental demand, they indicate that prior beliefs about suppression do influence the experienced and actual (in terms of intrusion frequency) efficacy of this coping style. Thus, positive expectations might be a precursor of successful suppression.

Christianson and Bylin (1999) conducted an experiment that was not a typical thought suppression study, although it does bear relevance for the issue of successful suppression. These authors introduced the fact that in a substantial number of criminal investigations (i.e., in 25% to 45% of the cases), the suspect claims to be amnestic for the crime. Although perpetrators may develop amnesia for their crimes (e.g., due to extreme stress, or alcohol or drug consumption), it also has to be acknowledged that some suspects may feign amnesia. This may be so because they find it easier to claim amnesia than to discuss their crime in full detail. In addition, claiming amnesia may contribute to the judge's perception of a decreased responsibility for the crime. Christianson and Bylin sought to investigate what the effect of such simulated amnesia is on the actual subsequent recollection of the crime. To test this, they instructed 54 undergraduates to read a case vignette, and to identify with the perpetrator in that story. The story was about two young men who are walking home at night, and encounter an elderly couple. The men ask the couple for a light, or a cigarette. Soon afterward, a fight commences. In the course of this fight, one of the young men (with whom the participants had to identify) stabs the elderly man with a knife. Next, the men run away. Some time later, they are arrested by the police in a nearby subway station. After a 30-minute delay, participants were instructed to recall the story in the "I"-form (i.e., participants had to pretend that they were the perpetrator). After this free recall, a cued recall consisting of 25 open-ended questions was carried out. While half of the participants underwent these recall tasks per se, the other half was instructed to simulate amnesia, "so as to evade responsibility for the crime" (Christianson & Bylin, 1999, p. 500). One week later, participants returned to the laboratory, and were given the same recall tasks. This time, all participants were instructed to genuinely recall the story to the best of their ability, whether or not they had previously simulated amnesia. In general, recall of participants who were genuine at both times, slightly declined from T1 to T2. In contrast, the performance of those who had simulated amnesia at T1 and were genuine at T2 increased significantly. Interestingly however, the performance of the latter group of participants never reached the level of those who were genuine at both times. That is, even when all participants were genuine (T2), those who had previously simulated amnesia had significantly poorer memory than those who had not feigned amnesia at T1. This pattern of results was found with free recall as well as with cued recall. Figure 5.2 presents the mean performances of the two groups of participants, averaged over the free and cued recall tasks. The data are presented as percentages of the maximum possible recall score.

The conclusion to be drawn from these findings is that simulating amnesia (cf. suppression of recollections) actually results in a small but significant decrease of memory. Thus, these findings suggest that the suppression of recollections can be somewhat successful after all. However, it is important to address several methodological specifics. First, it remains to be seen whether simulating amnesia is the same as

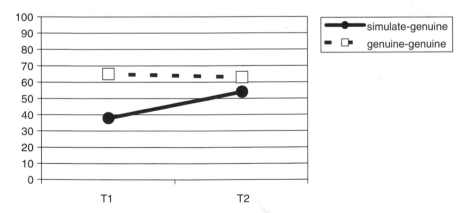

Figure 5.2: Percentages of recalled details as a function of condition and time. (From Christanson, S.A. & Bylin, S. (1999). Does simulating amnesia mediate genuine forgetting for a crime event? *Applied Cognitive Psychology, 13*, 495–511.)

suppressing recollections. The act of suppression entails a blocking of information from consciousness. If one wants to simulate amnesia (i.e., to withhold information), one does not necessarily suppress that information. It might be so that the to-be-withheld information is not suppressed but carefully considered in the process of feigning amnesia. Another important issue pertains to the dependent variable in the Christianson and Bylin (1999) study. These authors were interested in the quality and quantity of their participants' recollections. In contrast, in a typical thought suppression study, the number of intrusions (e.g., thoughts about white bears) is the main dependent variable. Given that the latter variable is rather discrete, the effect of suppression on memory is impossible to study in a typical thought suppression experiment. That is, one either remembers the word white bear or one does not. It is only when more elaborate stimuli (such as a story) become the target of suppression attempts, that possible memory undermining effects can be detected. In other words, the effect of suppression on intrusion frequency has to be distinguished from the effect on the quality of recollections. As to the explanation of the findings by Christianson and Bylin (1999), it is important to note that participants in the simulation condition had to do without a rehearsal of their recollection at T1, at which time they simulated amnesia. This lack of rehearsal may have caused the decreased performance at T2 compared to participants who did rehearse their recollection at T1.

A last factor with possible consequences for the efficacy of suppression pertains to individual differences in the technique on which one relies to suppress an unwanted thought. From the original study by Wegner and colleagues (1987; exp. 2), it has become clear that unfocused distraction (i.e., seeking an unlimited number of environmental distracters) will yield a larger rebound effect than focused distraction (i.e., thinking of just one distracter, e.g., a red Volkswagen, whenever the target thought intrudes consciousness). Apparently, the precise strategy can influence the efficacy of suppression attempts. Indeed, Wells and Davies (1994) stipulate the importance of differential suppression techniques. They even argue that suppression "is defined in terms of its goals rather than in terms of the strategy or strategies used to achieve this goal" (Wells & Davies, 1994, p. 871). Against this background, Wells and Davies introduced the Thought Control Questionnaire (TCQ), which contains 30 items measuring five distinct control strategies. Items are answered on a 4-point scale (1 = *never*; 4 = *almost always*). The development of this scale started with asking a sample of clinical (mainly anxiety disorder and hypochondriasis) and non-clinical respondents how they react when experiencing an unwanted intrusive thought. After factor analyses, the authors ended up with the following five main strategies: distraction (items 1, 9, 16, 19, 21, and 30), social coping (items 5, 8, 12, 17, 25, and 29), worrying (items 4, 7, 18, 22, 24, and 26), punishment (items 2, 6, 11, 13, 15, and 28), and re-appraisal (items 3, 10, 14, 20, 23, and 27). Three of these five strategies can be construed as suppression strategies (viz. distraction, worrying, and punishment), because they imply an attempt to mentally turn away from the intrusion. The remaining two strategies (social coping and re-appraisal) are no suppression strategies, because they imply a thorough analysis of the intrusive thought at hand (see also McKay & Greisberg, 2002). In the case of social coping, the respondent tends to discuss intrusive thoughts with peers, while re-appraisal pertains to attempts to try to think differently about the intrusion and its meanings. Hence, in these two strategies, suppression is not involved. All items of the TCQ are shown in Table 5.3 (items 5, 8, and 12 are reversed).

Interestingly, the five subscales have been proven to correlate differently with measures of psychopathological complaints. For starters, Wells and Davies (1994) found in a sample of 50 respondents that worrying and punishment (but none of the other three control strategies) correlated significantly with scores on the STAI, scores

---

Table 5.3   The Items of the Thought Control Questionnaire

When I experience an unpleasant/unwanted thought ...

---

1. I call to mind positive images instead
2. I tell myself not to be so stupid
3. I focus on the thought
4. I replace the thought with a more trivial bad thought
5. I don't talk about the thought to anyone
6. I punish myself for thinking the thought
7. I dwell on other worries
8. I keep the thought to myself
9. I occupy myself with work instead
10. I challenge the thought's validity
11. I get angry at myself for having the thought
12. I avoid discussing the thought
13. I shout at myself for having the thought
14. I analyze the thought rationally
15. I slap or pinch myself to stop the thought
16. I think pleasant thoughts instead
17. I find out how my friends deal with these thoughts
18. I worry about more minor things instead
19. I do something that I enjoy
20. I try to reinterpret the thought
21. I think about something else
22. I think more about the more minor problems I have
23. I try a different way of thinking about it
24. I think about past worries instead
25. I ask my friends if they have similar thoughts
26. I focus on different negative thoughts
27. I question the reason for having the thought
28. I tell myself that something bad will happen if I think the thought
29. I talk to a friend about the thought
30. I keep myself busy

From Wells, A. & Davies, M.I. (1994). The thought control questionnaire: A measure of individual differences in the control of unwanted thoughts. *Behaviour Research and Therapy*, *32*, 871–878.

on a scale measuring obsessive-compulsive complaints (the PADUA inventory; Sanavio, 1988), and with scores on the Penn State Worry Questionnaire (PSWQ; Meyer, Miller, Metzger, & Borkovec, 1990; i.e., a scale measuring excessive worrying). Some of these findings are obvious, but others may be quite surprising. An example of an expected finding is that worrying as measured by the TCQ is associated with the PSWQ. By contrast, the most unexpected finding seems to be that distraction was not associated with the STAI, PADUA, or PSWQ. As discussed previously, distraction, or at least failing, unfocused distraction, is hypothesized by Wegner et al. (1987) to be the vehicle behind the paradoxical effect of thought suppression. Hence, positive correlations between distraction as measured by the TCQ and scales measuring psychopathological complaints are to be expected. However, such correlations were not confirmed by the data of Wells and Davies (1994). Interestingly, this absence of associations between distraction and pathology has been replicated in several studies in which the TCQ was used. In fact, distraction scores have been found to be negatively correlated with indices of psychopathological complaints. Amir, Cashman, and Foa (1997) compared TCQ scores between a sample of 55 OCD patients and 27 healthy controls. Compared to controls, OCD patients relied more on all strategies except for distraction. Distraction was more frequently employed by the non-clinical participants than by the OCD patients. Recently, Abramowitz, Whiteside, Kalsy, and Tolin (2003) sought to replicate and extend the findings of Amir and colleagues (1997). In the study by Abramowitz and colleagues, a clinical non-OCD sample was included to test the OCD-specificity of various strategies. In addition, participants in this study completed the TCQ before and after treatment. Hence, three groups were included: An OCD sample ($n = 28$), an anxious control group (mainly panic disorder, $n = 12$), and a non-anxious control group ($n = 25$). When comparing the TCQ scores of these three samples, OCD patients seemed to rely more on worrying and punishment, and less on distraction than did participants in the other two groups. Comparison of pre- and post-treatment scores suggested that therapy had resulted in a decrease of punishment and an increase of distraction. All in all, these data indicate that punishment and worrying are associated with psychopathological complaints, while distraction is just the opposite, namely negatively correlated with pathology.

Further evidence for the differential efficacy of the various control strategies tapped by the TCQ comes from a study by Myers (1998), who compared TCQ scores of repressors (i.e., high defensive and low anxious individuals) with those of non-repressors. Results suggested that repressors (who are considered to be successful in their attempts to ignore and forget unpleasant information) rely more on distraction, and less on punishment, compared to non-repressors. Finally, Rassin and Diepstraten (2003) computed correlations between the TCQ and the WBSI, to investigate which TCQ strategies are associated with thought suppression as measured by the WBSI. In a sample of 47 OCD patients, we found that punishment was the only strategy that correlated significantly with the WBSI ($r = .49$). In addition, punishment correlated with the MOCI and the SCL-90. By contrast, distraction correlated negatively with the SCL-90. Hence, this negative correlation between distraction and the SCL-90, as well as the non-correlation between distraction and the WBSI is in contradiction with Wegner and colleagues' (1987) theoretical notion that distraction, suppression, and intrusions should be associated with each other. Compared to the experimental studies by Wegner and colleagues, one flipside of the TCQ studies is that they are all correlational in nature, and thus do not allow for firm causal inferences. For example, while a negative correlation between distraction and the MOCI may indicate that distraction is a fruitful control strategy, it may just as well indicate that people who have strong obsessive-compulsive complaints are reluctant to engage in distraction because they know that distraction is not fruitful in reducing their complaints. In other words, the correlation may reflect that distraction is a poor strategy, and is therefore only used by individuals who have just a few complaints. In an attempt to evade this methodological problem, De Bruin, Rassin, and Muris (2004) submitted 60 under-graduate students to a suppression procedure. All participants subsequently under-went a think-of-anything period, a suppression period (during which white bear thoughts had to be suppressed), and a final think-of-anything period. All three periods lasted 5 minutes each. Before the second period, participants not only were instructed to suppress white bear thoughts, but also received instructions about how they were to achieve this suppression. One group of participants ($n = 20$) had to use distraction, another group had to engage in worrying ($n = 20$), and the third group was given punishment instructions ($n = 20$). The idea was to test the efficacy of these three TCQ strategies experimentally. Unfortunately, analysis of the manipulation check indicated that participants had not sufficiently complied with the instructions. More specifically, participants in all three groups indicated to have engaged in distraction. Furthermore, participants in the punishment condition reported to have been unable to apply punishment conscientiously. Apparently, it is not easy to use specific control strategies on command. By means of alternative analysis, the number of white bear intrusions experienced during the experimental procedure was correlated with the previously completed TCQ. This analysis suggested that distraction was moderately correlated with intrusion frequency ($r = .31$). No other correlations were observed. Interestingly, these data are in line with the idea of Wegner and colleagues (1987) that distraction is associated with intrusions. In summary, while experimental studies have repeatedly yielded results suggesting that distraction (i.e., unfocused distraction) is an ineffective control strategy (Wegner et al., 1987), questionnaire studies relying on the TCQ seem to suggest that punishment and worrying are the most detrimental strat-egies, while distraction is not, or may even be effective. Apparently, the dynamics between distraction and psychopathology, as measured by self-report instruments, differ from those seen in experimental studies. One final consideration concerning distraction is that, next to the number of distracters that are used (i.e., unfocused vs. focused), the intensity of the distracter is likely to be important in determining suppression efficacy. It is intuitively plausible that random environmental distracters are not strong enough to keep one's attention for several minutes. Therefore, one has to skip from one distracter to the next. On the other hand, strong distracters may help to keep one's mind off an unwanted thought. Distracters can be strong in the sense that they are interesting and challenging.

All in all, there is some reason to believe that suppression attempts are not as doomed to fail as one might expect after reading the original thought suppression study by Wegner and colleagues (1987). Several factors seem to influence the efficacy of suppression attempts. From certain points of view, it can even be argued that suppression is effective. Factors possibly related to suppression efficacy include intelligence, personality, practice, cognitions about suppression, and the precise suppression strategy. These factors might function as confounders in suppression studies, and may thus explain why not all studies to date have succeeded in obtaining evidence for the paradoxical effects of suppression.

The Thought Suppression Inventory

When summarizing the literature discussed previously, the WBSI can be argued to suffer from two related flaws. First, there is an osmosis between suppression and intrusion items. Some items do not seem to tap thought suppression but rather the experience of intrusions. Unfortunately, different studies have yielded slightly different results as to which items construe suppression or intrusion questions. Indeed, some items have been found to load simultaneously on both factors. When using total WBSI scores, it must be acknowledged that these scores reflect both suppression and intrusions, and thus measure what could be called failing suppression attempts. This latter conclusion brings us to the second flaw inherent in the WBSI. That is, while recent studies suggest that suppression might, under some circumstances, be successful after all, this successful suppression dimension is evidently not tapped by the WBSI.

To compensate for these flaws, Rassin (2003) developed an alternative suppression questionnaire. This Thought Suppression Inventory (TSI) consists of 15 items to be answered on a 5-point scale (1 = *strongly disagree*; 5 = *strongly agree*; see Table 5.4).

Unlike the WBSI, the TSI is meant to measure three related but separate constructs: five items specifically address intrusions (items 1, 4, 7, 10, and 13), five items address suppression attempts (2, 5, 8, 11, and 14), and five items pertain to successful suppression (3, 6, 9, 12, and 15). Hence, the TSI yields three subscales, while there is no point in calculating total scores, because the intrusion scale is opposite to the successful suppression scale. In a factor analysis ($N = 161$ undergraduates), the three constructs were reproduced. However, the Cronbach's alphas of the three scales were not impressive (i.e., they ranged between .64 and .71). In the process of validating the TSI, its three scales were entered as predictors in several regression analyses. Predicted variables were the WBSI, TCQ, MOCI, and SCL-90. Table 5.5 presents the standardized betas obtained in these regression analyses.

Several of the findings displayed in Table 5.5 deserve some comment. First of all, both TSI intrusion and suppression were significantly correlated with the WBSI, while the successful suppression scale was negatively correlated with the WBSI. This pattern of results delivers further support for the notion that the WBSI addresses both suppression and intrusion, and is thus focused on unsuccessful suppression. Second, the suppression attempts scale correlated positively with TCQ distraction, suggesting that suppression attempts do take the form of distraction seeking. In addition, intrusion was negatively correlated with TCQ distraction, which suggests that distraction can be a fruitful thought control strategy. Furthermore, none of the other TCQ scales were related with TSI suppression attempts. Third, while intrusion was correlated with

Table 5.4   The Items of the Thought Suppression Inventory

1. I have many unpleasant thoughts
2. I always try to forget unpleasant events as fast as possible
3. I am able to keep a problem out of mind until I have time to deal with it
4. I experience many emotions that are too intense to control
5. I always try to put problems out of mind
6. I am able to suppress unpleasant thoughts
7. I have thoughts which I would rather not have
8. If I have an unpleasant thought, I try to think about something else
9. I am able to put aside problems and worries
10. I regularly "hear" unexplainable things inside my head, such as my own voice, or the voices of people who are not present
11. Sometimes I stay busy just to prevent having certain thoughts
12. I am able to suppress unpleasant experiences to the point that I hardly remember them
13. I am unable to concentrate
14. I try to avoid certain thoughts
15. I can keep the lid on my feelings if letting them out would interfere with what I am doing

From Rassin, E. (2003). The White Bear Suppression Inventory (WBSI) focuses on failing suppression attempts. *European Journal of Personality*, *17*, 285–298.

Table 5.5   Standardized Betas in the Regression Analyses

	TSI intrusion	TSI suppression attempts	TSI successful suppression
WBSI	.51*	.41*	−.24*
TCQ-Distraction	−.21*	.40*	.11
TCQ-Social coping	.27*	.02	−.03
TCQ-Worrying	.30*	.16	−.02
TCQ-Punishment	.39*	.08	−.10
TCQ-Re-appraisal	.00	−.11	.05
MOCI	.47*	.01	−.06
SCL-90	.70*	.04	−.14

*$P < .05$.
From Rassin, E. (2003). The White Bear Suppression Inventory (WBSI) focuses on failing suppression attempts. *European Journal of Personality*, *17*, 285–298.

MOCI and SCL-90, suppression attempts was not. Apparently, suppression per se is not necessarily associated with psychopathological complaints. In that sense, these findings stipulate the need for further research into the concept of successful suppression.

Conclusion

Although the bulk of the suppression literature suggests that suppression is an ineffective and even counterproductive coping style, there are exceptions. First, not all researchers have succeeded in discovering paradoxical suppression effects. Second, it seems that there are individual differences with respect to various suppression-related phenomena. One of the most obvious individual differences is that in suppression-proneness. Some people react to unwanted thoughts more often with suppression than others. The WBSI was introduced as a measure of such individual differences in suppression tendencies. However, there are reasons to believe that the WBSI is not completely neutral, but is biased toward unsuccessful suppression, because this scale contains several items addressing the occurrence of intrusive thoughts. An important, but so far somewhat neglected individual difference is that of suppression efficacy. There are several factors that may contribute to the success of suppression attempts. For example, optimism (as opposed to depression) may stimulate suppression efficacy. Also, fluid intelligence and working memory capacity aid in the struggle with unwanted thoughts. Furthermore, successful suppression may be achieved through practice. Next, a strong belief in the concept of successful suppression may actually help (the perception of) suppression efficacy. A last factor determining suppression efficacy seems to be the precise technique relied upon. Interestingly, several questionnaire studies, relying on the TCQ, have yielded results indicating that – contrary to the original theory of Wegner and colleagues (1987) – distraction may be a fruitful thought control strategy after all.

Chapter 6

Thought Suppression and Obsession

Introduction

A shallow analysis of Wegner et al.'s (1987) white bear study might invite the conclusion that this study specifically pertains to the Freudian idea of suppressing unwanted memories. Indeed, in the introduction of their article, the authors refer to Freud's work on the conscious and unconscious processes. However, in discussing their findings, they conclude that there are "many striking resemblances between the observed effects and the everyday observations people make about the tenacity of their worries, addictions, crushes, and obsessions" (Wegner et al., 1987, p. 12). In fact, the thought suppression paradigm has occupied a prominent place in the explanation of obsessions. Its spin-off in this field of research has by far exceeded that in the area of the suppression of recollections. This is likely because white bear thoughts are discrete, and thus resemble obsessions more closely than they do elaborate recollections.

This chapter will focus on the relation between suppression and obsession. First, obsession will be discussed in general terms. Next, the cognitive theory of obsession will be discussed in some detail. This theory focuses on individuals' cognitions about intrusive thoughts, and on the influence of such cognitions on the development of obsessional intrusions. Finally, the empirical evidence for the alleged detrimental effects of thought suppression on obsessions will be considered.

Obsessive-Compulsive Disorder

Daily, Harold takes the bus to work. While in the bus, he tries to not touch any of its steel interior. He wears leather gloves, so that in case touching is inevitable, his skin will not touch the steel. The reason for Harold's reluctance is his fear to catch a disease by touching "public" materials. He dislikes touching unfamiliar materials in general, but his fear of steel is extremely strong.

Kevin travels by car. Recently, he has developed a strange fear of having overrun a pedestrian on his way to work, without noticing. This fear becomes so strong that he sometimes drives back to check the whole route from home to work. He also fervently monitors the radio news broadcasts for reports of hit-and-run accidents. He even considers turning himself in for having killed someone with his car.

Charlene finds herself regularly fantasizing about strangling her 1-year-old baby. She realizes that these strange fantasies started after she had had a sexual fantasy while playing with her baby. Both the sexual and the aggressive fantasies are very confusing and disturbing to Charlene. Lately, she also thinks about what would happen if she jumped before a train, or how it would be to push someone else in front of a train.

People like Harold, Kevin, and Charlene may suffer from obsessive-compulsive disorder (OCD). Obviously, obsessions and compulsions are the key features of OCD. The precise DSM-IV-TR criteria (APA, 2000) are displayed in Table 6.1. Evidently, obsessions can be construed as mental intrusions in the sense that they appear automatically. As to the content of obsessions, most patients with OCD suffer from fear of contamination, aggressive thoughts, sexual thoughts, somatic fears, and a need for symmetry or exactness. The most prevalent compulsions are checking, washing, repeating, counting, ordering, and hoarding (Antony, Downie, & Swinson, 1998). Although, according to the DSM-IV (APA, 1994) the diagnosis of OCD requires obsession or compulsion, most OCD patients suffer from both. Rasmussen and Tsuang (1986) found that in a sample of 44 OCD patients, only two individuals suffered from obsession in the absence of compulsion, or vice versa. These authors also concluded that most patients with OCD simultaneously suffer from multiple obsessions and compulsions. According to Bebbington (1998), the point-prevalence of OCD in the general population is approximately 1% for men and 1.5% for women (Kessler et al., 1994). The average age of onset is approximately 20 years for men and 23 for women (Antony et al., 1998). Although OCD reacts fairly well to medication (especially antidepressants) and cognitive behavior therapy, it tends to have a chronic course if left untreated (Van Balkom & Van Dyck, 1998). Based on the clinical picture, OCD has been related to several other disorders, including Tourette's disorder, impulse control disorders, body dysmorphic disorder, eating disorders, and paraphilias. Some researchers refer to these disorders with the umbrella term "obsessive-compulsive spectrum disorders" (Goldsmith, Shapira, Phillips, & McElroy, 1998).

Causes of Obsessive-Compulsive Disorder

The causes of OCD can be studied at various levels. The most obvious question would be where the intrusive thoughts come from. Katz (1991) offers a "biological Freudian" explanation for the occurrence of intrusions. According to this theory, numerous unconscious thoughts are constantly active in currently not accessed regions of our mind. A neurotransmitter called serotonin is involved in the regulation of these unconscious dynamics (i.e., keeping them unconscious). If, for some reason, a serotonergic deficiency occurs, the brain is no longer able to prevent irrelevant thoughts and impulses from entering consciousness. Thus, a cognitive disinhibition occurs. A lack of serotonin may also explain the occurrence of compulsions, in that repetitive behaviors may help to restore serotonergic activity. In this line of reasoning, compulsions are a means to reach a serotonergic equilibrium. Jacobs (1994) concludes: "Since our results show that repetitive motor-acts increase serotonin neuronal activity, patients with this disorder may be engaging in repetitive rituals such as hand washing or pacing as a means of self-medication. In other words, they have learned to activate their brain

Table 6.1 DSM-IV-TR Criteria for Obsessive-Compulsive Disorder

A. Either obsessions or compulsions
   Obsessions are defined as:
   1. Recurrent and persistent thoughts, impulses, or images that are experienced, at some time during the disturbance, as intrusive and inappropriate and that cause marked anxiety or distress.
   2. The thoughts, impulses, or images are not simply excessive worries about real-life problems.
   3. The person attempts to ignore or suppress such thoughts, impulses, or images, or to neutralize them with some other thought or action.
   4. The person recognizes that the obsessional thoughts, impulses, or images are a product of his or her own mind (not imposed from without as in thought insertion).
   Compulsions are defined as:
   1. Repetitive behaviors (e.g., hand washing, ordering, checking) or mental acts (e.g., praying, counting, repeating words silently) that the person feels driven to perform in response to an obsession, or according to rules that must be applied rigidly.
   2. The behaviors or mental acts are aimed at preventing or reducing distress or preventing some dreaded event or situation: however, these behaviors or mental acts either are not connected in a realistic way with what they are designed to neutralize or prevent or are clearly excessive.
B. At some point during the course of the disorder, the person has recognized that the obsessions or compulsions are excessive or unreasonable.
C. The obsessions or compulsions cause marked distress, are time consuming (take more than one hour a day), or significantly interfere with the person's routine, occupational (or academic) functioning, or usual social activities or relationships.
D. If another Axis 1 disorder is present, the content of the obsessions or compulsions is not restricted to it (e.g., preoccupation with food in the presence of an eating disorder, hair pulling in the presence of trichotillomania, concern with appearance in the presence of body dismorphic disorder, preoccupation with drugs in the presence of a substance use disorder, preoccupation with having a serious illness in the presence of hypochondriasis, preoccupation with sexual urges or fantasies in the presence of a parphilia, or guilty ruminations in the presence of major depressive disorder).
E. The disturbance is not due to the direct physiological effects of a substance (e.g., a drug of abuse, a medication) or a general medical condition.

Reprinted with permission from the *Diagnostic and Statistical Manual of Mental Disorders, Fourth Edition, Text Revision, (Copyright 2000)*. American Psychiatric Association.

serotonin system in order to derive some benefit or rewarding effect, perhaps the reduction of anxiety" (p. 462).

Although the serotonin hypothesis may contribute to our understanding of OCD, there are several problems with this account. For example, serotonin deficiency is not specific for OCD, but is also associated with depression and aggression (Jacobs, 1994). Our current scientific techniques do not allow us to distinguish between possible differential manifestations of serotonergic malfunctions. Furthermore, the idea that repetitive behaviors should be construed as self-medicating motor activities is not in line with the notion that compulsions generally occur as voluntary reactions to obsessive intrusions. Self-medicating movements are more reminiscent of apparently pointless and more automatic behaviors as seen in Tourette's disorder and trichotillo-mania (APA, 2000).

A different research line, addressing the origin of compulsions, focuses on possible memory deficits in patients with OCD. The basic hypothesis is that people who check excessively may do so because they cannot remember whether they actually checked previously or whether they just imagined doing so (McNally & Kohlbeck, 1993). There are some indications that obsessive-compulsive checking is associated with (neuro-psychological) memory impairments (Tallis, 1997; Tallis, Pratt, & Jamani, 1999; Wilhelm, McNally, Bear, & Florin, 1997). However, there is no evidence to suggest that these memory impairments are causal factors in the development of compulsive behaviors (Tallis et al., 1999). McNally and Kohlbeck (1993) argue that patients with OCD do not suffer from memory impairment per se, but rather from decreased confidence in their memory (MacDonald, Antony, MacLeod, & Richter, 1997; Van den Hout & Kindt, 2003b). A possible mechanism behind the decrease in confidence was nicely illustrated by Van den Hout and Kindt (2003a). These authors argued that repeated checking may cause the individual to start doubting his or her recollection about having checked the pertinent item. More precisely, it is argued that people generally process memories of their actions episodically. However, if certain behaviors are repeated frequently, semantic processing will occur, thus overriding the original episodic recollection. Unlike episodic memories, semantic memories relatively lack clarity and detail. Subsequently, this lack of clarity decreases the confidence that one has actually carried out the recalled action. Van den Hout and Kindt (2003a) exposed 39 undergraduates to a virtual gas stove, and instructed them to turn on and off several gas rings by using their computer mouse. Next, participants had to indicate on a VAS how vivid their recollection of their actions was, and how sure they were that the gas stove was now really turned off. After this, half of the participants were given the same instruction 20 times, while the other half had to turn on and off virtual light bulbs. After these 20 trials, all participants were asked one last time to turn on and off gas rings of the virtual stove, and to rate the vividness and certainty of this last action. As expected, participants who had done nothing else than handle gas rings had a less vivid recollection of their 22nd trial and were less certain that the stove was actually turned off eventually compared to ratings made after the first trial. By contrast, there was no decrease in VAS scores in the group of participants who had handled the gas stove only during the first and 22nd trial, and had spent 20 trials in between handling light bulbs. These findings indeed suggest that repeatedly carrying out the same action decreases the vividness of the recollection of that action, and consequently the confidence that the action was really carried out.

Whereas decreased memory function or decreased confidence in memory may play a role in the development or continuation of compulsions, the relation between memory and obsession is a different story. While the findings by Wilhelm and colleagues (1996) might invite the conclusion that patients with OCD suffer from memory lapses, Radomsky and Rachman (1999) found evidence to suggest that patients with OCD have a better than average memory when it comes to phobic stimuli. They showed 40 participants a set of 50 items (such as a shoelace, pen, scissors). Next, the participants witnessed the experiment leader contaminate half of the items by rubbing them with a tissue that had allegedly been found on the floor of a hospital. The remaining items were touched with a clean tissue. Some time later, participants were asked to recall all 50 items. Notably, 10 participants had OCD, 10 participants suffered from other anxiety disorders, and 20 were healthy undergraduate students. Patients with OCD were very accurate in recalling contaminated items. This was so in comparison to both other groups as well as compared to the number of recalled uncontaminated items. These data suggest not only that there is no reason to doubt the memories of patients with OCD, but also that these patients have a memory bias as to obsession-relevant stimuli.

Clinical and Normal Obsessions

Meanwhile, the question arises whether looking for causes of intrusions is a fruitful endeavor. Rachman and De Silva (1978) asked several patients with OCD what their most frequent and disturbing intrusions were. Next, they invited 40 non-clinical participants to their laboratory and gave them a definition of unwanted intrusive thoughts. These participants were then asked whether they had ever experienced an unwanted intrusion, and if so, how frequently. It seemed that approximately 80% of the healthy volunteers in this study regularly (i.e., at least several times per week) experienced intrusive thoughts that met the criteria for obsession. Thus, it seems that the experience of obsessive intrusions is not an exclusive feature of OCD. Most of us have unwanted obsession-like thoughts. Furthermore, the content of obsessive intrusions experienced by "normal" participants did not seem to differ from that of obsessions experienced by patients with OCD. To illustrate this, Rachman and De Silva (1978) invited six experts (five psychologists and one psychiatric nurse), and asked them to classify 81 obsessive thoughts that were written on separate pieces of paper. Some of these thoughts are displayed in Table 6.2.

On average, the experts misclassified half of the clinical obsessions as obsessions of healthy volunteers, while they mistook approximately 17% of the normal obsession for clinical ones. As to Table 6.2, numbers 1, 4, 7, 8, and 10 stem from patients with OCD, while the other thoughts were reported by healthy volunteers.

The Rachman and De Silva (1978) study illustrates that most of us suffer from unwanted intrusive thoughts that cannot be discriminated from obsessions as experienced by actual patients with OCD (see also Salkovskis & Harrison, 1984; something

Table 6.2 Examples of Intrusions Reported by Patients With Obsessive-Compulsive Disorder and by Healthy Volunteers

1. To jump out of window
2. To jump off the platform when a train is arriving
3. To hurt or harm someone
4. To harm children with physical violence
5. To sexually assault a female, known or unknown
6. An accident occurring to a loved one
7. "I wish he/she were dead" with reference to persons close and dear
8. That he will get / has got cancer
9. That she, her husband, and baby would be harmed because of exposure to asbestos, with conviction that there are tiny asbestos dust particles in the house
10. "Did I commit this crime?" when reading or hearing reports of crime

From Rachman, S. & De Silva, P. (1978). Abnormal and normal obsessions. *Behaviour Research and Therapy, 16,* 233–248.

similar goes for the conducting of non-clinical rituals vs. clinical compulsions, see Muris, Merckelbach, & Clavan, 1997). Given that most of us are able to function normally, and do not need therapy, the clinically relevant difference between patients with OCD and other people cannot be the experience of intrusive thoughts per se. Therefore, the search for causes of obsessive intrusions may be theoretically interesting, but clinically less so. Rather, scientific attention should focus on characteristics of obsessions that do differ between "clinical" and "normal" obsessions. Rachman and De Silva found that, compared to healthy volunteers, patients with OCD experienced their obsessions as occurring more frequently, longer lasting, more intense, more disturbing, and more strongly, but more difficult to resist. Hence, the clinically relevant question is: "How do everyday intrusions turn into (more frequent, longer lasting, and intense) clinical obsessions?" The thought suppression paradigm provides an answer to precisely that question. So does a different research line that has become known as the cognitive theory of obsession. The subsequent paragraphs will address this theory in some detail.

Inflated Responsibility

In 1985, Salkovskis argued that the relative lack of successful cognitive-behavioral interventions for obsession, up to then, was due to the absence of a solid theoretical basis. According to Salkovskis, much of Beck's (1976) cognitive theory of depression could and should be translated to the study of obsession. The central argument in Beck's theory is that many depressions can be construed as a state of continual misinterpretation of normal phenomena. For example, many depressed people seem temporarily prone to emphasize the negative side of everything. Something comparable might be the case with patients with OCD, according to Salkovskis (1985). Given that the work of Salkovskis and others builds on Beck's theory, it is referred to as the cognitive theory of obsession. It is noteworthy that, recently, many cognitive researchers have applied Beck's theory to their own area. Thus, several cognitive theories have been introduced, including cognitive theories of panic disorder (Kamieniecki, Wade, & Tsourtos, 1997), social phobia (Van Niekerk, Möller, & Nortje, 1999), schizophrenia (Jensen & Kane, 1996), eating disorders (Shafran, Teachman, Kerry, & Rachman, 1999), and posttraumatic stress disorder (PTSD) (Ehlers & Clark, 2000).

Salkovskis' (1985) theoretical account begins with a differentiation between intrusions and (negative) automatic thoughts. Salkovskis observed that many patients who suffered from intrusions interpreted these intrusions in an extremely fast and peculiar way. These interpretations were so logical and beyond discussion for the patients that they were seemingly automatic, although objectively, the interpretations were clearly flawed. Table 6.3 presents several intrusions with their associated automatic interpretation, as observed by Salkovskis.

From these automatic thoughts, Salkovskis (1985) inducted several, more general dysfunctional assumptions. These assumptions share a sense of inflated responsibility for one's own thoughts. Therefore, the dysfunctional assumptions to which Salkovskis refers are called cognitive biases (Mineka & Sutton, 1992), or more specifically, responsibility biases. In the context of the cognitive theory of obsession, responsibility bias can be defined as "the belief that one has power which is pivotal to bring about or prevent subjectively crucial negative outcomes. These outcomes are perceived as essential to prevent. They may be actual, that is, having consequences in the real world, and/or at a moral level" (see Salkovskis, 1999, p. S32). Salkovskis (1985), and others (Rachman, 1993, 1997, 1998) argue that people who suffer from a responsibility bias will misinterpret certain intrusions in a manner that they feel over-responsible for having these intrusions and for the anticipated consequences of the intrusions. In this way, the presence of a responsibility bias results in increased intensity and unpleasantness of intrusions; in feelings of responsibility, guilt, and anxiety; and in an urge to

Table 6.3 Intrusive Thoughts and Associated Automatic Thoughts

Intrusive thought	Automatic thought
1. This hand cream might be contaminated	I will get cancer, and that is my own fault
2. I might not have switched the light off	I will get into trouble, and lose my job
3. My superior will find out that I told rumors about him	I will get into trouble, and lose my job
4. I wish that my friend gets harmed	Having this wish might make this really happen, and then I will have harmed someone I care about
5. Did I lock the door?	These doubts make my life unenjoyable

From Salkovskis, P.M. (1985). Obsessional-compulsive problems: A cognitive-behavioural analysis. *Behaviour Research and Therapy, 23,* 571–583.

Table 6.4   Examples of Cognitive Biases Relevant to Obsessive-Compulsive Disorder

1. Having a thought about an action is morally equivalent to performing the action
2. If a thought comes to mind, this means that this thought is likely to come true
3. If a thought repeatedly comes to mind, it must have special meaning
4. Failing to prevent harm is the same as having caused the harm in the first place
5. One can and should exercise control over one's thoughts
6. Responsibility is not attenuated by other factors (e.g., low probability of occurrence)
7. Not neutralizing after an intrusion is the same as wanting the intrusion to come true
8. If I feel anxious, this means that I must be in danger
9. Intrusive thoughts unveil my real self

engage in compulsive behaviors aimed at undoing the intrusion. In other words, a responsibility bias suffices to add to an intrusion all the characteristics of a clinically relevant obsession. In Table 6.4, examples of responsibility biases are shown.

The obsessive-generating power of biases such as those presented in Table 6.4 becomes clear when we consider their influence on the interpretation of an intrusive thought about having violent sex, experienced in church. While for most people whose thinking is bias-free, this intrusion may be strange but not very alarming, people who suffer from responsibility biases might become very upset. The first bias will lead one to believe to be immoral for having such a thought. The second bias may result in fear that the thought might come true. Bias 5 makes one fear that he or she is losing control and going insane. The seventh bias will force one to engage in a neutralizing compulsion (e.g., in this case, saying a prayer). Bias 9 will make one worry about his or her true nature. It is obvious that people who live by high cognitive standards (cf. responsibility biases), will activate automatic thoughts extremely fast in reaction to an intrusion, and will consequently misinterpret that intrusion, resulting in anxiety, guilt, urges to neutralize, and so on.

Of all biases presented in Table 6.4, the first two seem to be especially associated with obsessional problems (Emmelkamp & Aardema, 1999; Rachman, Thordarson, Shafran, & Woody, 1995). The first bias implies a high moral standard, in that having immoral thoughts is considered to be just as bad as carrying out immoral behavior. Therefore, this bias is termed the "morality" bias. The second bias implies a kind of magical thinking, in that thoughts are considered to have predictive value. Although many people would like the idea that having certain thoughts increases the likelihood that those thoughts become reality, this bias produces stress if one experiences unpleasant thoughts such as "I wish my mother dies," or "I am going to strangle my baby." This bias has been called the "probability" or "likelihood" bias. Because the morality and the probability bias share the notion that thoughts and actions are spuriously intertwined, both biases together are referred to as "thought-action fusion" (TAF) (Rachman, 1993; Rachman & Shafran, 1999; Rachman et al., 1995; Shafran, Thordarson, & Rachman, 1996).

The Cognitive Theory of Obsession

Although the cognitive theory of obsession boils down to the simple notion that obsessive characteristics of intrusions are caused by a flawed interpretation of intrusions, the theory deserves to be discussed in more detail (see, for extensive discussions, Frost & Steketee, 2002). Figure 6.1 displays a schematic overview of the cognitive theory. This schema begins with possible causes of cognitive biases (i.e., breeding ground). Salkovskis, Shafran, Rachman, and Freeston (1999) describe several processes that can result in the acquisition of a responsibility bias. First, developmental antecedents, in which one's thoughts appear to contribute to a serious misfortune, can promote the development of a bias. For example, a child may wish someone dead, while soon afterward, this person actually dies. This incident may lead the child to believe that his or her thoughts possess predictive value. Second, certain personality traits, such as perfectionism, may foster irrational cognitions, which stimulate catastrophic interpretations of intrusions. For example, the idea that the occurrence of unwanted intrusions predicts loss of mental control and development of serious mental illness can be interpreted as a perfectionistic bias with obsession-provoking effects (Shafran & Mansell, 2001). Finally, cultural influences can contribute to the development of cognitive biases. For example, certain religious dogmas are reminiscent of responsibility biases. Shafran and colleagues (1996) give the example of the Catholic notion that blasphemous, adulterous, and aggressive thoughts are sinful. In fact, teaching people that such thoughts are bad implies imposing cognitive standards that are nearly impossible to live up to (Rassin & Koster, 2003).

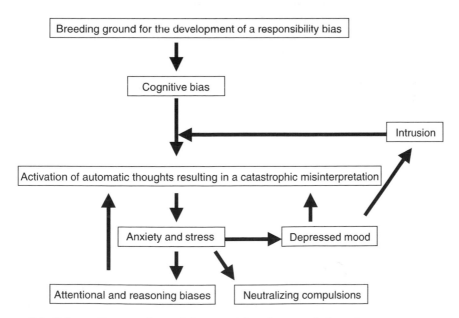

Figure 6.1: Schematic overview of the cognitive theory of obsession.

Once a cognitive bias is active, certain intrusions (e.g., violent fantasies) will activate a corresponding automatic negative thought, resulting in a catastrophic misinterpretation. A crucial element in this misinterpretation is that the individual feels responsible for having the intrusive thought and for any anticipated consequences of that thought. The resulting inflated sense of responsibility leads to the experience of tension, stress, and fear. This anxiety may have several consequences, such as attentional bias (Clayton, Richards, & Edwards, 1999; Salkovskis, Forrester, & Richards, 1998) and depressed mood. These altered mood states may initiate positive feedback loops. For example, depression may strengthen the misinterpretation of intrusions, and may, at the same time, result in an increased intrusion frequency (Rachman, 1997). Anxiety will also have consequences at the behavioral level, in that the individual will be tempted to engage in neutralizing compulsions. Hence, the cognitive theory does not only explain the increased intensity of intrusions, but also addresses the occurrence of compulsions. Notably, carrying out compulsions prevents exposure to the anticipated consequences of the intrusion, and thus perpetuates the symptoms.

Experimental Evidence for the Cognitive Theory of Obsession

Producing experimental evidence for the core hypothesis of the cognitive theory (i.e., the assumption that the interpretation of an intrusion determines its aversiveness) is somewhat difficult, because it requires that the researcher influence the participant's interpretation of an intrusion, which is, evidently, not so easy. To date, a handful of published studies have conjured up evidence for the responsibility hypothesis. In this section, some of these experiments will be discussed.

Lopatka and Rachman (1995) invited 30 patients with OCD who primarily suffered from checking compulsions to participate in their experiment. First of all, participants were interviewed to establish their checking concerns. The experimental induction entailed that participants were brought in situations in which they normally would check (e.g., a participant who had indicated that he normally checked the door lock repeatedly, had to close a door, without checking). At this point, the participant completed several VASs (range: 0 to 100) pertaining to perceived responsibility, discomfort, likelihood that something bad might happen, anticipated severity of this consequence, urge to check and so on. Every participant was placed twice in the same checking-behavior–provoking situation, once under conditions of low responsibility, and once under high responsibility conditions. The degree of responsibility was manipulated through the following instructions. In the high responsibility condition, responsibility was increased by stating that the participant was and remained completely responsible for his or her behavior, including all possible consequences. In the low responsibility condition, participants were told that the experimenter took all responsibility for any consequences of the participant's omission to check, as well as for anything else that might happen during the experiment. These instructions were encoded in a written contract, to increase their weight. Mean VAS scores in the low and high responsibility conditions are shown in Figure 6.2. As can be seen in this figure, participants, indeed, felt less responsible if they were allowed to shift

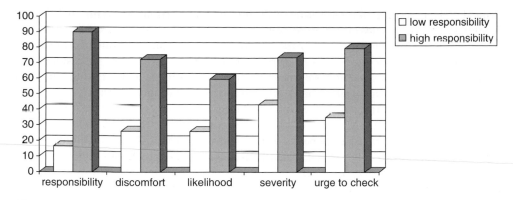

Figure 6.2: VAS scores in the low and high responsibility condition. (From Lopatka, C. & Rachman, S. (1995). Perceived responsibility and compulsive checking: An experimental analysis. *Behaviour Research and Therapy, 33,* 673–684.)

responsibility to the experimenter. Furthermore, decreased responsibility seemed to be associated with decreases in VAS scores measuring obsessive complaints.

Ladouceur and colleagues (1995) used a different design to study the effect of perceived responsibility. These authors invited 40 healthy volunteers to participate in a color perception task. Participants were placed in front of a glass pot filled with 200 pills. They had to sort these pills by color; there were 10 different colors, 20 pills per color. In the low responsibility condition, participants were told that this assignment was nothing more than practice, and that their performance would not even be analyzed. In the high responsibility condition, it was said that the study was conducted by request of a pharmaceutical company that wanted to know whether these colors were easily distinguishable. The colored pills were to be used to fight a virus in an Asian country. Because inhabitants were poorly educated, colors might be used to identify the different pills. Therefore, it was important that participants did their best. Several objective (e.g., hesitations, checks, total time) and subjective (e.g., anxiety, preoccupation with errors, doubts) variables were recorded. As expected, participants in the high responsibility condition scored higher on most variables than did those in the low responsibility condition.

Rachman, Shafran, Mitchell, Trant, and Teachman (1996) were interested in the effects of TAF, and came up with the following daring design. Sixty-three undergraduate students were asked to think of a friend or relative close to them. They were, then, given a piece of paper, and were asked to insert the name of that person into the typed sentence "I hope . . . is in a car accident." Next, several VASs were completed addressing anxiety, responsibility, guilt, likelihood, moral wrongness and so on. Half of the participants were given the opportunity to do whatever they wanted to undo the sentence (i.e., neutralization), after which the same VASs were completed (time 2). After a 20-minute delay, the VASs were completed for the third and last time (time 3). The other half of the participants were not allowed to neutralize immediately (time 2), but only after a 20-minute delay (time 3). With this design, Rachman and colleagues (1996) were able to study the effects of the TAF-like sentence (a model of an intrusion), neutralization, and passing of time without neutralization (cf. response prevention). The scores on the VAS measuring anxiety are displayed in Figure 6.3. As can be seen, completion of the sentence induced a substantial degree of anxiety, but neutralization decreased this anxiety. Interestingly, passing of time had the same effect as neutralization (see time 2). This pattern was virtually the same for all variables.

One of the self-admitted drawbacks of this study was that T2 fell at different times for the two conditions. That is, in the neutralization first group, T2 was approximately 2 minutes after the provocation. By contrast, in the delay first condition, T2 was 20 minutes after provocation, right before the opportunity to neutralize. Hence, the measurement at T2 constitutes a comparison between immediate neutralization and 20-minute delay. Van den Hout, Van Pol, and Peters (2001) adapted the design by Rachman and colleagues (1996) in a way that the effects of immediate neutralization could be compared with those of a 2-minute delay (a 2-minute delay was chosen because that much time was given to participants in the neutralization first condition to carry out their neutralization). The adaptation made by these authors simply dictated that participants in the delay first condition were asked to complete a VAS scale 2 minutes after the delay period had commenced. Interestingly, anxiety levels of participants who had merely waited for 2 minutes were similarly decreased compared to after provocation as those of participants who had used these 2 minutes to carry out neutralization. Based on this finding, Van den Hout and colleagues (2001) concluded that "the neutralization instruction seemed to have considerably less psychological impact than originally suggested" (p. 1448). That is, while in theory neutralization is a fruitless activity because it perpetuates anxiety in the long run, people continue their

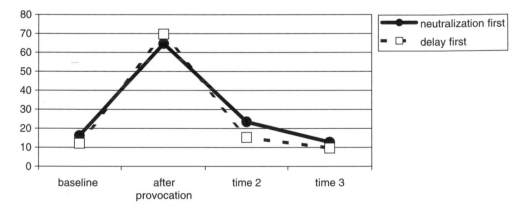

Figure 6.3: VAS scores measuring anxiety. (From Rachman, S., Shafran, R., Mitchell, D., Trant, J., & Teachman, B. (1996). How to remain neutral: An experimental analysis of neutralization. *Behaviour Research and Therapy, 34,* 889–898.)

neutralizing behavior because it decreases short-term feelings of anxiety. However, the data by Van den Hout and colleagues (2001) suggest that short-term relief can also be obtained by simply doing nothing.

Another study on neutralization was done by Salkovskis, Thorpe, Wahl, Wroe, and Forrester (2003). These authors instructed 29 patients with OCD to record their most disturbing obsession on an audiotape. Next, they underwent two experimental periods. During the first period, the audiotape was played 16 times. Half of the participants were instructed to think a neutralizing thought in reaction to every presentation of their self-recorded obsession (i.e., mental neutralization), while the other half were instructed to continually count backwards from 20 to 0 (i.e., distraction). Every fourth presentation, participants had to indicate their discomfort on a 100-mm VAS. During the second period, the audiotape was played another 16 times, while participants in both groups were instructed to merely sit and listen. Neutralization and distraction were not necessary and even unwanted during this second period. During the first session, neutralizing resulted in a quicker decrease of discomfort than did distraction. Interestingly however, during the second period, this rapid decrease had to be paid with an increase of discomfort, while participants who had previously engaged in distraction now felt less discomfort (Figure 6.4). These findings suggest that neutralization may not only be ineffective in the long run, but also counterproductive. Hence, the findings are reminiscent of the rebound effect observed in thought suppression studies.

Rassin and colleagues (1999) explored the possibility of inducing a probability bias in healthy volunteers and sought to test whether this newly acquired bias would change

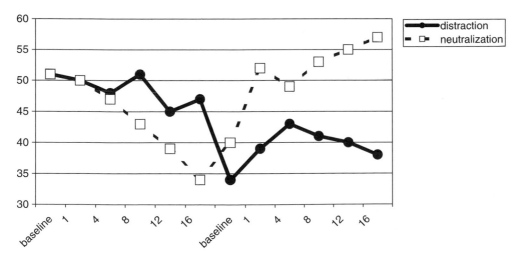

Figure 6.4: VAS scores measuring discomfort. (From Salkovskis, P.M., Thorpe, S.J., Wahle, K., Wroe, A.L., & Forrester, E. (2003). Neutralizing increases discomfort associated with obsessional thoughts: An experimental study with obsessional patients. *Journal of Abnormal Psychology, 112*, 709–715. American Psychological Association. Reprinted with permission.)

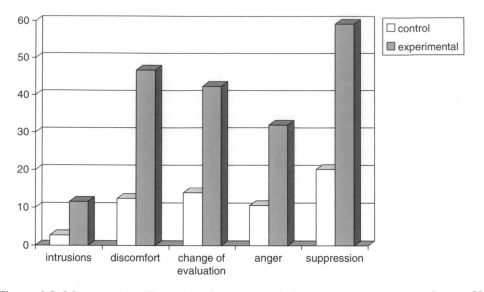

Figure 6.5: Mean scores. (From Rassin, E., Merckelbach, H., Muris, P., & Spaan, V. (1999). Thought-action fusion as a causal factor in the development of intrusions. *Behaviour Research and Therapy*, *37*, 231-237.)

the interpretation of a theretofore neutral thought. To achieve this, 45 high school students were connected to a bogus electroencephalography apparatus. They were told that the apparatus was able to detect certain discrete thoughts such as "apple." However, half of the participants were also told that if they thought of an apple, the apparatus would not only detect that thought, but would also transmit a signal to a computer that would apply an electrical shock to a co-participant who was in an adjacent room (i.e., an external consequence of having a target thought). After having spent 15 minutes in the laboratory, participants completed VASs pertaining to experienced discomfort, efforts to suppress thoughts of apple, changed evaluation of the target thought, and internally directed anger. They also had to estimate the number of target thoughts. The results are summarized in Figure 6.5. Clearly, the experimental induction had resulted in an increase of all variables.

To summarize, there is growing evidence for the core thesis of the cognitive theory of obsession. Relying on different experimental setups, researchers have succeeded in manipulating participants' perceived responsibility for their behaviors and thoughts. Overall, findings indicate that increases in perceived responsibility are accompanied by the hypothesized increases in obsessive complaints.

Intermezzo: Susceptibility and Severity

In health psychology literature, it is quite common to differentiate between perceived likelihood and anticipated consequences. For example, if a government wants to discourage certain health-endangering behaviors (e.g., unsafe sex), it is important to recognize that people use at least two parameters in their decision whether or not to engage in the discouraged behavior; namely, the perceived likelihood of a negative outcome (in this example, catching a sexually transmitted disease), and the anticipated severity of that negative outcome (i.e., how bad the disease is considered to be; see Sarafino, 1998). It seems likely that something similar might apply to the context of responsibility biases, in particular the probability bias. For example, people who suffer from a probability bias fear that their ugly thoughts will become reality. But which element of this idea is the most fear-provoking: the experience of having uncontrollable thoughts, the chance that these thoughts might become real, the severity of the imagined event, or plainly the perception of responsibility and guilt? Only a few studies have investigated the precise cognitive mediators of perceived responsibility.

Jones and Menzies (1997) sought to explore which cognitive mediators are most strongly correlated with obsessive anxiety. These authors invited 27 patients with OCD (i.e., obsessive handwashers) to place their hands in a container filled with dirt, hair, and meat. On several occasions during this test, cognitive mediators (perceived probability of catching a disease, anticipated severity of that disease, perceived responsibility for transmitting the disease to other people, and self-efficacy to complete the experiment), as well as obsessive complaints (anxiety, urge to wash their hands, time spent in the container, and time spent washing their hands, after the experimental task) were measured. It seemed that the danger expectancies (i.e., perceived probability and anticipated severity) were the most reliable predictors of the obsessive complaints. However, Jones and Menzies (1997) failed to find a differential effect of probability and severity.

Using a different research design, Menzies, Harris, Cumming, and Einstein (2000), tried to differentiate between probability and severity. Participants in this study were given 10 case vignettes, and were subsequently asked to indicate the probability that the described case might result in an unpleasant situation, and the degree of that unpleasantness. Some participants received case vignettes in which a third party played a crucial role (e.g., "Your father forgets to lock his car in a shopping centre car park. Later, while, shopping, you worry that the car may have been stolen"), while other participants received vignettes in which they themselves played the crucial role ("You forget to lock your father's car in a shopping centre car park. Later, while, shopping, you worry that the car may have been stolen"). Results suggested that regardless of the framing of the case vignettes ("third party responsible" versus "personally responsible"), participants rated the probability of the unpleasant outcomes evenly high (i.e., on a VAS ranging from 0 to 100, 24.6 and 27.9, respectively). But, as to severity, participants estimated the severity of the unpleasant outcomes worse when the vignettes were phrased in the personally responsible manner (67.5) than in the third party responsible manner (56.0; $P < .05$). This finding suggests that the anticipated severity of the feared situation may be the most important element in the overinterpretation of intrusive thoughts.

Individual Differences in Responsibility Bias

Just as people differ in suppression-proneness, there are also individual differences in responsibility biases. Rachman and colleagues (1995) came up with an 18-item questionnaire measuring individual differences in four responsibility attitudes: physical harm (e.g., "When driving, it is up to me to make sure that my passengers are wearing safety belts"), social context (e.g., "I should not turn down an invitation from a friend"), positive outlook (e.g., "I would welcome the opportunity to be put in charge of the safety of buildings"), and TAF (e.g., "For me, having a mean thought is as bad as doing something mean"). This so-called Responsibility Appraisal Questionnaire (RAQ) was completed by more than 200 undergraduates. Correlational analyses indicated that only TAF was correlated with obsessive complaints, while the other responsibility manifestations were not.

Soon after the publication of the RAQ, Shafran and colleagues (1996) introduced a refined version merely addressing TAF. This TAF-scale consists of 19 items that are answered on a 5-point scale ($0 = disagree strongly$; $4 = agree strongly$). The items are displayed in Table 6.5. The scale taps both the morality (items 1, 2, 3, 5, 7, 8, 10, 11, 13, 15, 16, and 17) and the probability bias. The latter bias is divided into a probability-for-self (items 6, 12, and 18) and a probability-for-others factor (items 4, 9, 14, and 19). This distinction has proven to be important because probability-for-self has some rational fundament, in that people might live up to their intrusion and, thus, actually suffer the foreseen consequences (cf. self-fulfilling prophecy). For example, the intrusion "I will have a car accident" may be followed by reckless, or dangerously slow and careful driving, increasing the risk of actually being in an accident. The probability-for-others factor, on the other hand, lacks such fundamental rational basis and may therefore be more exclusive to obsessional thinking. Shafran and colleagues' (1996) psychometric study of the TAF-scale, indeed, indicated three factors (morality, and two probability factors, i.e., for-self and for-others). Interfactor correlations were moderate (rs ranged between .32 and .35). The total score as well as the subscales correlated well with measures of obsessive complaints (e.g., MOCI). Furthermore, obsessive samples seemed to score higher on TAF than normal controls. This latter finding is especially true for the probability-for-other subscale. With respect to the morality and probability-for-self subscales, normals are not always found to score lower than obsessionals (see also Rassin, Merckelbach, Muris, & Schmidt, 2001). In short, TAF, as measured by the TAF-scale, appears to be a clinically relevant and "highly reliable construct" (Shafran et al., 1996, p. 387).

Although the TAF-scale is the best-documented questionnaire pertaining to responsibility bias, recently, several questionnaires have been introduced that are not limited to TAF, but address a wider range of responsibility biases. For example, Cartwright-Hatton and Wells (1997) introduced their Meta Cognition Questionnaire (MCQ) that addresses general attitudes regarding thoughts, worries, and mental control. Several items pertain to inflated responsibility beliefs (e.g., "Not being able to control my thoughts is a sign of weakness"). However, the MCQ is construed in such a way that it contains no subscale exclusively pertaining to responsibility biases. Salkovskis and

Table 6.5   The Items of the Thought-Action Fusion Scale

1. Thinking of making an extremely critical remark to a friend is almost as unacceptable to me as actually saying it
2. Having a blasphemous thought is almost as sinful to me as a blasphemous action
3. Thinking about swearing at someone else is almost as unacceptable to me as actually swearing
4. If I think of a relative/friend losing their job, this increases the risk that they will lose their job
5. When I have a nasty thought about someone else, it is almost as bad as carrying out a nasty action
6. If I think of myself being injured in a fall, this increases the risk that I will have a fall and be injured
7. Having violent thoughts is almost as unacceptable to me as violent acts
8. When I think about making an obscene remark or gesture in church, it is almost as sinful as actually doing it
9. If I think of a relative/friend being in a car accident, this increases the risk that he/she will have a car accident
10. If I wish harm on someone, it is almost as bad as doing harm
11. If I think about making an obscene gesture to someone else, it is almost as bad as doing it
12. If I think of myself being in a car accident, this increases the risk that I will have a car accident
13. When I think unkindly about a friend, it is almost as disloyal as doing an unkind thing
14. If I think of a relative/friend being injured in a fall, this increases the risk that he/she will have a fall and be injured
15. If I have a jealous thought, it is almost the same as making a jealous remark
16. Thinking of cheating in a personal relationship is almost as immoral to me as actually cheating
17. Having obscene thoughts in a church is unacceptable to me
18. If I think of myself falling ill, this increases the risk that I will fall ill
19. If I think of a relative/friend falling ill, this increases the risk that he/she will fall ill

From Shafran, R., Thordarson, D.S., & Rachman, S. (1996). Thought-action fusion in obsessive compulsive disorder. *Journal of Anxiety Disorders, 10,* 379–391.

colleagues (2000) introduced two responsibility scales. Their Responsibility Attitude Scale (RAS) measures general beliefs about responsibility (e.g., "To me, not acting to prevent disaster is as bad as making disaster happen"). Their Responsibility Interpretation Questionnaire (RIQ) addresses the strength and frequency of responsibility biases. For example, respondents are asked to indicate how often certain beliefs (e.g., "It would be irresponsible to ignore these thoughts") enter their mind, as well as how strongly they believe these beliefs. Like Cartwright-Hatton and Wells (1997), Salkovskis and colleagues (2000) found that their scales correlated with measures of obsessive complaints.

Thought Suppression and the Cognitive Theory of Obsession

Both the thought suppression paradigm and the cognitive theory of obsession provide an answer to the question how an everyday intrusion can become inflated into a clinically relevant obsession. The core argument of the thought suppression paradigm is that suppressing the pertinent intrusion makes it paradoxically hyperaccessible, resulting in an increased frequency. Other obsessional characteristics (e.g., discomfort, anxiety, and neutralization attempts) are largely left unexplained. These characteristics are, thereby, secondary to the increased frequency of intrusive thoughts. The cognitive theory postulates that the misinterpretation of an intrusion directly makes it more adverse. Thus, the original focus of the two explanations differs: Thought suppression pertains to intrusion frequency, while the cognitive theory addresses the emotional valence of the intrusion. The two accounts also differ with respect to other character-istics. Most importantly, the scopes of the accounts differ. Wegner (1989) distinguishes two kinds of intrusions: traumatic intrusions (which are rooted in an experienced traumatic event) and synthetic intrusions (which lack an obvious cause; see also Lee & Kwon, 2003). According to Wegner, both kinds of intrusions can develop into an obsession, merely due to thought suppression. In Wegner's (1989) words: "The obses-sions we develop from traumas, for instance, are clearly there prior to our desires for avoidance. The ruminations we may have that recall past traumas, then, are often suppressed after they occur. But when no obvious trauma is present, there is the good possibility that the obsession has crept up on us slowly, synthesized over time by a series of our own acts of suppression" (p. 173), and: "What this means is that the development of a synthetic obsession is totally dependent on suppression as the first step" (p. 173). In short, according to Wegner (1989), the thought suppression para-digm is relevant to any obsession, regardless of its content. Although it has been argued that suppression of unpleasant thoughts results in even larger rebound effects compared to neutral thoughts, the bottom line is that any thought is a potential obsession if it is suppressed long enough (Abramowitz et al., 2001). Hence, Wegner's words: "an obsession can grow from nothing but the desire to suppress a thought" (1989, p. 167).

In this respect, the cognitive theory of obsession differs from the thought suppres-sion paradigm. Several researchers have argued that OCD can be subdivided into different categories based on content and symptoms. For example, Calamari, Wiegartz, and Janeck (1999) propose that obsessive thoughts of patients with OCD can be grouped into five clusters: harming, hoarding, contamination, certainty, and rumination. Summerfeldt, Richter, Antony, and Swinson (1999) performed a factor analysis on data obtained from 203 patients with OCD and concluded that a multilevel four factor model described the symptoms in this sample best. These authors reported symptoms ranging from aggressive, religious, and somatic obsessions to repetition, counting, and hoarding compulsions. Interestingly, the cognitive theory of obsession does not pretend to be applicable to all of these differential manifestations of OCD. The core assumption of this theory is that the patient experiences some kind of inflated responsibility for his or her thoughts, resulting in feared anticipated consequences.

Thus, this theory may explain symptoms related to harming, aggressive, and contamination obsessions, as well as compulsive checking and cleaning. On the other hand, the cognitive theory may be of lesser importance in case of hoarding and somatic obsessions, and repetition and counting rituals. As mentioned previously, the thought suppression paradigm is somewhat less articulated when it comes to its explanatory power concerning differential manifestations of OCD.

While the thought suppression paradigm and the cognitive theory can be construed as alternative explanations for the exacerbation of intrusions, they can also be integrated into one "elaborated" cognitive theory. The simplicity and general applicability of the core thesis of the thought suppression paradigm ("an obsession can grow from nothing but the desire to suppress a thought", Wegner, 1989, p. 167) is elegant, but, at the same time, a weakness. That is, the motivation to engage in suppression is irrelevant in the suppression literature because the paradoxical effect is likely to occur anyway, regardless of the motivation of participants. The instruction to suppress a target thought is reason enough for the participant in a suppression experiment to actually engage in suppression. However, in real life, people must have a reason to suppress a specific thought. The most obvious reason to suppress a thought is that one does not want to think of it. Although unpleasant thoughts are more likely to become suppression targets, neutral or even pleasant thoughts can also be unwanted, under specific circumstances. For example, if one is engaged in a concentration demanding task (e.g., a test), one cannot afford to think about anything else during the completion of that task. Similarly, one may find it inappropriate to have sexual thoughts while attending a funeral, even though, in general, sexual thoughts are pleasant. Notwithstanding these examples of unwanted neutral or pleasant thoughts, most suppressed thoughts are considered to be unpleasant. But then, the question arises why some people find some thoughts unpleasant. Why is the impulse to push someone before a train for some people nothing more than a passing irrelevant and senseless thought, while others become intensely upset by this "insane and dangerous" impulse? Why do some people try to suppress every aggressive thought, while others do not? Although the thought suppression paradigm is not interested in these questions, it is worthwhile to acknowledge that the cognitive theory provides an eloquent answer. More specifically, the increased discomfort caused by the misinterpretation of an intrusion (cf. cognitive theory) constitutes a logical basis for suppression attempts. Therefore, it seems appropriate to incorporate thought suppression into the cognitive theory. In recent literature, the combination of interpretation and suppression has indeed become more current. In Rachman's (1998) words: "an inflated increase in the significance attached to an unwanted intrusive thought, such as an obsession, will lead to more vigorous and intense attempts to suppress such thoughts" (p. 393), and: "Given that patients can misinterpret the frequency with which they experience the obsession as evidence for the importance of the obsession (. . .), paradoxical increases in frequency that arise from attempts at suppression, may actually strengthen the catastrophic misinterpretation themselves. A vicious cycle is established" (p. 394). Purdon (1999) points out the generally accepted idea "that the development of obsessions results from negative appraisal of the thought and subsequent coping strategies" (p. 1043), and furthermore: "Suppression is particularly problematic because it will lead to an increase in thought frequency and subsequent need to neutralize" (p. 1043).

Figure 6.6 represents the cognitive theory of obsession (cf. Figure 6.1) with inclusion of thought suppression. According to this elaborated version (see Rachman, 1998), thought suppression occurs as a response to anxiety experienced as a result of the overinterpretation of an intrusion. Thought suppression initiates a positive feedback loop, because it will increase the intrusion frequency, which in turn leads to more discomfort and suppression attempts. Ultimately, Rachman's (1998) vicious circle will occur.

The possible interaction between the appraisal of intrusions, and suppression attempts has hardly been investigated (Warren, Zgourides, & Jones, 1989). One hint that the overinterpretation of intrusive thoughts promotes subsequent suppression attempts comes from the study by Rassin and colleagues (1999), in which participants were made to believe that thoughts of apple resulted in the application of an electrical shock to a peer participant. Participants who had been given this instruction scored 59 on a 100-mm VAS measuring suppression attempts, while control participants scored 20 ($P < .01$). In an attempt to manipulate both the interpretation of intrusions and suppression attempts, Rassin (2001a) submitted 40 undergraduates to the procedure described by Rachman and colleagues (1996). While all participants had to insert the name of a loved one into the typed sentence " I hope that... will soon be in a car accident," half were instructed to suppress any thoughts related to this sentence for 5 minutes. The remaining participants received no such suppression instructions. It was

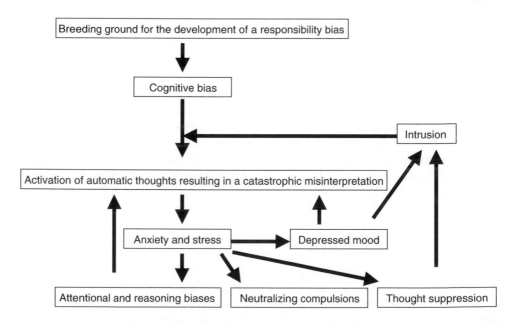

Figure 6.6: Schematic overview of the cognitive theory of obsession with suppression included.

hypothesized that after the 5 minutes, participants in the suppression condition would experience more discomfort, because both the TAF-like sentence and the suppression attempts should add to this, while in the control condition, participants' only source of discomfort was the TAF-like sentence. Contrary to expectation, suppression participants did not report greater discomfort. On the contrary, on some VASs, suppression participants scored lower than did controls (e.g., estimated probability, moral wrongness, time spent thinking about the sentence, responsibility, and guilt). This surprising finding suggests that suppression can be successful, and underlines the importance of future research in this, so far neglected, area.

Although Wegner (1989) claims that thought suppression may be a sufficient cause of obsessional problems, its role within the cognitive theory is more modest. In the cognitive theory of obsession, the (mis)interpretation of intrusive thoughts plays a crucial role in the development of obsessions. Thought suppression may increase the frequency of intrusions, and is therefore an ineffective reaction to intrusive thoughts, just like engaging in neutralization. However, the cognitive theory does not view thought suppression as a necessary causal factor, but rather as a maintaining or exaggerating one.

In summary, anxiety due to the misinterpretation of intrusions may provide a strong reason to suppress intrusions. Thus, the thought suppression paradigm can be assimilated by the cognitive theory of obsession. This combination of the thought suppression paradigm and the cognitive theory implies a twofold restriction of Wegner's (1989) claim that suppression can turn any intrusion into an obsession. First, the cognitive theory seems to pertain only to a subcategory of obsessional problems. Second, the role of thought suppression within the cognitive theory is not that of a primary causal factor, but rather that of a counterproductive reaction to anticipation anxiety, resulting in maintenance and strengthening of complaints.

Thought Suppression in Obsessive-Compulsive Disorder

As mentioned previously, the original white bear experiment by Wegner and colleagues (1987) has been invoked as an explanation for clinical obsessions, as occurring in OCD (Wegner, 1989). To increase the validity of the suppression paradigm as a model of obsession, it would be important to find the claimed paradoxical effect in samples of patients with OCD. In this section, the empirical evidence for the detrimental effect of thought suppression in OCD will be reviewed.

The most obvious reason to suppress a specific thought is that one does not want to have this thought. Patients with OCD may have a second reason to suppress their obsession. Research has indicated that many patients strive to conceal their obsession. Such concealment may be rooted in a reluctance to talk about the "forbidden" thought, or in a fear of rejection if people close to the patient become familiar with the "dirty" thought (Newth & Rachman, 2001). Experimental work of Bouman (2003) suggests that to conceal a specific thought, people tend to suppress it. In the pertinent experiment participants were randomly classified as interviewer or interviewee. The interviewers were instructed to ask the interviewees about their trip to the zoo (this trip was merely imaginary). Half of the interviewees were instructed that they should not mention the elephants in the interview, while the other half received no such instruction. After the interview, interviewees had to indicate how tense they had felt, how many times they had thought about elephants, and to what extent they had tried to suppress thoughts of elephants. The interviewers were asked to indicate to what extent the interviewees appeared to be tensed and discomforted. Comparison of interviewees in the concealment and those in the neutral condition suggested that concealment had led to tension, discomfort, increased elephant thought frequency and increased suppression attempts. Interestingly, interviewers were not able to differentiate between concealing and non-concealing interviewees. The latter finding is in line with the literature on deception detection, suggesting that nonverbal cues of deception are generally very hard to interpret or even nearly impossible to detect (Vrij, 2000).

To study the effect of thought suppression on obsessions, several researchers have modelled obsessions in analogue samples. Smári, Sigurjónsdóttir, and Saemundsdóttir (1994) asked 73 female undergraduates to tallymark every thought about a previously read story during two subsequent experimental periods. For half of the participants, the instruction was that they could think of whatever they wanted during both periods. The other half received a suppression instruction during the first period, and a liberal instruction during the second period. In addition, participants completed the MOCI (a scale tapping obsessive-compulsive complaints). Contrary to expectation, the authors found no evidence for an immediate enhancement or a rebound effect. More importantly, scores on the MOCI correlated negatively with the number of intrusions as well as with self-reported suppression attempts. Thus, these data do not support the notion that OCD is associated with increased suppression proneness or with failing suppression attempts.

Smári, Birgisdóttir, and Brynjólfsdóttir (1995) conducted a comparable study with 85 female undergraduate students. However, the to-be-suppressed thought in this study was a personally relevant intrusion that bothered participants in daily life. These authors did find that participants high on the MOCI suffered more intrusions during suppression attempts than did low scoring individuals. A similar experiment was conducted by Rutledge (1998). Her 109 undergraduates underwent three subsequent 9-minute periods: An expression, suppression, and another expression period. The target thought was a personally relevant intrusion. The findings were quite differentiated. The number of intrusions during suppression correlated significantly with scores on the MOCI, for female participants ($r = .25$). For male participants on the other hand, there was a negative correlation ($r = -.25$). Lastly, the MOCI did not correlate with intrusion frequency during the third period (cf. rebound). Based on these data, Rutledge concluded that the association between immediate enhancement and obsessionality is unclear and that the rebound effect is unrelated to obsessionality.

The studies presented above do not yield much reason to believe that thought suppression is specifically associated with obsession. The designs of these studies share the notion that the degree of obsessionality of nonclinical participants was correlated with the number of target intrusions during a thought suppression experiment. Another approach would be to study suppression in actual OCD samples. Given the claim that suppression can transform a normal intrusion into a clinical obsession (Wegner, 1989), surprisingly few studies have investigated suppression in OCD samples. Rassin, Diepstraten, Merckelbach, and Muris (2001) gathered WBSI scores of 24 patients with OCD before and after treatment. These scores dropped from 58 to 54. Although this change in WBSI-score was significant ($P < .01$), it should be acknowledged that the four points represent only a tiny drop (the total range of the WBSI being 15 to 75). Furthermore, the obtained decrease in WBSI-scores seemed to be present in a control sample of 20 patients with non-OCD anxiety (mainly panic disorder, social phobia, and PTSD). In that sample, pre-treatment scores were comparably high (60), and post-treatment scores were 51 ($P < .01$). The similarity in the pattern of results in both groups suggests that suppression is not exclusively linked to OCD. More importantly, as discussed before, the WBSI does not solely address suppression, but also intrusive thinking. Therefore, the results in this study may not reflect suppression dynamics, but rather changes in experienced symptoms.

Janeck and Calamari (1999) conducted one of the rare suppression experiments published to date in which patients with OCD served as participants. Individuals participating in this study were first asked to identify a recent intrusive thought that would be used as the suppression target. All participants underwent three 5-minute periods: a baseline "think-of-anything" period, an experimental period (either suppression, or think of anything), and a final think-of-anything period. With this design, Janeck and Calamari were able to compare suppression effects between subjects (period 2), as well as within subjects (period 2 vs. period 3). Thus, some participants subsequently underwent a control, suppression, and control period, while others merely went through three control periods. Furthermore, the design dictated that both conditions were run with patients with OCD as well as with normal controls. The results of the study, in terms of self-reported intrusion frequency, are displayed in Figure 6.7. The only significant difference observed by Janeck and Calamari (1999)

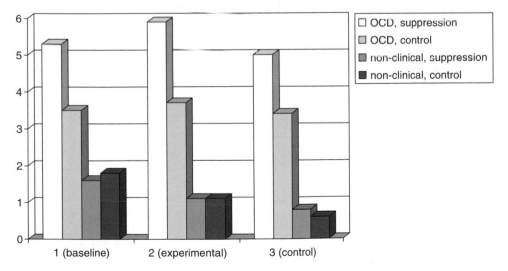

Figure 6.7: Intrusion frequency during three periods. (From Janeck, A.S. & Calamari, J.E. (1999). Thought suppression in Obsessive-Compulsive Disorder. *Cognitive Therapy and Research, 23*, 497–509.)

was that patients with OCD, regardless of experimental condition or period, reported more intrusions than did non-clinical controls. Hence, the authors found no support for the detrimental effect of thought suppression, neither within nor between groups.

Janeck and Calamari (1999) proceeded with a calculation proposed by Rutledge and colleagues (1996). For every participant, an immediate enhancement (intrusion frequency during period 2, divided by the sum of intrusions during periods 1 and 2), and rebound (intrusion frequency during period 3, divided by the sum of intrusions during periods 1 and 3) computation was run. Participants with a score equal to, or higher than 0.6 were categorized as "immediate enhancers," or "rebounders," respectively. In this additional analysis, there seemed to be more individuals suffering from an immediate enhancement in the OCD sample (i.e., 31%) than in the non-clinical sample (19%). Likewise, a greater percentage of patients with OCD was categorized as rebounder (25%), compared to non-clinical controls (0%). In short, while Janeck and Calamari (1999) found no direct experimental suppression effect when looking at their original variable (intrusion frequency), they did find that, compared to nonclinical controls, more patients with OCD suffered from paradoxical effects of thought suppression.

Another experimental study using an OCD sample was conducted by Tolin, Abramowitz, Przeworski, and Foa (2002). These authors criticized the study by Janeck and Calamari (1999) because of the following considerations. First, there was no control anxious sample. Second, the study exclusively relied on self-reports. Third, the use of personally relevant thoughts as suppression targets introduced a possible confounder, in that these thoughts are likely to individually differ in severity, discomfort, and so on. Furthermore, it can be argued that patients with OCD by definition suppress their personally relevant intrusions. Hence, the experiment, and the experimental instructions may not have been all that controlled. To evade these flipsides, Tolin and colleagues (2002) came up with the following design. Participants underwent three subsequent 5-minute periods: baseline control, suppression, and think-of-anything control. The original white bear was used as target thought. The experiment was run with three samples: 15 patients with OCD, 16 patients suffering from other anxiety disorders, and 14 non-anxious controls. Analysis of self-reported thought frequency yielded only one significant finding, that is, only patients with OCD suffered from an immediate increase of thought frequency. In the other samples, no immediate enhancement effects were observed. None of the samples displayed a rebound effect.

Tolin and colleagues (2002) conducted a second experiment in which three similar samples underwent a reaction time procedure. All participants were instructed to suppress thoughts of bears for 5 minutes. During these 5 minutes, they had to carry out the following assignment. They were repeatedly shown a number of words (e.g., scar, gown, and also the target, i.e., bear) on a computer screen, in reaction to which they had to press the A key as rapidly as possible. The series of words also contained a number of non-words (e.g., rekm, bloy, and wati), after which the L key had to be pressed. After the initial task, the same procedure was run a second time, with the exception that, during the second time, the suppression instructions were withdrawn. It was hypothesized that the paradoxical effect of suppression would lead to a hyper-accessibility of the target, and therefore to decreased reaction times, compared to other words and nonwords. Results indicated that the hypothesized decrease of reaction time for the target word was observed in the OCD sample, but not in the other two samples, during the first period. During the second period, no significant differences were found within or between groups.

All in all, the studies of Tolin and colleagues (2002) allow for the conclusion that OCD seems to be marked by a deficit in the ability to suppress neutral thoughts. This deficit manifested as an immediate increase in intrusion frequency, rather than as a rebound effect. Tolin and colleagues interpret their findings as suggesting that there may be important individual differences, not in suppression proneness, but in suppression ability. The fact that the results of Tolin and colleagues in study 2 were similar to those of study 1 decreases the likelihood that the finding can be attributed to self-report artefacts. Thus, Tolin and colleagues also delivered results supportive of the notion that self-reports can be reliable.

Two studies that were discussed previously (Abramowitz et al., 2001; Amir et al., 1997) did not focus on thought suppression per se, but on suppression techniques as indexed by the TCQ. Amir and colleagues found that, compared to 27 non-clinical volunteers, 55 patients with OCD scored higher on all TCQ subscales except distraction. Hence, OCD was concluded to be associated with increased self-punishment, reappraisal, social coping, and worrying in response to experiencing intrusive thoughts. Abramowitz and colleagues (2003) extended this design by including a non-OCD anxiety disorder group. These authors found that self-punishment and worrying were suppression techniques most typical for OCD. By contrast, patients with OCD relied less on social coping and distraction compared to the other groups of participants. The authors also found that after therapy, the use of self-punishment decreased while that of distraction increased.

To summarize, there is only little experimental evidence for the claim that thought suppression plays a role in OCD. That is, so far, only a handful of published studies have used patients with OCD as participants. One of these studies failed to find support for the alleged paradoxical effect of suppression (Janeck & Calamari, 1999), while another found support for an immediate enhancement effect, but not for the rebound effect (Tolin et al., 2002). Plainly, experimental evidence is meagre. Of course, it can be argued that this scarcity of evidence does not necessarily down rate the validity of the thought suppression paradigm, because the core thesis is that suppression increases intrusion frequency, and thus intensifies intrusions. Hence, it may be the case that suppression is not prominent once OCD has developed, while it does play an important role in a prior developmental stage. Admittedly, this ad hoc argument appears somewhat thin.

Conclusion

The main idea borne out by the experiment of Wegner and colleagues (1987) is that suppression of a target thought paradoxically increases the frequency with which that target thought intrudes consciousness. This notion has developed into an important model for the development of obsessions as occurring in OCD. Some theoretical accounts of OCD focus on the origin of obsessions and compulsions. However, there is reason to argue that that approach is clinically less relevant. That is to say that earlier research has indicated that most of us experience intrusions and compulsions regularly (Muris et al., 1997; Rachman & De Silva, 1978). Given that only a percentage of the general population experiences these phenomena as clinically relevant, the important question seems to be how everyday intrusions develop into clinical obsessions. The thought suppression paradigm can answer precisely that question. But so can the cognitive theory of obsession. In this chapter, it is argued that although the thought suppression paradigm and the cognitive theory may be construed as concurrent and alternative explanations, both accounts can be integrated into an elaborated cognitive theory. Such an integration reduces the explanatory power of thought suppression, because within the elaborated cognitive theory, thought suppression is a contributing but not a necessary factor in the development of obsessive-compulsive symptoms.

Another limitation of the thought suppression paradigm, is that despite the frequently uttered claim that suppression fosters obsession, relatively few studies have investigated suppression and its effects in OCD samples. To date, only a handful of thought suppression studies have used actual patients with OCD as participants. Moreover, the results of those studies are – like the bulk of other thought suppression research – not unanimously favorable for the claimed immediate and rebound effects of suppression.

Chapter 7

Thought Suppression and Trauma

Introduction

As discussed in the previous chapter, the thought suppression paradigm has had an important impact on theories concerning the development of obsessive-compulsive disorder (OCD). By now, a number of studies have also addressed the effects of thought suppression on traumatic intrusions. Indeed, it seems logical that individuals who suffer from intrusive recollections (cf. flashbacks) may attempt to suppress those recollections. Hence, the thought suppression paradigm may not only be relevant to theories of OCD, but also to accounts of disorders in which traumatic intrusions are crucial (e.g., posttraumatic stress disorder [PTSD]). Traumatic intrusions differ from obsessions in at least two ways. First, traumatic intrusions are rooted in the experience of a traumatic event, while obsessions are not necessarily so. Second, while obsessions are relatively discrete and possibly verbal, traumatic intrusions are probably (at least partly) visual and relatively elaborated. Therefore, the question arises whether targets such as white bears are suitable as laboratory models of traumatic intrusions. In addition, given the elaborateness of traumatic intrusions, thought suppression may not only affect intrusion frequency, but also the quality (i.e., content) of the intrusion. This chapter focuses on the effect of thought suppression on traumatic intrusions. First, trauma-related psychiatric syndromes and their similarities with OCD will be briefly discussed. Then, the few experimental studies pertaining to the suppression of recollections will be discussed.

Trauma-Related Psychiatric Disorders

In the DSM-IV-TR, two trauma-related anxiety disorders are distinguished: Acute stress disorder (ASD) and PTSD. Evidently, both disorders share their traumatic origin. The clinical pictures of both syndromes are similar. The most important difference is that ASD occurs rapidly after experiencing a traumatic event, while PTSD occurs after a delay of at least one month. The exact diagnostic criteria of ASD and PTSD are displayed in Tables 7.1 and 7.2, respectively.

The prevalence of ASD and PTSD in the general population is not known. Given that the two disorders occur by definition in reaction to trauma, prevalence can best be expressed as a percentage of those who experienced a traumatic event. Research indicates that ASD or PTSD develop in a significant minority of individuals who

Table 7.1   DSM-IV-TR Criteria for Acute Stress Disorder

A. The person has been exposed to a traumatic event in which both of the following were present:
  1. The person experienced, witnessed, or was confronted with an event or events that involved actual or threatened death or serious injury, or a threat to the physical integrity of self or others.
  2. The person's response involved intense fear, helplessness, or horror.
B. Either while experiencing or after experiencing the distressing event, the individual has three (or more) of the following dissociative symptoms:
  1. A subjective sense of numbing, detachment, or absence of emotional responsiveness.
  2. A reduction in awareness of his or her surroundings (e.g., "being in a daze").
  3. Derealization.
  4. Depersonalization.
  5. Dissociative amnesia (i.e., inability to recall an important aspect of the trauma).
C. The traumatic event is persistently reexperienced in at least one of the following ways: recurrent images, thoughts, dreams, illusions, flashback episodes, or a sense of reliving the experience; or distress on exposure to reminders of the traumatic event.
D. Marked avoidance of stimuli that arouse recollections of the trauma (e.g., thoughts, feelings, conversations, activities, places, people).
E. Marked symptoms of anxiety or increased arousal (e.g., difficulty sleeping, irritability, poor concentration, hypervigilance, exaggerated startle response, motor restlessness).
F. The disturbance causes clinically significant distress or impairment in social, occupational, or other important areas of functioning or impairs the individual's ability to pursues some necessary task, such as obtaining necessary assistance or mobilizing personal resources by telling family members about the traumatic experience.
G. The disturbance lasts for a minimum of 2 days and a maximum of 4 weeks and occurs within 4 weeks of the traumatic event.
H. The disturbance is not due to the direct physiological effects of a substance (e.g., a drug of abuse, a medication) or a general medical condition, is not better accounted for by brief psychotic disorder, and is not merely a exacerbation of a preexisting axis I or axis II disorder.

From American Psychiatric Association (APA) (2000). *Diagnostic and Statistical Manual of Mental Disorders, 4th edition, Text Revision (DSM-IV-TR)*. Washington, D.C.: APA.

experience a traumatic event. Estimates range between 14% and 33% (APA, 2000). Risk factors for the development of posttraumatic symptoms include complaints in reaction to previous trauma, personal psychiatric history in general, family psychiatric history, low career achievement, and rigid thinking style (Seligman, Walker, & Rosenhan, 2001). As to the natural course of ASD, the syndrome is likely to develop

Table 7.2 DSM-IV-TR Criteria for Posttraumatic Stress Disorder

A. The person has been exposed to a traumatic event in which both of the following
   were present:
   1. The person experienced, witnessed, or was confronted with an event or events
      that involved actual or threatened death or serious injury, or a threat to the
      physical integrity of self or others.
   2. The person's response involved intense fear, helplessness, or horror.
B. The traumatic event is persistently reexperienced in one (or more) of the following
   ways:
   1. Recurrent and intrusive distressing recollections of the event, including images,
      thoughts, or perceptions.
   2. Recurrent distressing dreams of the event.
   3. Acting or feeling as if the traumatic event were recurring (includes a sense of
      reliving the experience, illusions, hallucinations, and dissociative flashback
      episode, including those that occur on awakening or when intoxicated).
   4. Intense psychological distress at exposure to internal or external cues that
      symbolize or resemble an aspect of the traumatic event.
   5. Physiological reactivity on exposure to internal or external cues that symbolize
      or resemble an aspect of the traumatic event.
C. Persistent avoidance of stimuli associated with the trauma and numbing of general
   responsiveness (not present before the trauma), as indicated by three (or more) of
   the following:
   1. Efforts to avoid thoughts, feelings, or conversations associated with the trauma.
   2. Efforts to avoid activities, places, or people that arouse recollections of the
      trauma.
   3. Inability to recall an important aspect of the trauma.
   4. Markedly diminished interest or participation in significant activities.
   5. Feeling of detachment or estrangement from others.
   6. Restricted range of affect (e.g., unable to have loving feelings).
   7. Sense of a foreshortened future (e.g., does not expect to have a career, marriage,
      children, or a normal life span).
D Persistent symptoms of increased arousal (not present before the trauma), as
   indicated by two (or more) of the following:
   1. Difficulty falling or staying asleep.
   2. Irritability or outbursts of anger.
   3. Difficulty concentrating.
   4. Hypervigilance.
   5. Exaggerated startle response.
E. Duration of the disturbance (symptoms in criteria B, C, and D) is more than
   1 month.
F. The disturbance causes clinically significant distress or impairment in social,
   occupational, or other important areas of functioning.

From American Psychiatric Association (APA) (2000). *Diagnostic and Statistical Manual of Mental Disorders, 4th edition, Text Revision (DSM-IV-TR)*. Washington, D.C.: APA.

into PTSD, given that the symptoms of both disorders show considerable overlap. If left untreated, spontaneous recovery from PTSD occurs within three months, in half of the cases. However, in some cases PTSD can take a chronic and seemingly lifelong course (APA, 2000).

Similarities Between Obsessive-Compulsive Disorder and Posttraumatic Stress Disorder

Although there are marked differences between obsessive and traumatic intrusions, there are also similarities between both kinds of intrusions. Indeed, several studies have yielded evidence to suggest that the criterion "traumatic memories are rooted in trauma, while obsessions are not" may be an oversimplified rule of thumb. For example, Bryant and Harvey (1998) argued that posttraumatic intrusions and obsessive intrusions may not always be readily distinguishable. More specifically, they argued that traumatic recollections are susceptible to posthoc alterations to the extent that they no longer represent the actual event but are replaced by fantasies (e.g., people may imagine worst case scenarios of the experienced event). To test this possibility, the authors asked patients with PTSD about their trauma, and about their recollections thereof. These recollections were compared to third party accounts and, if available, objective reports. Strikingly, participants seemed to be convinced of the veracity of their own intrusive recollections, regardless of correspondence with third party accounts. In the words of Bryant and Harvey (1998): "... even participants who were amnestic of their trauma and whose imagery was documented to be inconsistent with objective accounts of the trauma attributed historical accuracy to their intrusive imagery" (p. 85). This finding is somewhat counterintuitive, because traumatic recollections are generally characterized by intensity, vividness, and intrusiveness, while such characteristics are often considered to indicate veracity.

Lipinski and Pope (1994) took this line of reasoning one step further. These authors presented the following case: "Mr. B, a 45-year-old man with longstanding diagnoses of bipolar disorder and OCD, experienced intrusive images of dead animals, corpses lying in blood, or bodies crushed or cut in half by a train. The images were repetitive and severely distressing; the patient was compelled to think specific opposing thoughts to drive away the images. He stated that he 'saw' the images vividly but fleetingly 'like a picture.' During a recent hospital admission, the patient was rediagnosed as having posttraumatic stress disorder, borderline personality disorder, and multiple personality disorder. These diagnoses were based largely on the images, which, were interpreted as flashbacks. Treatment with insight-oriented psychotherapy directed at uncovering the traumas responsible for the flashbacks was recommended. However, the patient experienced resolution of the images over a period of approximately 2 months with clomipramine treatment alone" (p. 245). A second case is described as follows: "Ms. A, a 25-year-old woman, displayed a 10-year history of severe obsessive and compulsive symptoms including constant obsessions of dirt and contamination, rituals of washing her hands 100 to 125 times per day, and compulsive cleaning of her kitchen, eating utensils, and bathroom for 4 to 8 hours daily. She also experienced intrusive images of violent or frightening scenes. For example, she was herself as a child with her father about to stab her, and then herself sitting in a pool of blood. (This never actually occurred in her childhood.) Even more commonly, she saw her house burning down and her children burning, smothering, or being stabbed in the chest. She described these experiences a 'seeing them in my mind's eye, very vividly, like a picture . . . like a slide show changing from one picture to another.' Upon experiencing these images, she would compulsively check and recheck her children and her house. During several psychiatric admissions, the patient's images were interpreted by treatment personnel as flashbacks of repressed childhood trauma, and a diagnosis of posttraumatic stress disorder was recorded. The patient states that she was encouraged to enter insight-oriented psychotherapy to discover the past traumas underlying her flashbacks. However, treatment with fluoxetine 20 mg daily led to virtual disappearance of her obsessions, compulsions, and images within 6 weeks. Indeed, the patient briefly developed manic symptoms on fluoxetine" (p. 245). In these cases, and others, what were thought to be intrusive memories, turned out to be obsessive fantasies. Hence, the misdiagnoses of PTSD were replaced by OCD. Apparently, it is not always easy to distinguish intrusive memories from obsessive intrusions.

Another interesting case was presented by Pitman (1993). The 46-year-old B.A. entered the mental health care as a Vietnam veteran. He had served two Vietnam tours during which he had been in hundreds of combat missions, for which he received two Purple Hearts. The traumatic experiences (e.g., seeing many corpses, and being shot at) were accompanied by symptoms of depersonalization and alienation. In times of extreme danger, he felt as if his mind left his body. He protected himself from mental collapse by thinking of his colleagues as "pieces of meat," rather than humans. He also developed OCD-like routines, such as counting (fired rounds, feet of dead soldiers), checking (his cigarettes), and doubting (whether he had really chambered a round in his rifle). When B.A. returned home, it became clear that he had developed multiple psychiatric symptoms, including OCD, PTSD, dysthymia, and panic disorder. For him, there was no difference between his intrusive recollections and his obsessions. Whereas Lipinski and Pope (1994) argue that obsessions might be mistaken for flashbacks, Pitman (1993) argues that the reverse might also occur: obscene intrusions may sometimes be actual recollections instead of obsessions. For example, B.A. patrolled his property for signs of intrusion, and was scared by visits from the mailman. This patrolling can be construed as compulsive checking, although it might also be reexperiencing Vietnam activities. Not only does this case illustrate the osmosis of OCD and PTSD, it also proves that trauma can cause OCD. Pitman even speaks of a possible shared "pathogenic role of anxiety" in OCD and PTSD (1993, p. 105).

Further support for the causal role of traumatic experiences in the development of OCD was obtained by Khanna, Rajendra, and Channabasavanna (1998), who interviewed 32 patients with OCD about all major negative life events they had ever experienced. The results suggested that, compared to a sample 32 nonclinical participants, patients with OCD had experienced significantly more life event in the 6 months preceding the onset of their obsessive-compulsive complaints. More recently, De Silva and Marks (1999) presented eight further examples of patients in whom OCD developed following a traumatic incident. Generally, the content of the OCD symptoms was traceable to the trauma (e.g., checking door locks after being assaulted, and washing and cleaning after being raped). In some cases however, there was no obvious link between the OCD symptoms and the preceding trauma (e.g., praying after being robbed, cleaning after having been in a road accident, and experiencing upsetting intrusive imagery after being witness to a crime, while this imagery was not linked to the crime). The authors discussed several mechanisms by which PTSD can transform into OCD. For one thing, overt behavior directly caused by an experienced traumatic event (e.g., checking the door lock after being robbed in one's own house) may in time develop into ritualistic activity. Much the same is true for mental activities. For example, pleasant mental images deliberately created in reaction to an intrusive memory of a traumatic event, may become intrusive themselves, and thus satisfy criteria for obsessions. Alternatively, people may acquire misinterpretations in reaction to experiencing traumatic intrusive memories (e.g., "These flashbacks indicate that I am losing control"). In turn, these misinterpretations foster obsessional thinking. All in all, De Silva and Marks (1999) emphasize the intertwinement of PTSD and OCD, and recommend that therapists routinely enquire about possible traumatic events when assessing patients with OCD.

Gershuny, Bear, Radomsky, Wilson, and Jenike (2003) argue that OCD may be functional in reducing distress caused by PTSD. That is, obsessive-compulsive symptoms can constitute the avoidance of trauma-related emotions. They illustrate this with four cases. In one of these cases, the patient (a single female in her early forties) had developed the compulsion to wash her hands whenever she had contact with the "unlucky" number 54. In her youth, she had been repeatedly traumatized by her father (e.g., sexual abuse). He killed his wife (the patient's stepmother) and ordered the patient to help him clean the blood from the carpet. The stepmother was 54 years old. The compulsive washing after confrontation with the number 54 was in effect a way to avoid thoughts or feelings associated with the trauma (i.e., the killing of the patient's stepmother). By this line of reasoning, a reduction of compulsive behavior prevents the patient from avoiding trauma-cues, which results in a (temporary) increase of posttraumatic stress. Indeed, in the cases presented by Gershuny and colleagues, decrease of OCD was associated with increase of PTSD, while an increase of OCD lessened PTSD severity. Hence, in some tenacious cases, patients stumble from one seemingly treatment-resistant disorder to another.

So far, it has been argued that obsessions can be mistaken for recollections, and vice versa. Hence, the line between OCD and PTSD is not always clear. Scott and Stradling (1994) further elaborated on the arbitrariness of current diagnoses. They presented the following case: "Charles, a middle manager in a large organization, was subject to 18 months of persistent 'dumping' of work on him by a superior driven by the anticipation of a merger with a rival organization. His boss never said 'No' to his superiors, and delegated all the extra work to Charles and his staff.... Charles prided himself on his fairness as a manager, but was denied the resources for his staff to do an adequate job. He became nauseous at the sight of his work and avoided it. He had flashbacks to a number of encounters with his boss over the previous 18 months. At home, he was uncharacteristically irritable with his family. When assessed after being off work for 6 weeks, he had all the hallmarks of PTSD—save the trauma—and was also severely depressed" (1994, p. 72). Accordingly, Scott and Stradling (1994) argue that one can develop PTSD without having experienced a single discrete traumatic event. Therefore, the requirement of a "traumatic event outside the range of usual human experience" as explicitly stated in the DSM-III-R (APA, 1987), but no longer in the fourth edition, denied individuals like Charles a fitting diagnosis. To fill this gap, the authors proposed a new diagnosis called prolonged duress stress disorder (PDSD).

Suppression of Elaborated Stimuli: Effects on Frequency

Evidently, the intrusive traumatic recollections characteristic of ASD (see Table 7.1, criterion C) and PTSD (see Table 7.2, criterion B) are likely to become targets of suppression attempts. Indeed, attempts to avoid trauma-related thoughts, feelings, and external stimuli are hallmarks of ASD (criterion D) and PTSD (criterion C). As mentioned before, the elaborateness of traumatic recollections raises not only the question of the effect of suppression on target frequency, but also that of possible effects on the quality of memory. Several studies have addressed the former issue. Bryant and Harvey (1995) carried out a survey of 56 survivors of motor vehicle accidents. This survey was done approximately 1 year after the accident, and included among others, perceived severity of the accident scales, a scale measuring avoidant coping style, and the IES. To test the effect of suppression on intrusion frequency, the authors conducted a regression analysis in which avoidant coping, and perceived and actual severity of the accident served as predictors. The dependent variable was the intrusion subscale of the IES. It was found that avoidant coping was the strongest predictor of intrusion frequency ($r = .56$, $P < .001$). Although these findings support the notion that avoidance (cf. suppression) fosters intrusions, it must be acknowledged that the data are cross-sectional in nature, and therefore do not justify causal inferences. Amir, Kaplan, Efroni, Levine, Benjamin, and Kotler (1997) compared three groups of participants with respect to their habitual coping styles: 46 PTSD patients, 42 non-PTSD anxiety disorder patients, and 50 nonclinical individuals. Participants completed the IES and the Coping Style Questionnaire (Plutchik, 1989). The latter scale taps eight distinct coping styles: suppression, help-seeking, replacement, blame, substitution, mapping, reversal, and minimization. One finding was that PTSD patients scored significantly higher on suppression than both the non-PTSD anxiety group and the healthy control group. Next, Amir et al. computed correlations between the eight coping styles on the one hand, and the IES on the other hand. These correlations were limited to the PTSD group. Interestingly, of the eight coping styles, suppression was the only strategy that correlated with the IES. Hence, these data support the notion that suppression and intrusion are associated. Again, the cross-sectional nature of the correlation precludes strong conclusions as to causality.

Harvey and Bryant (1998b) subjected 48 participants to three subsequent 5-minute periods. All participants were survivors of motor vehicle accidents. Half developed ASD, while the other half did not. The target thoughts during all three periods were thoughts about the accident. Some participants underwent three suppression-free liberal periods, while others were instructed to suppress trauma-related thoughts, only during the second interval. During every period, the participants had to indicate the occurrence of target thoughts by pressing a button that was connected to a computer. The number of button presses is displayed in Figure 7.1. As can be seen, compared to controls, ASD patients experienced more trauma-related thoughts during all three periods. In addition, ASD-patients who had suppressed the target thoughts during the second period, experienced more intrusions during the third, compared to their nonsuppressing peers. Hence, these ASD patients experienced a rebound effect, while no such effect was evident in the non-ASD groups. These data support the idea that suppression of traumatic intrusions can have the same paradoxical effect as the suppression of trivial thoughts like white bears. Interestingly, the paradoxical effect merely occurred with ASD patients, and not with nonclinical participants.

Guthrie and Bryant (2000) adapted the design of Harvey and Bryant (1998) to explore the longer term effects of suppressing trauma recollections. In this study, 40 motor vehicle accident survivors were included, 20 of whom had developed ASD. The participants underwent three subsequent periods. Half went through three liberal periods, while the other half underwent a liberal-suppression-liberal combination. However, every period lasted 24 hours, instead of 5 minutes. Trauma-related thoughts had to be monitored for 3 days, and for the occurrence of every target a tick had to be put on a piece of paper. Guthrie and Bryant found, like Harvey and Bryant, that ASD patients experienced more target thoughts (i.e., 10.87) per day than did non-ASD

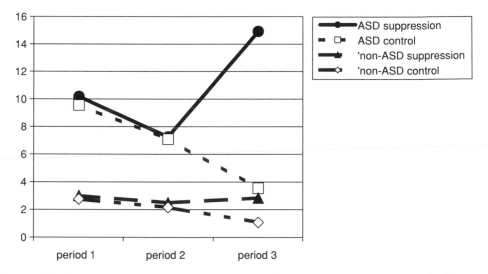

Figure 7.1: Target thought frequency as a function of condition and period. (From Harvey, A.G. & Bryant, R.A. (1998b). The effect of attempted thought suppression in acute stress disorder. *Behaviour Research and Therapy, 36*, 583–590.)

participants (3.50 per day). However, in the present study, no effect of suppression was observed, which suggests that the paradoxical effect of suppressing traumatic intrusions may be short-lived.

In another study, Shipherd and Beck (1999) invited 36 women to participate in a thought suppression experiment. All women had been sexually assaulted. Seventeen women met the criteria for PTSD as a consequence of the assault, while 19 did not, although they did experience posttraumatic stress symptoms at a subclinical level. Participants underwent three 9-minute periods: a liberal period, a suppression period, and another liberal period. During the suppression period, participants were instructed to try not to think about the sexual assault. During all periods, participants had to write down the contents of the thoughts that went through their minds. Afterward, the transcripts were analyzed, and the number of thoughts about the assault as a percentage of all thought topics was calculated. Hence, for every period a percentage was calculated for the PTSD and for the non-PTSD participants. The percentages for the latter group of participants were 15, 7, and 5, respectively. Those for the PTSD patients were 31, 8, and 21. Apparently, PTSD patients had more traumatic thoughts during the liberal periods (1 and 3), while they had relatively few intrusions during suppression attempts (period 2). Furthermore, although there was no significant rebound effect, PTSD patients reported an increase in intrusion frequency from period 2 to 3, while non-PTSD participants did not. In reference to the PTSD group, Shipherd and Beck summarize the findings as "indicating both successful suppression and a rebound effect" (1999, p. 106).

Davies and Clark (1998) modelled a real life event (and possible thought suppression target) by showing participants a film clip, a manipulation that was introduced by Wegner, Quillian, and Houston (1996). Davies and Clark wanted to differentiate between the effects of suppression of a neutral recollection and that of a traumatic recollection. To that end, participants were shown two film clips of 3 minutes duration each. The traumatic clip was a fragment of a fire safety video in which a large building was on fire and in which several people were killed. The neutral film showed a polar bear in its natural setting. The order in which the film clips were shown was counterbalanced. After each film clip, participants underwent two 2-minute periods. During the first period half of the participants ($n = 16$) were instructed not to think of the film clip, while the other half were given liberal instructions. Before the second period, all participants received liberal instructions. During both periods, participants had to verbalize their stream of consciousness and had to press a button whenever film-related thoughts entered their consciousness. The verbalizations were recorded and analyzed afterward to obtain target thought frequencies as percentages of all thoughts. The findings are presented in Table 7.3. As can be seen in this table, there was no increase in button presses during the second period, regardless of whether participants saw a neutral or traumatic film. However, when looking at the percentages, such an increase was present in the suppression condition, but not in the control condition. Although the increase appeared to be stronger in case of the traumatic film, statistical analyses revealed that this difference was not significant. Nonetheless, Davies and Clark concluded that "there was a rebound effect for analogue traumatic intrusions although not for polar bear thoughts" (1998, p. 571).

Table 7.3 Film-related Thoughts

		Polar bear film suppression	Control	Disaster rilm suppression	Control
Period 1	Button presses	2.5	3.0	2.8	3.6
	Percentage	14.3	44.9	27.7	72.8
Period 2	Button presses	2.1	2.4	1.5	2.6
	Percentage	36.4	25.2	52.3	36.4

From Davies, M.I. & Clark, D.M. (1998). Thought suppression produces a rebound effect with analogue posttraumatic intrusions. *Behaviour Research and Therapy*, *36*, 571–582.

Like Davies and Clark (1998), Harvey and Bryant (1998a) sought to explore the effects of suppressing recollections with differential emotional valence. These authors invited 72 undergraduate psychology students to participate in their experiment. Participants were allocated to one of six experimental conditions. These conditions were formed based upon instruction (suppression versus liberal) and film valence (neutral, distressing, or humorous). Hence participants were shown a 3-minute fragment of a neutral film ("The Lilac Bus"), a distressing film ("Taxi Driver"), or a humorous film ("Mr. Bean"). After having seen the film clip, participants underwent two 3-minute periods. During the first period, half of the participants were instructed to suppress recollections of the film, while the other participants were free to think of anything. During the second period, all participants received liberal instructions. During both periods, thoughts of the film, if any, had to be indicated by pressing a button. The number of film-related thoughts in the various conditions is displayed in Table 7.4. The findings indicated that the distressing film caused more intrusions than did the neutral and humorous films. In addition, suppression during period 1 was followed by a significant increase in intrusion frequency in period 2 regardless of film valence. Thus, these data suggest a rather robust rebound

Table 7.4 Film-Related Thoughts

		Period 1	Period 2
Neutral film	Suppression	3.5	6.3
	Control	5.7	4.1
Distressing film	Suppression	8.0	11.8
	Control	10.9	7.1
Humorous film	Suppression	4.7	7.7
	Control	8.3	5.5

From Harvey, A.G. & Bryant, R.A. (1998a). The role of valence in attempted thought suppression. *Behaviour Research and Therapy*, *36*, 757–763.

effect. The fact that this rebound effect also occurred with the neutral and humorous film clips, lessens the validity of the thought suppression paradigm as a model of PTSD, according to the authors. In their words: "the present findings suggest that ironic effects of attempted suppression are not limited to distressing stimuli, and thus question the utility of the thought suppression paradigm as an explanation of clinical intrusions" (Harvey & Bryant, 1998a, p. 763). Despite this conclusion by the authors, the fact remains that they found thought suppression to result in a thought rebound. Evidently, a rebound of trauma-related recollections is more likely to be termed clinically relevant, than is a rebound of humorous recollections (e.g., of an encounter with Mr. Bean).

In summary, findings from various studies have indicated that the suppression of recollections can result in the same paradoxical target increase as does the suppression of white bear thoughts. This seems to be so with personally relevant (idiosyncratic recollections) as well as with personally irrelevant recollections (e.g., thoughts of a film). Likewise, there is some evidence to suggest that the paradoxical effect is not limited to traumatic recollections, but also affects the frequency of neutral or even humorous memories.

Suppression of Elaborated Stimuli: Effects on Memory

As mentioned previously, whereas the original white bear experiment (Wegner et al., 1987) focused on the effect of thought suppression on intrusion frequency, it would also be worthwhile to explore the effect of suppression on the quality of recollections. In other words, in addition to the question of frequency, the content of the suppressed recollection is an important topic of scientific research. However, surprisingly few studies have addressed this issue. Only recently, Wegner and colleagues (1996) came up with an adaptation of the original Wegner and colleagues (1987) thought suppression paradigm, which was especially developed for the study of the effect of suppression on episodic memory. The authors were interested in the effect of suppressing recollections, because they noticed that "victims of traumatic events often describe their recollections of these episodes as fragmentary, more like snapshots or slides than the replay of a continuous experience" (Wegner et al., 1996. p. 680). They hypothesized that this snapshot likeness is caused by suppression. Justly, they argue that their new study fundamentally differed from previous thought suppression research: "the memory disorder hypothesis is not an obvious extension of experimental studies of thought suppression to date. In fact, these studies indicate that people have trouble even eliminating a thought from consciousness, much less erasing it from memory," (Wegner et al., 1996, p. 680) and: "the traumatic experiences that people might suppress thoughts about are not white bears or concrete nouns, of course, but rather are temporally extended sequences of events with a range of sensory aspects, many personal implications, and multiple forms of potential memory representation" (p. 681).

In their first experiment, Wegner and colleagues (1996) showed participants a 10-minute film clip "that was selected to be interesting but nontraumatic" (p. 682).

Next, participants were sent home for five hours with differential instructions. Some participants were instructed to suppress film-related thoughts, if any ($n = 22$), others were instructed to think about the film clip as much as possible ($n = 24$), and a last group of participants ($n = 21$) received liberal instructions. Five hours later, participants returned to the laboratory, and completed several questionnaires and assignments. For example, they had to indicate how often they had thought about the film. Also, they rated the vividness (e.g., "How vivid is your memory of the film clip?") and fluency (e.g., "Can you replay the clip in your mind from beginning to end?", and "Do your memories of the film look like snapshots or a rolling film?") of their recollection of the film. Their actual memory was tested by means of cued recall (i.e., 21 questions). Lastly, participants had to put five fragments from the film clip in the correct chronological order. It was found that participants in the expression group had thought more often about the film ($M = 8.12$) than those in the suppression ($M = 3.27$) and liberal conditions ($M = 2.57$). The latter two conditions did not differ significantly from each other. Participants in the suppression condition experienced their recollection of the film clip as more fragmented, snapshot-like than did participants in the other two conditions. Furthermore, suppression participants' performance on the fragment ordering assignment was worse than that of other participants. Hence, the data supported the notion that suppression results in a decline of memory, more specifically in an experienced and actual loss of chronological accuracy.

In a second experiment, participants were shown a 35-minute film clip that again was not particularly emotional or traumatic, and were subsequently divided over suppression ($n = 53$), expression ($n = 52$), and liberal ($n = 52$) conditions. Five hours later, participants returned to the laboratory and completed various questionnaires and assignments, including a free recall test. As in study 1, expression participants reported to have experienced more film-related thoughts ($M = 5.98$) than suppression ($M = 2.34$) and liberal ($M = 2.29$) participants. In this case, there was no significant difference between groups with respect to clip ordering performance. The authors employed a formula to estimate sequence memory by analyzing participants' free recall. ANOVA indicated a nonsignificant ($P = .08$) group difference on this new sequence memory variable. Subsequently, Wegner and colleagues (1996) conjoined the expression and liberal groups, and compared this new group with the suppression group. With this additional analysis, suppression participants were proven to perform worse on chronology than other participants ($P = .03$). As to perceived snapshot likeness, ANOVA yielded no group differences. Again, the authors conducted a subsequent planned comparison analysis in which the suppression group was compared to the expression-plus-liberal group. The former group scored 3.17 on the 5-point snapshot likeness scale, while the latter scored 2.95. This difference was marginally significant ($P = .05$).

Wegner and colleagues (1996) discuss several possible explanations for their findings. One explanation might be experimental demand. Participants in the suppression condition might have feigned a loss of memory because they expected that the researchers hoped to find just that. However, this explanation raises the question why participants would exclusively have performed worse on sequence memory and not on the more obvious measures of cued and free recall. A second explanation could be distractor association. The act of suppression might have caused suppressed pieces of memory to become associated with certain external distractors—that in turn had come to function as retrieval cues during the day. At the memory test, however, these cues were no longer available, which might have resulted in a loss of memory. As with the demand explanation, the question arises why the effect would be limited to sequence memory. The findings might also be attributed to rehearsal interruption. That is, participants in the suppression group were prevented to rehearse the film clip because they suppressed film-related thoughts once they came up in consciousness. The lack of rehearsal might have created the memory loss. However, Wegner and colleagues argue that if this explanation is valid, participants in the expression condition should be expected to perform better than those in the liberal condition. The data yielded no support for this expectation. A related explanation is retrieval inhibition, which implies that suppression prevented film-related thoughts from entering consciousness in the first place. Given that participants in the suppression condition reported some film-related intrusions, this explanation does not seem to apply to the present data. The explanation that the authors seemingly prefer is termed scene activation, and boils down to the following. The to-be-suppressed stimuli in the studies were fairly elaborated (i.e., film clips of 10 and 35 minutes respectively). Therefore, film-related intrusions are likely to pertain to specific scenes of the film rather than to the complete clip. These scenes (which were probably the most impressive anyway) are subsequently suppressed and paradoxically strengthened. These specific, suppressed scenes may become so hyperaccessible that they compromise the overall memory of the film clip, thus deteriorating memory of the chronology of the filmed events. This explanation is elegant because it reconciles the paradoxical effect of suppression with a memory undermining quality.

Indeed, Wegner and colleagues interpreted their findings as supportive of the notion that memories can be repressed: "The snapshot effect of suppression suggests that people might indeed do something that resembles the effect attributed to classical repression" (1996, p. 689). They also argue that the memory fragmentation caused by suppression may foster the development of false memories. By this view, the snapshots may no longer represent a meaningful event, and gaps in the recollection may be filled with post hoc information. If this post hoc information is false, but credible, the individual is likely to incorporate the information in his recollection. In the words of Wegner and colleagues: "the snapshots would seem meaningless until they were assembled into a sensible sequence, and the invented sequence could be compelling only because it is meaningful...false recovered memories might be embraced, then, because they bring scattered snapshots back into an understandable order" (1996, p. 690).

Notwithstanding the far going interpretation of Wegner and colleagues' (1996) findings, several methodological comments on their studies are in line. First, the nature of the stimuli deserves some comment. Of course, it is an important achievement that the authors used a film as target stimulus, instead of a discrete (obsessional) thought. By using a film clip, the authors increased the validity of their study as a model of suppressing traumatic recollections. However, it is somewhat unfortunate that the film clips were specifically chosen to be nontraumatic. Given this nontraumatic nature of the stimuli, it can not be excluded that the findings by Wegner and colleagues merely pertain to neutral recollections and not to traumatic ones. Another comment is that the findings were "modest," or "not particularly strong" (Wegner et al., 1996, p. 688). In study 1, the memory undermining effect of thought suppression was limited to experienced and actual fragmentation, leaving other memory characteristics (e.g., cued recall) unaffected. Thus, the effects were very specific. In study 2, these findings were almost not replicated. There was no group difference in clip ordering. The authors made quite a stretch to obtain an effect of suppression on sequence memory. That is, they had to analyze free recall in order to gather information on sequence memory, and still found only a nonsignificant effect in the ANOVA ($P = .08$). Only after making two groups instead of three, the difference attained significance. The same reduction of groups was needed to find an effect ($N = 157$, $P = .05$) on perceived snapshot likeness. Thus, the effects were very modest, to say the least. Lastly, the scene activation hypothesis can be criticized as an explanation for the findings. This hypothesis implies that specific suppressed scenes become hyperaccessible, thus disrupting overall sequence memory. Therefore, it implies a paradoxical increase of thoughts about these specific scenes. However, in neither experiment, such an increase of target thoughts was observed. In both studies, suppression participants reported an equal number of film-related thoughts as did participants in the liberal condition. In addition, suppression participants experienced fewer film-related thoughts than did their expressing peers.

In summary, the studies by Wegner and colleagues (1996) have opened the door to the idea that suppression of elaborated stimuli results in depressed memory. More specifically, actual and perceived sequence memory may be affected. These findings are reminiscent of the Freudian idea of repressing memories. However, it is important to note that the findings by Wegner and colleagues are rather small. In addition, some important critiques can be made, pertaining to the nontraumatic nature of the stimuli, and the lack of a satisfactory explanation. Hence, it still remains to be proven that traumatic experiences can actually be repressed from memory, as posited by Freud.

To date, a handful of studies have built on the work by Wegner and colleagues (1996). Rassin, Merckelbach, and Muris (1997) sought to replicate the findings by Wegner and colleagues, but used a traumatic film clip instead of a neutral one. The stimulus in this study was a 3-minute film clip of a "faces-of death" video in which a tourist is attacked by a grizzly bear. From a previous study, it was known that this fragment was generally experienced as emotional and fairly aversive. After having seen the film fragment, participants were sent home for 5 hours. Half of the participants ($n = 26$) received instructions to suppress film-related thoughts, if any, while the other half ($n = 24$) received no further instruction. During the afternoon session, participants completed a questionnaire that addressed several aspects of their recollection. Among other things, they had to indicate the number of film-related thoughts they had experienced during the past five hours. In addition, they underwent a cued recall test. Some of these items pertained to the content of film (e.g., "Did the deer walk from left to right, or from right to left?"), while others specifically address sequence memory (e.g., "In the film two animals were shown, a deer and a grizzly; which animal was shown first?"). Furthermore, several items of the Memory Characteristics Questionnaire (Johnson et al., 1988) were completed. These items address the clarity, contextual embedding, and perceived intensity of one's recollection. Findings suggested that suppression did not result in a decrease of memory accuracy, including sequence memory. Furthermore, suppression participants experienced their recollection of the film clip as clearer than did control participants. Lastly, suppression participants experienced more film-related thoughts ($M = 3.5$) during the day than did controls ($M = 2.1$). Hence, these findings are more in line with the bulk of the thought suppression literature suggesting that suppression paradoxically makes thoughts hyperaccessible. The difference between these findings and those of Wegner and colleagues (1996) may be attributed to the differences in the to-be-suppressed stimuli. While Wegner and colleagues used 10- to 35-minute neutral film clips, Rassin and colleagues relied on a 3-minute traumatic film clip. In summary, the present findings cast doubt on the claim by Wegner and colleagues that suppression of traumatic recollections results in a decline of memory. Perhaps then, suppression has some desired (i.e., memory undermining) effects in case of neutral memories, but not with emotional recollections.

Rassin (2001b) studied the effect of thought suppression on memory by using the Gudjonsson Suggestibility Scale (GSS) as memory test. The GSS (Gudjonsson, 1984) was introduced as a test of interrogative suggestibility. It is administered as follows. First, a short story is read to the respondent. Next, the respondent is asked to reproduce the story as accurately as possible. This free recall test can take place immediately or after a delay period. After this, the respondent is asked a set of 20 questions about the story, 15 of which are leading in that they imply information that was not in the original story. Following this, the interrogator retreats briefly and returns to tell the respondent that he/she made several mistakes and, therefore, must answer all questions once more. Administered in this way, the GSS renders information about memory and confabulation. Furthermore, the tendency to accept posthoc misinformation can be expressed by summing the number of times that the respondent gives in to leading questions during the first questioning. This number can range from 0 to 15 and is referred to as the "yield" score. The number of changed answers during the second round as compared to the first is referred to as "shift." The shift score ranges from 0 to 20 and is thought to indicate the extent to which the respondent is susceptible to social pressure. A total suggestibility score can be computed by summing up the yield and shift score. Consequently, total scores range form 0 to 35. The psychometric qualities of the GSS have been proven to be satisfactory (Gudjonsson, 1997b, 2003; Merckelbach, Muris, Wessel, & Van Koppen, 1998), and, thus, this scale can be considered a standardised measure of memory and suggestibility. Apart from the fact that the GSS provides a good memory index, there was a second reason to use this scale to investigate the effects of thought suppression on memory. Note that, according to the "trace strength hypothesis" (see Coxon & Valentine, 1997), decreased memory is likely to be accompanied by increased suggestibility. The reason for this may be that a poor memory hinders the detection of discrepancies between misleading information and the original event. Given this hypothesized relationship, thought suppression may not only have memory-undermining effects, but may consequently also increase suggestibility.

In the Rassin (2001b) study, participants listened to the GSS story and were subsequently divided over three conditions: A suppression ($n = 20$), an expression ($n = 19$), and a liberal ($n = 17$) condition. Participants in the suppression condition were instructed to suppress story-related thoughts for 5 minutes, after which they were given a pause of 5 minutes. Following this break, they were again instructed to suppress story-related thoughts. All in all, participants underwent five experimental 5-minute periods separated by four 5-minute breaks. The same procedure was followed in the expression and liberal conditions. During the experimental periods, participants had to tally mark the number of story-related thoughts. The idea behind this inter-changing procedure was that it made possible a relatively long experimental period, during which the instruction could be repeated four times. In addition, it seems logical that in real life, suppression periods are also interchanged with suppression-free episodes (see Wegner, 1989). After this induction, participants were asked several meta-memory questions, completed a free recall assignment, and were asked the 20 questions of the GSS twice.

The number of story-related thoughts is displayed in Figure 7.2. As can be seen, suppression participants reported fewer intrusions than those in the other conditions during most of the periods. As to the other variables, the only differences were that suppression resulted in a worse free recall performance compared to expression but not compared to liberal instructions, and suppression resulted in a perceived snapshot likeness of the recollection of the story, compared to expression.

These findings are somewhat reminiscent of those by Wegner and colleagues (1996). Interestingly, like those authors, Rassin (2001b) used a fairly neutral suppression target (i.e., a story about a woman who is on vacation in Spain and gets robbed). Hence, these findings underline the idea that suppression may be somewhat effective (i.e., memory-undermining) in case of nontraumatic recollections.

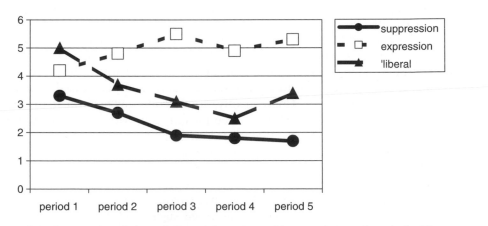

Figure 7.2: Story-related thoughts as a function of instruction and period. (From Rassin, E. (2001b). Thought suppression, memory, and interrogative suggestibility. *Psychology, Crime & Law, 7*, 45–55. Used with acknowledgement of Taylor & Francis Ltd., http: // www.tandf.co.uk/journals.)

A previously discussed study by Rassin and colleagues (2003) bears relevance on the issue of suppressing memories. The participants in that study listened to an audiotaped story based on Wenzlaff and colleagues (1988). This story is fairly adverse: It is about a person who is late for an important job interview, and has to speed in his car to get there in time. Then he causes a car crash in which a baby gets killed. After hearing this story, participants were sent home with different instructions. Some participants ($n = 20$) were told to suppress any thoughts about the story, while those in the control condition received no further instructions ($n = 20$). The authors were interested in the effects of manipulating beliefs about the efficacy of thought suppression. Therefore, two additional suppression conditions were included. Participants in both conditions had to suppress story-related thoughts, if any. However, they were given different information about the efficacy of suppression. One group of participants ($n = 20$) were told that suppression is generally effective (the "suppression-works" condition), while another group of participants ($n = 25$) were told that suppression is generally found to have paradoxical effects (i.e., the "suppression-does-not-work" condition). Two hours later, participants returned to the laboratory, where they completed several questionnaires including memory tests. First, they had to estimate the number of story-related thoughts that they had experienced during the 2 hours. They also had to evaluate the success of their suppression attempts on a VAS from 0 (*not at all*) to 100 (*very*). Similar VASs were completed for meta-memory, snapshot likeness, and the unpleasantness of the story. Finally, they had to recall the story to the best of their knowledge. The observed scores of the four groups are displayed in Table 7.5. As can be seen, the additional instructions did not affect the actual accuracy of recollections (neither did suppression per se), but there were effects on target thought frequency, perceived suppression efficacy, and emotional valence of the story. More specifically, negative instructions resulted in an increase of intrusions, and in a reduction of perceived suppression efficacy. Positive instructions resulted in a decrease of perceived aversiveness of the story. To sum up, these data suggest that suppression may affect the

Table 7.5   Mean Scores in the Four Groups

	Control	Suppression	Suppression works	Suppression does not work
Thought frequency	3.2[a]	3.5[a]	2.9[a]	6.3[b]
Suppression success	62.1[ab]	69.0[ab]	79.8[a]	59.6[b]
Meta-memory	62.8	64.6	58.1	59.5
Snapshot likeness	38.9	48.5	45.4	52.1
Unpleasantness of story	53.7[a]	52.0[a]	38.3[b]	57.0[a]
Correctly reproduced details	31.2	30.5	30.9	32.0

Note: Scores in the same row that do not share superscripts differed at $P < .05$.
From Rassin, E., Van Brakel, A., & Diederen, E. (2003). Suppressing unwanted memories: Where there is will, there is a way? *Behaviour Research and Therapy, 41*, 727–736.

content, or rather the perceived emotional valence, of recollections, depending on prior beliefs held by the individual.

Another previously discussed study with relevance to the issue of suppressing recollections was conducted by Christianson and Bylin (1999). These authors noted that in murder cases, suspects regularly claim to suffer from amnesia for their offense. They further hypothesize that in some cases, this claimed amnesia may not be genuine. That is, suspects may feign amnesia to prevent discussing their crime in detail. Christianson and Bylin were interested in the effect of feigned amnesia on actual memory. They instructed 54 undergraduates to read a story about a violent assault. The participants were instructed to identify with the main character, that is, the person who commits the assault. After being thoroughly familiarized with this story, participants were interrogated about it as if they had actually committed the assault. This interview took place 30 minutes later. In addition, participants were questioned 1 week later. While one group of participants had to answer all questions truthfully on both occasions, the other group of participants had to feign amnesia for the crime during the first interrogation, but had to be truthful during the second. Evidently, during the first interview, amnesia simulants performed worse on the free recall than did genuine participants. One week later, the performances of the to groups displayed a regression to the mean effect. Genuine participants did lightly worse compared to the first interview, while the performance of simulators had now increased because they no longer had to simulate amnesia. Interestingly however, the recall accuracy of the latter group never reached that of the genuine group. Apparently, the simulation of amnesia had prevented them to recall the story as accurately as did participants who had never engaged in the simulation of amnesia. This finding can easily be explained if one considers that participants in the simulation condition had to do without a rehearsal opportunity on the first occasion, while those in the genuine condition did have such an opportunity. However, it appears also fair to conclude that the suppression of recollection during the first interrogation deteriorated the memory accuracy one week later. By this view, suppression of memory was indeed found to be slightly (though far from perfectly) effective.

A last study that is noteworthy in the discussion about suppression effects on memory is that by Wagenaar and Groeneweg (1990). These authors described the memories of individuals who were imprisoned in Camp Erika, a penal colony camp during the World War II. A man whose last name was De Rijke was a particularly cruel camp leader who was accused of war crimes. At the end of the war, several camp survivors were interviewed about their stay in the camp and about De Rijke specifically. Interestingly, these approximately 20 survivors were interviewed again in 1984 to 1987. Hence, their recollections at these two points in time could be compared to each other. Overall, the recollections of the camp survivors were rather consistent, despite the 40 year delay. However, some individuals seemed to have forgotten crucial information in the 1980s that they had mentioned 40 years earlier. For example, one person was beaten to the extent that he could not walk for days. While he reported this incident immediately after the war, he failed to mention it 40 years later. Another person seemed to have forgotten being witness to an execution. Some individuals no longer remembered the name of De Rijke, while others had forgotten him completely. When confronted with their earlier, more complete, statements, most of the camp survivors recognized their memory flaws. These data show that forgetting, not just of periphery details but also of crucial incidents, does occur. However, although the camp survivors were unlikely to enjoy discussing and remembering their stay in the camp, there is no evidence that the observed loss of memory should be attributed to actual suppression attempts.

Conclusion

In this chapter, the effect of suppression on traumatic intrusions was discussed. First, it is argued that there is reason to believe that the suppression of traumatic intrusions may have the same effects as the suppression of obsessive intrusions. For one thing, both kinds of intrusions share their aversiveness and by definition their involuntariness. In addition, OCD and PTSD seem to share a common pathogenesis. In some cases, the two disorders are even impossible to distinguish. When evaluating the empirical evidence for the effects of suppressing traumatic recollections, there indeed seems to be a considerable number of studies that support the notion that suppression paradoxically increases intrusion frequency. But as with obsessions, there are also nonsupportive findings. Given that, compared to obsessive intrusions, traumatic intrusions are elaborated, it has also become possible to study the effect of suppression on the quality of the recollection. This is an important topic because it taps on the old Freudian idea of repressing traumatic recollections. However, to date, only a handful of studies have addressed this issue. And again, the findings have been contradictory. While some researchers found that suppression indeed deteriorates memory, others found no support for the claimed memory undermining effect. The studies conducted so far give rise to the conclusion that memory undermining effects are more likely to occur when the recollection is less traumatic, while in case of more traumatic recollections, suppression does not seem to result in a decline of memory. Interestingly, whereas a paradoxical increase of intrusion frequency appears to be in contradiction with a decrease of memory accuracy, Wegner and colleagues (1996) proposed an explanation, that is the scene activation hypothesis, that succeeds in reconciling the two alleged effects of thought suppression. In any case, the effect of suppression on memory deserves further scientific study.

Chapter 8

Thought Suppression and Miscellaneous Targets

Introduction

In the previous chapters, the relevance of the thought suppression paradigm for theories of obsessive-compulsive disorder (OCD) and post-traumatic stress disorder (PTSD) has been discussed. In previous years, suppression has also been implicated in other anxiety disorders. The relevance of the paradigm even seems to exceed the area of anxiety. Depressing thoughts, addictive impulses, and hallucinations can all become the target of suppression attempts, and indeed, scientific research has addressed all these topics. In addition, paradoxical effects of suppression have also been observed in non-clinical contexts, thus entering the arena of cognitive and even social psychology. In this chapter, research of suppression of a variety of targets will be discussed.

Thought Suppression and Anxiety

Spinhoven and Van der Does (1999) asked a large sample of clinical participants to complete the WBSI and the SCL-90. Participants in this study were 254 outpatients suffering from various disorders such as depression, dysthymia, panic disorder, social phobia, and PTSD. The goal of the authors was to explore how suppression tendencies are related to various kinds of psychopathology measured by the SCL-90 in a mixed patient sample. Results suggested that suppression correlated significantly ($P < .001$) with all of the eight scales of the SCL-90 as well as with the total score. Correlations ranged from .33 for sleeping problems to .57 for depressive symptoms. Next, the authors computed correlations with a so-called corrected WBSI. As mentioned previously, the WBSI has been said to be biased toward unsuccessful suppression, because it includes a number of items referring to the experience of intrusive thoughts. Spinhoven and Van der Does excluded no less than ten items, leaving only five items in the corrected WBSI. These five items were argued to genuinely pertain to thought suppression attempts. Like the original WBSI, the corrected version correlated significantly with all of the SCL-90 subscales and with the total score (rs ranging from .24 for sleeping problems to .41 for depression). These data indicate that thought suppression is indeed associated with a number of psychopathological symptoms in a variety of populations.

   In their study with 122 healthy volunteers, Muris and Merckelbach (1994) found that suppression correlated negatively with trait anxiety ($r = -.33$, $P < .05$). However, these authors used the DSQ, which contains only two suppression items. In addition, these items are formulated in a positive manner (e.g., "I am able to keep the lid on my feelings, if the circumstances require so"). Hence, the DSQ is focused on successful suppression, in contrast to the WBSI. Perhaps then, people who are good at thought suppression are generally less anxious.

Koster, Rassin, Crombez, and Näring (2003) sought to explore the effect of suppressing thoughts about an upcoming threatening event. Thirty-four undergraduate students were told that they were to undergo a painful electrical stimulation. Before this electrical shock, participants underwent three 3-minute experimental phases. During the first and third period, participants were free to think of anything. During the second period, half of the participants were free to think of anything, but the other half were instructed to suppress thoughts about the electrical shock, if any. During all three periods, thoughts about the shock had to be monitored and indicated by pressing the spacebar on a computer keyboard. After each period, participants rated their anxiety on a scale from 0 (*not at all*) to 10 (*very much*). Results suggested that during the second period, suppression participants experienced as many thoughts about the shock as did controls (i.e., approximately 2.5). During the third period, suppression participants experienced a thought rebound (i.e., four target thoughts), while those in the control condition did not (two thoughts). This difference was statistically significant. A similar pattern was observed for self-reported anxiety. Hence, these data suggest that suppression of an anxiety-provoking thought produces a thought rebound as well as an increase of anxiety. Of course, participants did not really receive an electrical shock. By means of manipulation check, participants were asked whether they believed that they would actually receive a shock. Most participants reported to have done so; only three participants had to be excluded from the analyses.

De Jongh, Muris, Merckelbach, and Schoenmakers (1996) submitted 58 undergraduate students to the following procedure. First, they were instructed to imagine being in a dentist chair undergoing painful treatment (i.e., drilling and filling a tooth). Next, they had to rate the likelihood of occurrence of 24 negative thoughts, such as "this treatment will hurt," "the nerve will be touched," "everything goes wrong," "I will panic," and "I will die during treatment." Seventy percent of the participants reported that they would think that the treatment was going to hurt. The least often endorsed item was "I will faint" (1.3%). No participant endorsed the item about dying during treatment. After this, they had to try to suppress thoughts about the imaginary treatment and the rated 24 negative thoughts for 1 minute. Eventually, participants rated the successfulness of their suppression attempts on a scale from 0 to 100. It is important to note that before the experiment proper, participants completed the STAI and a dental fear questionnaire. The mean score on the suppression efficacy VAS was 79.2, indicating that participants were rather successful in their suppression attempts. Interestingly, the score on the suppression efficacy VAS correlated negatively with scores on the STAI ($r = -.31$, $P < .05$), and with the score on the dental fear questionnaire ($r = -.41$, $P < .01$). Based on these findings, De Jongh and colleagues concluded that anxiety undermines the capacity to suppress unwanted thoughts and thus cognitive control.

Muris, De Jongh, Merckelbach, Postema, and Vet (1998) studied the effect of suppressing dentist-related thoughts in a between-subject design. Two groups of participants were included in their study: A sample of 35 dental phobics, and a group of 49 non-phobic controls. All participants were followed during an invasive dental treatment (drilling and filling). Half of the participants were instructed to suppress negative treatment-related thoughts if any, during treatment, while the other half were instructed not to suppress such negative thoughts during treatment. Participants rated their anxiety before, during, and after treatment. After treatment, they rated their suppression effort, and the frequency of intrusive negative thoughts about the dental treatment. All these ratings were done on VASs ranging from 0 to 100. When exclusively looking at the sample of non-phobic participants, thought suppression seemed to produce various paradoxical effects. Suppression participants experienced more treatment-related intrusions, more discomfort, and were more anxious during and after treatment, compared to non-suppressing non-phobics. Within the phobic sample, however, there were no differences between suppressors and non-suppressors. For starters, non-suppressing participants reported to have spontaneously engaged in suppression attempts to an equal extent as those who had actually received suppression instructions. Thus, the manipulation failed. When comparing phobics with non-phobics, the former group of participants scored higher on virtually all variables (intrusion frequency, discomfort, and anxiety).

A last example of thought suppression in specific phobia is a study by Muris, Merckelbach, Horselenberg, Sijsenaar, and Leeuw (1997). Participants in this study underwent three 5-minute periods. During the first and third periods, all participants received "think of anything" instructions. Half of the participants received those instructions during the second period as well, while the other half had to suppress thoughts about spiders during period 2. During all three periods, participants had to indicate spider-related thoughts by pressing a button. In addition, they completed a VAS after each period indicating the amount of time that was consumed by spider-related thoughts. Half of the participants ($n = 41$) were officially diagnosed as suffering from specific phobia (spider phobia), while the other half consisted of non-phobic controls ($n = 40$). Results suggested that there was no effect of instruction: Thought suppression did not result in more spider-related thoughts during any of the periods. Suppression effects were absent in the phobic as well as in the non-phobic sample. However, there was a main effect of diagnosis: phobics (regardless of instruction) experienced more spider-related thoughts during all periods than did non-phobics. These findings yield no support for the idea that thought suppression is implicated in the development of specific phobia.

An anxiety disorder that deserves special attention is the generalized anxiety disorder (GAD; APA, 2000). GAD is characterized by excessive worrying which can be defined as anxiety provoking concerns about future events in which there is uncertainty about the outcome (Buhr & Dugas, 2002). Worries are to GAD what obsessions are to OCD. In fact, it is not so easy to distinguish worries from obsessive intrusions. Worrying about what happens if one's house burns down is very similar to obsessing about whether or not one has turned off the gas. Generally, worries are experienced as more ego-syntonic and at the same time as less intrusive than obsessions. In addition, certain meta cognitions are exclusive to worrying and not to obsessing. For example, the idea that worrying is a fruitful endeavour is predictive of excessive worrying but not of obsessing. Similarly however, the experience of being unable to control one's worrying is also exclusive to excessive worrying (Wells & Morrison, 1994; Wells & Papageorgiou, 1998). Coles, Mennin, and Heimberg (2001) explored whether the concept of TAF distinguishes obsessions from worries. They asked 173 undergraduate students to complete the TAF-scale, the PSWQ, and the Obsessive Compulsive Inventory (OCI; Foa, Kozak, Salkovskis, Coles, & Amir, 1998). The authors found that worry (PSWQ) and obsession (OCI) were moderately correlated ($r = .56$, $P < .001$). Furthermore, obsession was correlated with TAF-probability and with TAF-morality. However, worry was also correlated with both forms of TAF. Subsequently, Coles et al. conducted regression analyses in which TAF was to be predicted by the PSWQ and the OCI. In these analyses, the PSWQ failed to significantly contribute to the prediction of TAF, once the OCI was included. Therefore, it seems that TAF indeed differentiates between obsession and worry, in that it is an exclusive feature of the former.

In one of the previous chapters, it has been argued that, although classification systems such as the DSM-IV-TR are very important, the differences between various symptoms are sometimes trivial or somewhat artificial. For example, the difference between an obsession and a traumatic intrusion is not always clear. The fuzziness of taxonomies is especially evident with worrying. Not only are worries very similar to obsessions, but worries are both a symptom and a coping strategy at the same time. Admittedly, many psychiatric symptoms are considered to be coping strategies by patients (e.g., compulsions, avoidance), but in case of worrying, there even is a questionnaire that intends to measure the tendency to worry in reaction to the experience of unwanted thoughts, that is the previously discussed TCQ (Wells & Davies, 1994). The TCQ taps five control strategies, one of which is worrying. Research suggests that worrying as measured by the TCQ is far from fruitful (Wells & Davies, 1994). One hypothesized reason to engage in worrying is intolerance of uncertainty, that can be defined as a perceived unacceptability of a possible negative event, however small the probability of its occurrence (Buhr & Dugas, 2002). Intolerance of uncertainty has been found to be associated with excessive worrying. In addition, people high on intolerance of uncertainty require more than an average amount of information before they come to a decision (Ladouceur, Talbot, & Dugas, 1997).

Another cause of worrying may be the wish to avoid upsetting mental imagery (see Borkovec & Inz, 1990). Worrying generally takes a verbal form, and verbal cognitions yield less cardiovascular response than do visual images (Stöber, 1998; Peasley-Miklus & Vrana, 2000). Therefore, it can be expected that worrying in an abstract "what if" form is preferable for many people compared to concrete aversive visual imagery. However, Wells and Papageorgiou (1998) found that worrying is not a very fruitful way of avoiding mental imagery. They showed 70 healthy volunteers a distressing 8-minute film clip. Afterward, participants received one of the following five instructions: Worry about the film verbally, image about the film, distraction by means of a pen and paper task, worry about usual concerns, or settle down and do nothing. After having carried out these instructions for 4 minutes, participants were given a diary in which they had to report thoughts about the film if any, for 3 days. Results indicated that, compared to control, verbal worrying increased the number of visual images about the film both immediately as well as during the 3 days following the experiment. In fact, in the longer run, worrying resulted in more visual images about the film than did purposely imaging. This was true for worrying about the film as well as for worrying about usual individual concerns. To summarize, worry can be construed both as an intrusive cognitive activity (resembling obsession and hypochondriasis) and as a control strategy (in reaction to intrusive imaging), albeit a seemingly fruitless strategy.

Becker, Rinck, Roth, and Margraf (1998) examined the effect of suppression in GAD patients ($n = 29$), social phobics ($n = 25$), and non-anxious controls ($n = 28$). All participants underwent two periods. During the first period, they had to suppress white bear thoughts, while during the second period, they had to suppress their main personal worry, which had been identified beforehand. During both periods, intrusions (of white bears during period 1, and of the personal concern during period 2) had to be indicated by means of computer mouse clicks. As always, suppression was never perfect, the overall intrusion frequency being 7.2. Participants in the social phobia and non-anxious control groups, found it more difficult to suppress white bear thoughts than to suppress their main worry. Social phobics experienced 11.3 white bear intrusions and only 5.8 worries, while control experienced no more than 6.9 white bear intrusions and 3.3 worries. In the GAD group, the pattern of intrusions was inversed: These participants experienced 6.4 white bear intrusions and 9.3 worries. Hence, as can be expected, GAD patients found it harder to suppress thoughts about their recent worries than thoughts about white bears. The authors take this as evidence to conclude that "patients with GAD do indeed suffer from a lack of mental control regarding their worries", although "the results do not imply a complete lack of mental control in GAD (Becker et al., 1998, p. 51). But, of course, these findings do not show that thought suppression is the vehicle behind worries in GAD. For one thing, there were no no-suppression control conditions included in this study, which precludes firm conclusions about causality.

Mathews and Milroy (1994) made their participants worry about their main recent concern, suppress that concern, or think about a pleasant topic, for 5 minutes. After this, participants remained another 15 minutes in the laboratory without further instruction. Of course, intrusive worries and other unpleasant thoughts were monitored. Two participant groups were included in the study: A group of 30 excessive worriers and an equally large group of non-anxious controls. Results suggested a main effect of participant group, in that worriers experienced more worries and other unpleasant, unrelated intrusions than did non-worriers. However there was no effect of instruction.

In summary, thought suppression has been applied to specific phobia (e.g., dental fear and spider anxiety), worrying, and anticipation anxiety. Overall, results suggest that the paradoxical effect of suppression observed in the original experiment by Wegner and colleagues (1987) is only marginally relevant to theories about the development of phobia and excessive worry. The strongest conclusion to be drawn from the studies discussed (e.g., Becker et al., 1998; Koster et al., 2003) is that anxiety reduces the ability to suppress unwanted thoughts, thereby weakening cognitive control.

Thought Suppression and other Pathology

From the findings obtained by Spinhoven and Van der Does (1999), it can be concluded that thought suppression may not only be relevant to the development or maintenance of anxiety, but also to other psychopathologic conditions. Indeed, the authors found that the WBSI is correlated with scales of depression, delusions, sleeping problems, and even somatic complaints.

Wenzlaff and colleagues (1988) conducted a series of experiments to test whether depression, like anxiety, reduces the capability to suppress thoughts at will. According to these authors negative, depressive events and cognitions are especially likely targets of suppression attempts, because the exclusion of negative material from consciousness is pivotal for mental well-being, at least in Freud's view. However, depressed individuals may have difficulties in suppressing depressive cognitions. First, depressive cognitions are likely to trigger associated negative cognitions, thus creating a negative cognitive circle from which is it very hard to escape. Second, due to mood congruency, depressed individuals are extra likely to generate additional negative, depressive cognitions. In their first experiment, participants read either a positive or a negative story (e.g., about being late for a job interview and causing an accident on the way). Next, half of the participants had to suppress thoughts about the story for 9 minutes, while the other half received no suppression instructions. Fifty-six participants were selected because of their high score on a depression scale (BDI), while 56 others were included because of their low depression score. All participants who had read the positive story displayed a gradual decrease of story-related thoughts over the 9 minutes. Non-depressed participants who had read the negative story displayed a similar decrease, regardless of instruction. However, depressed participants who had read the negative story reported an increase of story-related intrusions whether or not they tried to suppress these intrusions. In their second study, Wenzlaff and colleagues asked 40 depressed and 40 non-depressed undergraduate students to rate the efficacy of nine distracters. These distracters differed in emotional valence from positive (e.g., thinking about winning the lottery) to negative (e.g., thinking about drowning). Interestingly, all participants reported that the best way to suppress a thought is to choose a distracter with an emotional valence that is opposite to that of the to-be-suppressed thought. In other words, suppressing a positive thought will work best by thinking of something unpleasant, while suppressing a negative thought can best be done by thinking of something pleasant. In their third study, the authors wanted to test whether depressed individuals not only know that thinking positive things is the best way to suppress depressive thoughts, but if they also actually use positive distractors. Ninety-one participants (of which 21 were subclinically depressed) were instructed to imagine being in a positive or negative situation. Next, they were instructed to suppress thoughts about this imaginary situation for 10 minutes. They were explicitly given the nine positive and negative distractors used in study 2. Afterward, participants had to indicate which distractors they had relied on during their suppression attempts. Overall, more positive than negative distractors were used. However, when looking at the participants who had to suppress a negative image, those who were depressed used more negative distracters both compared to positive distractors and compared to their non-depressed peers. These findings suggest that depression indeed hinders the capacity to suppress thoughts, particularly negative thoughts.

Similar findings were reported by Conway, Howell, and Giannopoulos (1991). In their first study, these authors made 23 dysphoric and 24 non-dysphoric participants undergo a small test after which they received (bogus) feedback about their performance. Some participants were given positive feedback (i.e., they were told that they had answered 18 of 20 items correctly), while others received unfavourable feedback (i.e., six of 20 correctly answered questions). Next, all participants were instructed to suppress thoughts about the test for 5 minutes, although they had to indicate test-related intrusions by means of bell pressing. Non-dysphoric participants displayed a minute-by-minute decrease of test-related thoughts, ranging from 1.9 in the first minute to 0.2 in the last. This decrease occurred regardless of the nature of the received feedback. Dysphoric participants, specifically those who had received negative feedback about their performance, were unable to put aside test-related intrusions. In the last minute, they still had on average one thought about the test. In a second study, dysphoric ($n = 32$) and non-dysphoric ($n = 32$) participants were simply instructed to suppress white bear thoughts for 5 minutes. Although the total number of intrusions did not differ significantly between dysphorics ($M = 1.58$) and non-dysphorics ($M = 1.48$), there was a difference when solely looking at the last minute. A minute-by-minute analysis revealed that non-dysphoric participants experienced only 0.4 intrusions in the last minute, while dysphoric participants reported 0.9 intrusions in the last minute. In summary, these studies yield some, though not particularly strong evidence for the deteriorating effect of depressed mood on cognitive control.

Wenzlaff and Bates (1998) argued that diminished cognitive control is typical of depressed states to the extent that it can actually be used to predict depression. Based on scores on the BDI, these authors selected 45 non-depressed participants, 23 depressive ones, and 22 individuals who scored in between and were thus classified as being "at risk" of developing depression. Participants were instructed to unscramble as many sentences as possible in 4 minutes, by numbering the words. In every assignment, there were more words than necessary to fit into one meaningful sentence. Some assignments were neutral, for example, "has green child the eyes blue." In this example, one has to choose between green and blue. However, some assignments forced the participants to choose between a positive and a negative solution (e.g., "am I ruining life improving my"). In addition, participants received differential instructions, that is, sometimes they were told to create whatever sentences they wanted, while at other times they had to create positive sentences, or negative sentences. A further variable was that half of the participants received increased cognitive load by memorizing a six-digit number. The authors calculated the percentages of negative sentences created by the participants. When given no specific instruction about the valence of the unscrambled sentences, only 5% of the statements created by non-depressed participants were negative. This percentage was 2% under the instruction to create positive sentences. When instructed to create negative sentences, 89% of the unscrambled sentences were negative. Cognitive load had virtually no effect on this group of participants. The percentages of negative sentences were higher in the depressed group: 44% in absence of instruction, 17% under positive instruction, and 99% under negative instruction, respectively. The "at risk" group produced 6% negative sentences in absence of instruction, 5% under the instruction to create positive sentences, and 94% when told to create negative statements. These figures resemble those of the non-depressed group. However, these percentages pertain to the non-load trials. Under high cognitive load, the at-risk participants created 23% negative statements in absence of any instruction, and no less than 17% in case of positive instruction. Hence, the at-risk group masked their depressive thinking in absence of cognitive load. But when load was increased, these participants were no longer able to mask their true, depressive thinking style, and displayed a pattern of results more reminiscent of that produced by depressed participants, rather than that of their non-depressed peers.

Thought suppression has not only been studied in relation to depression, but also against the background of addictive and eating disorders. For example, Haaga and Allison (1994) explored whether thought suppression predicts relapse in people who have recently stopped smoking. They invited 100 ex-smokers to their laboratory, where these participants had to verbalize their reactions to six imaginary stressful situations that might elicit the desire to smoke (e.g., being in the company of people who smoke and offer a cigarette). The responses were classified by two coders either as cognitive restructuring (e.g., "I would think about health hazards"), or as thought suppression (e.g., "I would put the urge to smoke out of my mind"). Twelve months later, all participants were invited to return to the laboratory. Ninety-six turned up, only sixteen of whom were still abstinent. Analysis revealed that these 16 successful quitters exceeded the relapsers at the use of cognitive restructuring. No group differences occurred for thought suppression however. Hence, suppression was not a counter-productive, yet not a particularly effective strategy to refrain from smoking. Salkovskis and Reynolds (1994) invited 62 volunteers to their laboratory who were trying to stop, or had recently stopped smoking. These participants were then primed by rating the frequency of experiencing several smoking-related thoughts. The to-be-rated thoughts were negative (e.g., "I would really enjoy a cigarette", or "There's nothing wrong with having just one cigarette"), or positive (e.g., "I am stronger than my addiction to smoking," or "I feel better now I have quit on smoking"). Next, participants were either instructed to merely monitor any smoking-related thoughts ($n = 20$), to suppress such thoughts ($n = 22$), or to suppress and simultaneously carry out breathing exercises (i.e., suppression plus distraction; $n = 20$). After having carried out these instructions for 5 minutes, participants underwent a second, monitor only 5-minute period. Analysis of intrusion frequency originally revealed that suppression participants experienced approximately seven thoughts during period 1, and six during period 2. Participants in the control condition experienced seven and four thoughts during the subsequent periods, respectively. Target thought frequencies for the distraction group were three and three. Hence, although there was no rebound effect, suppression did result in more intrusions during the second period, compared to the control and distraction groups. However, the authors discovered that some participants had not completely complied with the experimental instructions. That is, not all participants in the suppression and (suppression plus) distraction conditions had suppressed to a satisfactory extent, while some in the monitor only condition had engaged in spontaneous suppression. To solve this intertwinement, Salkovskis and Reynolds eliminated data from participants in the suppression and distraction groups who scored below 40 on the 0 to 100 suppression effort VAS. Likewise, participants in the monitor only condition scoring over 70 on the manipulation check were also excluded from the additional analysis. Analysis of the filtered data set revealed no rebound effect, but it was very clear that suppression was ineffective in reducing smoking-related thoughts in the short and longer run, compared to both no instruction and distraction. That is, during both periods, suppression participants experienced more intrusions than did those in the other two groups.

Findings by Palfai, Monti, Colby, and Rohsenow (1997) could be construed as evidence that suppressing the urge to drink alcohol paradoxically leads to greater readiness to think positively about consuming alcohol. These researchers included 40 heavy social drinkers in their teasing experiment. In this study, heavy social drinking meant an average consumption of 124 alcoholic drinks per month. Participants were exposed to their favorite beverage. They had to pick up the glass with their dominant hand, and put in under their nose, so that they were able to smell it. Of course, they were not allowed to drink from it. Half of the participants were explicitly instructed to completely suppress their urge to drink, while the other half received no such additional instruction. After this exposure, participants had to evaluate 36 alcohol expectancy items, some of which were positive (e.g., "alcohol makes me happy"), while others were negative (e.g., "alcohol makes me sick"). Each item appeared on a computer screen, and participants had to respond by pressing a yes or no button on the keyboard as quickly as possible. Overall, participants reacted faster to positive than to negative items (mean reaction times being 1,867 and 1,997 milliseconds, respectively). Interestingly, suppression participants ($M = 1,750$) were faster than controls ($M = 2,120$), suggesting that suppression paradoxically had activated alcohol-related cognitions. However, suppression participants did not endorse more positive expectancy items than did controls. Therefore, the findings merely indicate a paradoxical mental activation, but not an increased positive attitude toward the suppressed target. On the other hand, given the strong manipulation, it is quite impressive that suppression instructions produced an additional effect anyway.

Harnden, McNally, and Jimerson (1997) exposed 40 women, 19 of whom were fervent dieters, to two 5-minute experimental periods. Half were instructed to think about weighing themselves before both periods. The other half received the opposite instruction (i.e., suppressing thoughts about weighing) before the first period—but not before the second. During both periods, participants had to verbalize their thought stream. Analyses of the verbalizations revealed that overall, dieters experienced more weighing-related thoughts than non-dieters. In the first period, participants in the suppression condition reported fewer thoughts about weighing than did those in the expression condition, regardless of their tendency to weigh themselves. Interestingly, during the second period, a rebound effect occurred for the non-dieters, but not for the dieters. The authors concluded that their "findings suggest that thought suppression may play a greater role in the creation than in the maintenance of preoccupations" (Harnden et al., 1997, p. 289).

Johnston, Bulik, and Anstiss (1999) studied the effect of suppressing thoughts about chocolate. Forty-two women (half were self-admitted chocolate cravers) were instructed to think about planning a dessert menu for a large dinner party. However, half were additionally instructed to suppress thoughts about chocolate during the assignment. All participants had not eaten since a few hours before the experiment started. During the 5 minutes of thinking about the dessert, participants verbalized all their thoughts. Next, they played an apple picker game for 2 minutes. They were told that every scored apple could be exchanged for a chocolate bar. The analyses pertained to the number of chocolate thoughts during the first 5 minutes, and to the number of picked apples (and hence earned chocolate bars) during the following 2 minutes. Suppression participants succeeded in thinking significantly less often about chocolate compared to controls (means being 1.3 and 6.7, respectively). Interestingly however, they earned significantly more chocolate bars (26.5) than did controls (20.6). Hence, suppression was effective in the short run, but it produced a rebound effect in the longer run. The latter finding is particularly interesting because the rebound effect was manifested as a behavioral effect rather than a self-report. Johnston and colleagues concluded that "exerting mental control may not, then, be an effective strategy in achieving behavioral control" (1999, p. 26). The idea that suppression may have the same effect on thoughts about food as on obsessive intrusions is not so far-fetched as it may seem. Indeed, lay people regularly speak of food obsessions. There is also some scientific evidence for the notion that obsession and eating disorders are closely related. For example, Formea and Burns (1995) asked 1,703 undergraduate students to complete the PADUA and the BULIT-R, a measure of bulimic symptoms (Thelen, Farmer, Wonderlich, & Smith, 1991). They found a significant correlation between the scores on both measures, in male ($r = .43$) and female respondents ($r = .41$, both $P < .001$). There is another reason to argue that OCD and eating disorders are related. That is, while OCD is associated with the previously discussed cognitive bias of thought-action fusion, Shafran and colleagues (1999) found evidence to suggest that patients with anorexia as well as restricting bulimics suffer from a very similar bias which they termed "thought-shape fusion" (TSF). Apparently, some people feel fat, guilty, and anxious when they merely think about eating high calorie food. Also, people may think that thoughts of "forbidden" food can actually result in weight gains. Indeed, Radomsky, De Silva, Todd, Treasure, and Murphy (2002) found experimental evidence for the concept of TSF in a sample of 20 anorexia patients. These individuals were instructed to imagine themselves eating fattening food. This instruction sufficed to increase their feelings of guilt, anxiety, fatness, and their urge to neutralize the thoughts of food.

A publication that should not be left unmentioned here is that by Polivy and Herman (1985). Although their article stems from before Wegner and colleagues' (1987) white bear study, it addresses a phenomenon that is highly relevant for the thought suppression literature. First, Polivy and Herman noted that binge eating is seen in an impressive proportion of bulimia cases but also in an equally high percentage (i.e., approximately 50%) of patients with anorexia. Next, they argued that, even though many people claim that they diet to neutralize previous binging, laboratory as well as field studies indicate that generally, dieting precedes binging. They propose biologic and cognitive explanations for this causal mechanism. For example, the human brain (specifically the hypothalamus) may strive to keep the body weight at a certain desirable level – which is not necessarily the same as that desired by the individual. If the body weight drops below this setpoint weight, the body will try to restore its weight by taking in large quantities of food in short periods (cf. binging). Although this setpoint theory is appealing, its scientific drawback is that there is no way of knowing what a person's setpoint weight is. Hence, the setpoint theory cannot be proven to be false. For example, if mister A weighs around 130 pounds all his life, one may conclude that that is his setpoint weight. However, if he loses 20 pounds at the age of 50 years, one will be tempted to conclude that his setpoint was at 110 after all, even if it had appeared to be 130 for several decades. As to cognitive explanations, the authors argued that extreme dieting will cause a preoccupation with food and calories, and a dichotomous thinking style (e.g., good vs. forbidden food). Consequently, a dieter who believes that his diet is ruined for today anyway may therefore let go of all inhibitions and engage in binging. Hence, a little trigger (e.g., eating a small piece of a chocolate bar) can cause a dieter to indulge an excessive food intake, while such an effect will not occur with non-dieters. Regardless of the explanation for the association between dieting and binging, this causal path is to a great extent reminiscent of a paradoxical thought suppression rebound effect. That is, dieting (cf. suppression) may be somewhat effective in the short run, but is likely to backfire and produce increased food intake. Indeed, the authors speak of "the disinhibition of suppressed or restrained eating" (Polivy & Herman, 1985, p. 195).

An intrusion to which the thought suppression paradigm has yet hardly been applied is the (verbal) hallucination (Garcia-Montes, Perez-Alvarez, & Fidalgo, 2003). Although hallucinations significantly differ from obsessions and many other intrusions, and are traditionally associated with different psychiatric syndromes, they may resemble each other more than expected. For example, Morrison (1998) argues that the cognitive analysis of obsessions and panic attacks is also applicable to hallucinations. According to this analysis, most individuals experience hallucinations or illusions, from time to time. These hallucinations only become disturbing if one misinterprets them as indicating loss of control, messages from the devil, or commands that must be obeyed. By this view, hallucinations are not all that different from obsessive intrusions. In fact, the only remaining difference would be that obsessions are internally attributed, while hallucinations are externally attributed. Hence, the line between obsessions and hallucinations is quite thin. Accordingly, Morrison and Baker (2000) found that schizophrenic patients who suffer from auditory hallucinations experience more obsessive intrusions than hallucination-free schizophrenics. This finding indicates that hallucinations and obsessions not only are similar, but that they also tend to co-occur. This raises the question of the role of suppression in psychosis. Do people suffering from hallucinations try to suppress their hallucinations, and if so, what are the effects of these suppression attempts? To date, the latter question has only been addressed in one study. Rassin and Van der Heiden (2004) asked 50 undergraduate students to listen to a 3-minute noise file, through headphones. Participants were told that in the noise file, aggressive voices might be distinguishable that would utter swearwords. Specifically, the word "fucker" might occur. Half of the participants received the additional instruction to pay no attention to that swearword and to suppress it whenever they heard it. After this initial period, a second 3-minute period was spent listening to the (same) noise file, this time without further instruction. In the control condition, the number of target words was approximately four in both periods. In the suppression condition, however, the frequency increased from two in the first to eight in the second period. Hence, suppression was somewhat effective in the short run, but counterproductive in the longer run. Indeed, this pattern of results is reminiscent of that often found with other kinds of intrusive thoughts. As an aside, no less than 37 of the 50 participants (i.e., 74%) in this study were fooled into hearing the target word, which in fact was not included in the noise file. In addition, nine participants reported to have heard other swearwords as well (e.g., "piece of shit," "bitch," and "damn").

Yet another thought that can become the target of suppression attempts is the thought about pain. In the previously discussed study by Cioffi and Holloway (1993), participants were instructed to keep their hand in a container with ice water for as long as possible. During this pain tolerance procedure, they either distracted themselves, focused on their pain sensations, or suppressed pain-related thoughts. Results indicated that suppression participants reported more pain after the cold pressor task than did participants in the other two groups. By contrast, Harvey and McGuire (2000) did not find paradoxical effects of pain suppression. These authors submitted 39 patients with chronic pain (mainly back, neck, and hands) to the following procedure. Participants underwent three 5-minute periods. During periods 1 and 3, they all received think of anything instructions. During the second period, however, only 13 participants received such instruction, while 12 others received instruction to pay close attention to their pain, and 14 received suppression instructions. After every period, participants rated the frequency, discomfort, severity, and duration of pain-related thoughts, on scales from 1 (*not at all*) to 10 (*all the time*). Frequency ratings during the three subsequent periods were 5.5, 5.2, and 5.0 in the control group, 5.9, 9.2, and 6.8 in the attention group, and 5.7, 3.7, and 5.8 in the suppression group. Similar patterns were observed for the other variables. Hence, suppression did not produce divergent results compared to control, while attention resulted in increased frequency, discomfort, severity, and duration, compared to the two other groups. The notion that suppression might actually affect the perception of pain is not that exotic, given the study by Petrie and colleagues (1998) in which it was found that expression of emotions can improve the functioning of the immune system (as indexed by the number of T lymphocytes), while suppression can undo this beneficial effect.

Whereas Ansfield and colleagues (1996) studied the effect of suppression on sleep onset latency, Harvey (2003; see also Harvey, 2002) took this line of reasoning one step further, and argued that suppression of presleep worries might actually contribute to the development of insomnia. This author included 30 insomniacs and an equal number of non-clinical controls in her study. Participants had to identify a main thought or theme that was likely to be on their mind at night. Half of the participants were then instructed to suppress that thought once they went to sleep, while the other half were instructed to think whatever they wanted. Analysis of the self-estimated sleep onset latency revealed that insomniacs took longer to fall asleep (33.5 minutes) than did controls (10.9 minutes; $P < .001$). In addition, there was a main effect of instruction: Suppressors needed on average 29.8 minutes to fall asleep, while controls only needed 19.5 minutes ($P < .05$). In a further study, Harvey and Payne (2002) sought to differentiate between suppression by means of unfocused distraction or by visual imagery. Participants in this study were 50 undergraduate students with subclinical insomnia. They were assigned to one of three conditions: A general distraction condition in which they were instructed to distract themselves from their worries and other sleep inhibiting, arousing thoughts, an imagery condition, in which participants were told to distract themselves by thinking about a pleasant and relaxing leisure activity, and a no instruction control condition. Participants were asked to monitor the time spent falling asleep while employing the experimental instruction. The authors expected that imagery would be a successful strategy (resulting in decreased sleep latency), while general distraction would be ineffective. However, results indicated that while controls reported to have needed approximately 80 minutes to fall asleep, the latency was significantly reduced by imagery (to 30 minutes), but also by general distraction (to 45 minutes). Indeed, there was no significant difference between general distraction and imagery. In addition, the three groups did not differ in the number of pre-sleep worrisome cognitions. Hence, suppression seemed to be a fruitful strategy in this study.

In conclusion, the thought suppression paradigm has been applied to a variety of psychiatric symptoms, ranging from depressive rumination to hostile hallucinations. On the one hand, this broad application is quite unproblematic, because every thought or impulse that imposes itself can be defined as an intrusion, and can thus become the target of suppression attempts. Indeed, although different in some respects, intrusions are similar, if for no other reason, because of their shared involuntariness. On the other hand, differences in the to-be-suppressed targets may require different mental operations. As mentioned before, it is one thing to suppress a white bear thought, but quite another to suppress an elaborated traumatic memory. While white bear thoughts are discrete, verbal, personally irrelevant, and emotionally neutral, obsessive fantasies about strangling one's own baby are non-discrete, visual, personally relevant, and probably upsetting. Traumatic recollections may be even more elaborate, because they pertain to at least several minutes of an experienced event. Likewise, intrusions can be categorized based on their origin. That is, some intrusions can be traced to a single event, while others seem to develop gradually, without apparent cause (synthetic intrusions; Wegner, 1989). Abramowitz and colleagues (2001) used three target characteristics as independent variables in their meta-analysis of suppression studies, namely personal relevance, valence (neutral, negative, and positive), and discreteness. They found, that, overall, personal relevance and valence of the suppressed target do not influence the immediate or delayed effect of suppression. However, target elaborateness was found to promote the occurrence of a rebound effect. In the words of Abramowitz and colleagues (2001): "larger rebound effects were found with nondiscrete target thoughts (e.g., a story) than with discrete thoughts (e.g., a white bear)" (p. 700). Oddly, the effect of target valence has been studied quite frequently in single suppression experiments, unlike that of target discreteness. Meanwhile, the findings by Abramowitz and colleagues suggest that some targets might be easier to suppress than others. Apparently, target characteristics should not be overlooked when it comes to the efficacy of thought suppression. Differences in target characteristics may explain some of the differential effects found in the various studies described in this section.

Although the findings are hard to summarize, some conclusions can be drawn. First, it seems that although there is no reason to argue that thought suppression contributes to the development of depression, depressed mood seems to decrease cognitive control and thus contributes to the paradoxical effect of suppression attempts. Second, suppression does seem to be able to contribute to the development or maintenance of food- and drug-related disorders, because its paradoxical effect with these kinds of thoughts and impulses has been observed repeatedly. Third, the effect of suppression on pain perception is yet unclear, and deserves future study, as does the effect of suppression of hallucinations and sleep inhibiting cognitions.

Cognitive Operations and States

Reviewing the literature, it can be concluded that the paradoxical effect of suppression has been studied with quite an impressive number of intrusions and impulses, such as obsessive intrusions, traumatic intrusions, worries, phobic thoughts (e.g., spider-, or dentist-related), sexual thoughts, and addictive urges (e.g., to smoke, drink, or eat). Furthermore, suppression has been proven to affect a variety of variables, including stream of consciousness, reaction time, skin conductance, pain tolerance, sleep latency, stereotyped ideas, and the ability to keep a secret. But why stop there? Considering the seemingly broad applicability of the thought suppression paradigm, one might come to the conclusion that suppression (or, ignoring) of any mental or behavioral impulse will, in time, result in a rebound effect. Most of us are familiar with examples of children that cannot resist the temptation to engage in otherwise uninteresting behavior, once a parent has forbidden it. Likewise, we all know that the best way to start a rumor is to tell it under the pretence that it is, and must remain, a secret. Unfortunately, from a scientific stance, there is no evidence for the thesis that any behavior that is forbidden (cf. suppressed) will paradoxically be carried out more frequently, merely because of the prohibition. However, there are some studies that have yielded results to suggest that the relevance of the thought suppression paradigm is not limited to the domain of psychopathology.

One example is a study by Newman, Duff, and Baumeister (1997), who argue that suppression may foster another defence mechanism, namely projection. Their hypothesis is neatly summarized in the following quotation: "people are frequently faced with evidence suggesting that they might (at least to some extent) possess characteristics that make up their unwanted or undesired selves. One way of responding to this threat is to avoid or suppress thoughts about the possibility. Over time, repeated thought suppression may allow a person to maintain the belief that he or she does not possess the unwanted traits. Another consequence, though, will be that the trait concepts one is suppressing will become chronically accessible. Chronically accessible traits dominate people's interpretations of other's behavior. The final outcome of this defensive process, then, is that threatening traits will be projected onto others" (Newman et al., 1997, p. 983). The authors define projection as "the act of perceiving in other people those characteristics that one wishes to deny in oneself" (Newman et al., 1997, p. 980). They presented no less than six studies to prove their point. In one study, they first asked a sample of 48 undergraduate students to report their own undesirable characteristics. Results suggested that, among others, selfishness, laziness, rudeness, arrogance, and dishonesty were the most often mentioned undesirable traits. In the second part of this study, participants had to write about an occasion on which they had acted in an undesirable way. The precise nature of the undesirable behavior was varied per participant, in a way that every participant wrote about a situation is which he had acted in a way congruent with a self-reported unwanted trait, and about a situation in which the undesirable behavior was not one of the self-reported unwanted traits. For example, a participant who had reported to be lazy and dishonest was instructed to write about an occasion on which he had been lazy (i.e., a personally threatening trait), and about an occasion on which he had been arrogant (a personally non-threatening trait). During both writing assignments, the time actually spent writing was recorded. Half of the participants were preselected repressors (i.e., individuals scoring high on defensiveness and low on anxiety), while the other half was not. Analysis of the time spent writing suggested that non-repressors wrote for 781 seconds about the personally threatening trait and 571 seconds about the non-threatening trait. By contrast, repressors wrote 547 seconds about the threatening and 969 about the non-threatening trait. These data suggest that repressors indeed avoid thinking about their undesirable traits. In one of their other studies, the authors presented 32 undergraduates (16 of whom were repressors) with descriptions of ambiguous behaviors of others (e.g., a vignette about a girl who refuses to cheat with her friends on an examination). Participants had to rate the behaviors on four-point scales. In this example, the anchors might be "mean" (1) and "honest" (4). Hence, higher scores indicated that the behavior was interpreted positively. The vignettes were constructed in a way that they tapped personally threatening traits and non-threatening traits for each participant. On average, the score of repressors was higher (3.19) than that of controls (2.82) in case of non-threatening behaviors. However, in case of personally threatening behaviors, repressors were more likely to choose the undesirable interpretation (2.62), compared to controls (3.25). Apparently, repressors eagerly saw the traits that they disliked in themselves, in other people's behavior. Although the findings indeed suggest that repression may result in projection, it is important to note that the authors seemingly treat the concepts of repression and suppression interchangeably. However, as discussed before, there is good reason to argue that the two defenses should be distinguished.

A research area in which thought suppression may play a prominent role is that of secrecy. As argued by Bouman (2003), and Newth and Rachman (2001), patients with OCD are likely to conceal their obsessions and compulsions. Needless to say, secrecy is crucial in numerous other contexts. Therefore, the question arises whether people are able to keep a secret by suppressing the to-be-kept-secret information. Bouman (2003) found that participants in his experiment were indeed able to hide information during a conversation. Participants in this study were instructed to talk about an imaginary trip to the zoo. Some of them were additionally instructed not to mention elephants. Although the participants who received this additional instruction reported to be more tensed and discomforted and to experience more intrusions about elephants, this increased anxiety was not noted by their conversational partners. Interestingly, although participants had not received any specific guidelines as to how they should succeed in refraining from talking about elephants, they reported to primarily rely on thought suppression.

Lane and Wegner (1995) argued that compared to telling a lie, keeping a secret is even more difficult, because no particular story or lie is available to serve as a replacement. Therefore, suppression (with all of its dangers) of the to-be-kept-secret information is the only option one has. The authors conducted four studies to prove that keeping a secret by means of suppression will paradoxically result in a preoccupation. In one of their studies, 82 undergraduate students were instructed to verbally respond to 24 topics. After a topic (e.g., "date" or "alcohol") was presented to the participant, he/she had to react with two sentences. In some cases, participants were told to give a truthful reaction, in some cases, they had to make up a lie, and in other cases they were told to produce an irrelevant, senseless reaction (i.e., keep their real reaction secret). After some time, participants had to recall as many topics as possible. The authors hypothesized that topics in reaction to which participants had given an irrelevant reaction would be remembered best due to the paradoxical hyperaccessibility effect of suppressing their true reactions. Indeed, topics to which participants had reacted to truthfully ($M = 1.69$) as well as deceitfully ($M = 1.80$) were remembered less often than topics in reaction to which participants kept their true reactions secret by producing an irrelevant reaction ($M = 2.29$; $P < .01$). These findings are particularly interesting because they reflect a rebound effect, in the sense that the improved recollection of information kept secret was observed after the suppression instructions had stopped. In addition, the findings do not pertain to the custom measure of intrusion frequency but to actual memory effects. In another study, Lane and Wegner invited 237 undergraduate students to complete a questionnaire addressing 50 topics, ranging from masturbation to being bitten by a dog. Respondents had to rate these topics on three characteristics: how many intrusive thoughts they produced, how strongly participants tried not to think about them, and to what extent participants kept these topics secret from others. All ratings were done on a point scale ranging from 1 to 5. The most fiercely kept secret in this sample was masturbation, the most strongly suppressed thought was about failing a test, while being in love produced the most intrusive thoughts. Importantly, there were significant correlations between scores on intrusiveness, suppression, and secrecy (ranging from .23 to .32). Hence, these findings deliver further support for the idea that suppression and intrusion play a role in the process of keeping secrets.

Wegner and Gold (1995) investigated the effects of suppressing thoughts about a previous relationship (cf. hiding feelings about an old flame). First, they asked 119 undergraduates several questions about their old loves (e.g., "I still think about him/her a lot," "I would leave my other relationship, if he/she could come back into my life"). Based on the answers on these questions, participants were classified as hot flames (i.e., they still desired their previous relationship) or cold flames (i.e., they no longer did). Next, all participants underwent three 8-minute periods. During the first and last period, participants were free to think of anything. During the second period however, half of the participants were instructed to suppress thoughts of the old flame, while the other half were told to suppress thoughts about the Statue of Liberty. During all periods, participants verbalized their thought stream. In addition, their skin conductance level was measured as a way of determining their emotional state. The authors analyzed the data separately for hot and cold flames. When looking at the number of flame-related thoughts, there were no group differences during the second period (overall mean was 3.4 intrusions). During the third period, however, a differential pattern emerged. Within the cold flame group, suppressors experienced more thoughts (30) than controls (18). But in the hot flame group, the pattern was reversed, that is 26.1 intrusions for suppressors and 34.8 for controls. Hence, these data suggest that suppression of cold flame thoughts was paradoxically ineffective, but suppression of hot flame thoughts was not. To make things even more complex, the skin conductance level data displayed the opposite effect. Suppression of hot flame thoughts produced an increase of skin conductance, while suppression of cold flame thoughts produced a decrease of conductance. While these data may be difficult to interpret, they do suggest that hiding feelings about an old flame is likely to backfire in one way or another.

Gross and Levenson (1997) conducted a further experiment on the effects of hiding one's feelings. In their study, 180 female undergraduates watched three films: A neutral, pleasant, and sad film fragment. Ninety participants were instructed to hide their feelings about the films while they were being observed by raters. In addition to the observations of these raters, participants' physiologic reactions (e.g., heartbeat and skin conductance) were measured. Finally, participants self-reported the extent to which they had enjoyed the fragments afterward on a scale from 0 to 8. First, the data suggested that suppression of feelings was effective in the sense that the raters found that suppressors displayed significantly fewer emotional expressions such as smiling, crying, eye blinking, and movements, compared to non-suppressors. However, suppression significantly increased physiologic activity, especially cardiovascular functions, during the pleasant and neutral films. In addition to this effect on physiologic functioning, suppression significantly decreased the amusement ratings with approximately one point compared to control. Hence, while suppression seemed to be effective in hiding feelings, the costs of this were an increased physiologic activity, and a decreased ability to enjoy the observed film fragments. Richards and Gross (2000) further studied "the cognitive costs of keeping one's cool" (2000, p. 410). They showed a distressing film fragment about a man who admits to his wife an extramarital affair as a consequence of which the other woman is pregnant, to 53 participants. Some participants were instructed to hide their (mostly negative) feelings during this film clip, while the remainder received no such instruction. The participants rated their emotional involvement in the fragment, and were submitted to a memory test containing 24 questions about the film clip. While there was no group difference in emotional involvement, participants who had hidden their feelings scored significantly worse (i.e., 64% correct answers) on the memory test compared to controls (73% correct).

In summary, findings from the various studies discussed above suggest that thought suppression may be a fruitful way to keep secrets. While the keeping of secrets by means of suppression is generally effective, there is a pay off in that cognitive load and physiological activity increases. A last research line relevant to the present discussion is that on non-behavioral cues of deceit. Although thought suppression has hardly been referred to in this literature, there are some similarities. In their thorough analysis, Depaulo, Lindsay, Malone, Muhlenbruck, Charlton, and Cooper (2003) tested the discriminative power of over 100 alleged cues to deception. Surprisingly, several alleged deceit indicators do in fact not discriminate between truth tellers and liars. For example, a well-known – but incorrect – cue is eye contact: It is generally believed that people make less eye contact during lying. Research suggests however, that this is not true. Similarly, while many people think that excessive body movements (e.g., hand and foot movements) indicate deceitful behavior, the opposite seems to be the case. That is, people who tell a lie, make fewer movements compared to when they are telling the truth. The authors offer an interesting explanation for this. Specifically, they argue that liars know that they are likely to display increased movement due to nervousness. In a subsequent attempt to compensate for this hyperactivity, they completely suppress all movement. But this extreme suppression then makes them appear too stiff. This might be referred to as an "overcompensation" effect. This finding suggests that behavioral control is – like mental control – very hard under some circumstances.

As to this latter observation, that is the similarity between mental and behavioral control, there is an interesting literature suggesting that both kinds of control are indeed associated. Specifically, Baumeister, Bratslavsky, Muraven, and Tice (1998) argue that all voluntary behavior draws upon one common energy source. Therefore, there is a considerable competition between actions (whether overt behavioral or merely mental). The authors go on to argue that making the choice to carry out one act or another (a choice that consumes energy from the same source itself) constitutes who we are as individual. Hence, they termed the process of allocating the limited source of energy "self-regulation." In homage to Freud, they refer to the limited capacity of energy as "ego depletion." The notion of ego depletion implies some interesting hypotheses. For example, if the self-regulatory system is depleted by one process, subsequent self-regulation in another area is likely to fail. This would explain, why crimes predominantly occur at night – when people are tired, and why addictive relapses are prone to happen when people are stressed anyway (Baumeister, Muraven, & Tice, 2000). Indeed, Baumeister and colleagues (1998) produced some experimental evidence for the idea that seemingly unrelated acts of self-control in fact drain one common energy source. In one study, they included 67 undergraduate students in the following procedure. Participants were placed alone for 5 minutes in a room in which radishes and chocolate cookies were present. Participants had been instructed not to eat for at least 3 hours before the experiment commenced. Some participants were told that they were not allowed to eat chocolate cookies, while others were forbidden to eat radishes. It was hypothesized that those who were not allowed to eat cookies needed to engage in more self-control than those who were not allowed to eat radishes – simply because most people love chocolate cookies more than radishes. After this (for some more than others) demanding task, participants underwent a completely different assignment that implied persistence. In this subsequent test, participants had to trace geometric figures without retracing lines and without lifting their pencil from the paper. They were given as much time as they wanted to complete this test. In fact however, the assignments were made in a way that they were impossible to complete. The authors hypothesized that, if resisting chocolate cookies and persistence in a difficult task indeed draw from one common energy, those participants who had been told to refrain from eating cookies would give up the geometric task sooner than their chocolate eating peers. Indeed, analysis of the duration of working on the geometric assignments confirmed this idea. Participants who had eaten chocolate cookies spent 18.90 minutes at the geometric assignment, while those who had not, gave up after no more than 8.35 minutes. By comparison, a group of participants who had not gone through the food phase, but only underwent the geometric assignment lasted for 20.86 minutes before giving up. In another experiment, 30 participants were shown a 10-minute emotional film clip. Half of them were instructed not to feel and show any emotional involvement in the film fragment, while the other half received no additional instruction. Next, they all were given six minutes to complete 13-word unscramble assignments. It was hypothesized that suppressing emotional involvement in the film would decrease performance on the unscramble task. Indeed, those participants who had suppressed their emotions completed fewer word puzzles (4.94) than those who had not suppressed (7.29).

Muraven, Tice, and Baumeister (1998) gathered further support for the hypothesis that different kinds of self-control consume one common energy. They, again, sought to combine self-regulatory actions that have no apparent relation to each other. In their first study, sixty participants were shown a 3-minute emotional film clip. One third of them were instructed to "really get into the movie" (Muraven et al., 1998, p. 777), one third was instructed to suppress any emotional involvement, while the remainder received no involvement instruction. The subsequent task was a test of stamina: Participants had to squeeze a handgrip for as long as possible. It was hypothesized that both getting involved in the film and suppressing involvement would decrease physical strength, compared to simply watching the film. To control for interference, participants underwent the handgrip test before and after the film fragment. The eventual score was the difference in squeeze duration between the pre- and post-film test. As expected, the change score was only 1.57 seconds in the control group. That is, at T2, their squeeze was only 1.57 second shorter than at T1. In the experimental conditions, however, the differences were significantly increased to 25.1 in the involvement condition, and 18.49 in the suppression condition. Hence, the data support the hypothesis that the additional instructions during the film fragment phase negatively influenced the physical endurance during the subsequent test. In another study, Muraven and colleagues submitted 58 undergraduates to a thought suppression procedure and to an anagram test. First, participants were left alone in the laboratory for 6 minutes. Some of them were instructed to suppress white bear thoughts, some were given expression instructions, and a last group received liberal instructions. Two minutes later, all participants were given a number of (in fact unsolvable) anagrams. As in the previously discussed study, the dependent variable was the time spent working on these anagrams. As expected, suppression participants gave up sooner (i.e., after 563 seconds) than those in the expression (867 seconds) and control (758 seconds) conditions. These findings suggest that suppression is an effortful endeavor indeed, and that it makes subsequent actions susceptible to failure. Or in the words of Baumeister and colleagues (1998), suppression is one of the many processes that can result in ego depletion. In their third study, 49 participants either suppressed white bear thoughts, or worked on moderately difficult multiplications for 5 minutes. These two tasks were considered to be equally difficult, although the suppression assignment would involve more self-regulation. Next, all participants saw an 18-minute humorous film fragment under the instruction not to express any signs of amusement. Ratings of the participants' facial expressions indicated that those who had suppressed white bear thoughts expressed significantly more amusement than those who had completed mathematic calculations. Again, the act of suppression seemed to reduce self-regulatory power in a subsequent unrelated situation.

A last example is a study by Muraven, Collins, and Nienhaus (2002) that included 58 male volunteers who were social drinkers. Upon arrival at the laboratory, at which time they had not eaten or drunk for 3 hours, participants' alcohol level was tested by means of a breath sample. Next, they were randomly assigned to a white bear thought suppression condition, or to a simple arithmetic calculation condition. This phase lasted for 5 minutes. Afterward, they were told that they would undergo a simulated driver's test. While waiting for that test, they were placed in a bar. Although they were free to consume alcohol (beer), they were told to inhibit themselves because of the subsequent driving test. After having waited for 20 minutes, participants' alcohol level was measured again. In fact, there was no driving test. Analyses of the alcohol level, as well as that of the number of consumed bottles of beer, indicated that participants who had previously engaged in thought suppression consumed more alcohol than those who had completed mathematic assignments. Thus, controlling oneself in the first stage (i.e., suppressing white bear thoughts) deteriorated the self-control capacity in the second phase (i.e., resisting the temptation of drinking beer).

The ego depletion literature does not imply that thought suppression attempts are doomed to fail by definition. Rather, it suggests that suppression drains one common energy source, and thus is in competition with other acts of mental self-regulation, but also with acts of overt behavioral self-regulation. The insight from thought suppression literature, that suppression is particularly ineffective in case of increased mental load, fits in nicely with this ego depletion account. Hence, it might be argued that the thought suppression paradigm can be construed as a specific area of ego depletion research. Following this line of reasoning, the literature on ego depletion addresses some interesting issues that may also be relevant to the thought suppression paradigm. For example, a question following from ego depletion research is whether the ego energy source actually depletes as rapidly as seen in most studies (i.e., after one act of self-regulation of say 5 minutes duration), or whether there is an automatic internal feedback loop that seeks to conserve energy. In the former case, people are genuinely unable to perform subsequent acts of self-regulation, while in the latter, such self-regulatory acts are not impossible but merely more difficult to carry out. There is some reason to suggest that the observed ego depletion effect is often actually the result of a conservational process. For example, if participants are granted extra financial compensation for successful self-regulation during a second task, the normally observed depletion effect diminishes (Baumeister et al., 2000). Another issue is whether ego depletion can be avoided by training self-regulatory skills. Baumeister and colleagues use the analogy of a muscle, and then argue that training should increase mental stamina, and therefore performance on self-regulation tasks. Indeed, they conclude that success in one area of self-regulation can spin off success in other areas. For example, people who successfully stopped drinking are more likely to succeed in giving up smoking, compared to smokers who did not previously overcome an alcohol addiction (Baumeister et al., 2000).

If we assume that thought suppression is an act of self-regulation, and thus is a part of the literature on ego depletion, the applicability of the thought suppression paradigm is broadened tremendously. Self-regulation, and its inherent problem of ego depletion are implicated in virtually every aspect of human functioning. This broad applicability is illustrated in a recent book edited by Baumeister and Vohs (2004). In that book, self-regulation is defined as "1) establishing a goal, 2) engaging in actions that lead to obtaining this goal, and 3) monitoring progress toward the goal" (Faber & Vohs, 2004, p. 509). Although this definition may make self-regulation appear to be easy, the authors continue to say that many self-regulatory efforts fail due to the existence of conflicting goals, failure to monitor one's own behavior, and depletion of the source that permits goal-directed behavior (i.e., self-control). They further distinguish between temporary and chronic failures of self-regulation. When applied to buying stuff that one does not actually need, impulsive (i.e., a temporary loss of control) and compulsive (a chronic loss of control) buying can be distinguished. An area in which self-regulation is crucial is sexuality. Evidently, in a civilized society, individuals must inhibit many of their sexual impulses: "People are not free to go around doing whatever they care to do sexually" (Wiederman, 2004, p. 525). Sexual disinhibitions are likely to encounter severe criticism and rejection (cf. prostitution, homosexuality, child sexual abuse, and rape). Nonetheless, loss of sexual self-regulation is abounding. One explanation for this may be that sexual urges are strong motives, and thus readily constitute conflicting goals. Although lack of sexual self-control has received much attention, overinhibition of sexual impulses can also be quite a problem.

An important application of self-regulation theory is crime. Hirschi (2004) sees the bigger part of criminal activity as the result of failing self-regulation. In this view it is assumed that individuals are by default socialized, while criminal behavior is the consequence of temporarily engaging in immediate gratification at the cost of later gratification. Assuming that criminality is indeed an exception, rather than a natural activity that coincidentally is in conflict with laws superimposed by the state, the question arises who is responsible for criminal acts. Indulging the ego depletion theory, criminals may very well be law-obeying individuals who happen to have depleted their self-regulatory energy at some point. Moreover, if actual suppression of criminal urges has the same paradoxical effect as the suppression of mental contents, some criminal activities might be the result of attempts to comply with social and legal norms. By this line of reasoning, it is questionable whether criminals who do their best to refrain from criminal activity should receive punishment. To date, this topic has hardly been studied scientifically. In a preliminary investigation, Nagtegaal and Rassin (2004) asked 90 undergraduate students to complete several questionnaires including the WBSI, the aggression scale of the Eysenck Personality Profiler (EPP; Eysenck, Wilson, & Jackson, 1996), and the Minnesota Multiphasic Personality Inventory (MMPI-2; Butcher, Dahlstrom, Graham, Tellegen, & Kaemmer, 1989). Results suggested that scores on the WBSI were correlated with scores on EPP-aggression ($r = .37$, $P < .01$), and with scores on the Psychopathic deviate scale of the MMPI ($r = .34$, $P < .01$). Next however, the WBSI was split into a suppression and an intrusion subscale, based on factor analysis (Blumberg, 2000; Höping & De Jong-Meyer, 2003; Rassin, 2003). These additional analyses indicated that intrusion was correlated with EPP-aggression ($r = .39$, $P < .01$) and with Psychopathic deviation ($r = .35$, $P < .01$), but suppression was not (rs being .28 and .26, respectively, ns). Hence, these data do not yield support for the notion that suppression of aggressive impulses paradoxically increases the likelihood that these impulses will result in actual aggressive behavior. A study by Johnston, Hudson, and Ward (1997) did not address the association between impulses and behavior, but it did address the suppression of a specific criminal thought, namely the thought of child sexual abuse. The authors included 30 convicted child molesters and 30 non-sexual offenders in their study. Participants were first primed to sexual thoughts. This was done by instructing them to write for 5 minutes about the last time they had had sex. Next, they were left alone in the laboratory for another 5 minutes, during which half of them had to suppress any sex-related thoughts. To trace a possible rebound effect, participants completed five Stroop test cards, each of which contained 100 stimuli. First, there was a color card containing lines printed in five different colors. Second, there was a standard interference card containing color names printed in five different colors. Third, there was a sex card containing words like penis, naked, and bum. Next, a child card contained words like school, park, infant, and children. Finally, there was a control card containing words unrelated to sex and children (e.g., river, and chain). In their analyses, the authors not only differentiated between child molesters and non-sexual delinquents, but they furthermore divided the former group into a situational and preferential subgroup. A situational molester is a single offense delinquent, while a preferential molester is known for having molested more than one child. Analysis of the participants' verbalized thought stream indicated that those given suppression instructions indeed thought less about sex than their non-suppression colleagues. This was true for non-sexual delinquents as well as for the two types of molesters. The analysis of the Stroop test first of all suggested no group differences on the color, interference, and control cards. For the child card, there was no effect of suppression instruction. However, preferential molesters were as a group slower (and hence more distracted by the child-related words) than situational molesters and non-sexual offenders. For the sex card, there were again no suppression effects in the situational and non-sexual groups, but there was a significant difference in the preferential group, in that prior suppression resulted in slower responses. Based on these data, the authors make some interesting remarks. First, it seems that thought control is possible for sex offenders, if only for a few minutes. They even think that findings like these are "encouraging for the use of suppression as a therapeutic technique" (Johnston et al., 1997, p. 314). However, they go on to argue that the rebound effect observed in the preferential offender group leads "one to question the utility of thought suppression as a therapy technique" (p. 316). They further argue that the loss of control, of which the observed rebound effect is reminiscent, is the breeding ground for actual sexual offences. That is, the experience of no longer being in control of one's thoughts and impulses may be construed by offenders as a sign that they now must indulge their sexual fantasies. Hence, the authors argue that "a loss of control may even be a desirable state, for example, as a means of avoiding self-censure" (Johnston et al., 1997, p. 306). Finally, the authors make an interesting methodological remark about the use of the Stroop test as a measure of thought rebound. Specifically, they argue that the Stroop test inherently implies the suppression of the natural tendency to pay attention to word content. In that sense, participants are required to engage in suppression during the Stroop test, and therefore, this may not be a good measure of rebound, because rebound implies that the suppression attempts have ceased.

In a sublime and unique study, Wegner, Ansfield, and Pilloff (1998) delivered direct support for the hypothesis that the suppression of an overt behavior paradoxically increases the chance that the individual will carry out that specific behavior. Eighty-three undergraduate students were invited to perform a midget golf test. They had to aim for a putt that was 2 meters away. In the control trial, they were merely instructed to make the ball land in the putt. In the experimental trial, they were additionally instructed to be particularly careful not to hit the ball past the putt, that is, not to overshoot. Half of the participants were given an additional mental load in that they had to remember a six-digit number. The order of control and experimental trial was randomized. The dependent variable in this study was the extent of overshooting in centimeters during the experimental trial minus the overshooting range during the control trial. Results indicated that participants without mental load performed better during the experimental trial than during the control trial (overshooting in the experimental trial controlled for the control trial was—11.43 cm). However, participants who had received additional mental load performed worse during the experimental trial (controlled overshoot was 20.79 cm). This implies that trying not to overshoot under mental load paradoxically resulted in overshooting more, compared to the condition in which overshooting was not specifically prohibited. In their second study, 84 participants were instructed to hold a pendulum (a pointed crystal attached to a 50-cm nylon line) still for 30 seconds. Traditionally, movements of a pendulum are attributed to unconscious processes or even external forces (Wegner & Wheatley, 1999). Participants in the study by Wegner and colleagues (1998) held the pendulum in their dominant hand over a glass plate under which a video was placed to record any movements of the pendulum. On the glass plate, a grid was painted with an x- and y-axis. Some participants were simply told to keep the pendulum over the center of the grid (the hold steady condition). Others were additionally instructed to specifically avoid any movements along the x-axis. Half of the participants received additional load, either by counting backward from 1000 by three (i.e., cognitive load), or by holding a 2.2-kg brick in their non-dominant hand (i.e., physical load). The dependent variably was the ratio of movements along the x-axis to the total number of movements. This proportion is displayed in Figure 8.1 as a function of instruction and load. As can be seen in this figure, the instruction to avoid movement along the x- axis paradoxically resulted in relatively more such movements, and this effect was stronger if participants were under additional load. Interestingly, the type of load (mental vs. physical) was indifferent to this effect, which underlines the ego depletion theory. These findings suggest that suppression is as ineffective in controlling behavior as it

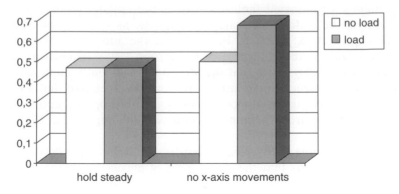

Figure 8.1: Proportion of x- axis movements. (From Wegner, D.M., Ansfield, M., & Pilloff, D. (1998). The putt and the pendulum: Ironic effects of the mental control of action. *Psychological Science, 9*, 196–199.)

is in controlling thought streams. In the words of Wegner and colleagues: "Trying not to perform simple actions under load can prompt the occurrence of those actions," and: "it appears that distraction can undermine motor control to produce not only erroneous movement, but precisely the least wanted movement" (1998, p. 199).

In summary, this section started with the hypothesis that the implications of the thought suppression research may exceed far beyond the borders of clinical psychology, and indeed, there is evidence to suggest that suppression is implicated in a wide range of cognitive states. Interestingly, the self-regulation theory, including the notion of ego depletion, allows for predictions about the situations in which thought suppression will be particularly ineffective. Specifically, the idea that all self-regulatory actions, whether mental or physical, consume one common energy, suggests that suppression will be less fruitful if other self-regulations have been carried out soon before the act of suppression. Another interesting consequence of the self-regulation theory is that the suppression of (overt) behavioral impulses is likely to have the same paradoxical effect as observed with the suppression of cognitive contents. Indeed, a study by Wegner and colleagues (1998) delivered findings suggesting that we sometimes do exactly what we try not to do.

Thought Suppression in Social Psychology

In the previous paragraphs, the thought suppression paradigm has been applied to a variety of contexts. In this section, the relevance of the paradigm in social psychology will be dealt with. Specifically, social psychologists have studied the effects of attempts to suppress stereotype ideas. In the previously discussed study by Macrae and colleagues (1994), undergraduate students were found to be able to suppress stereotyped ideas about skinheads. In their description of how they thought that a skinhead spends a regular day, fewer stereotypes (e.g., sleep long, use drugs) occurred if participants were instructed to avoid them (i.e., 5.6), compared to when no suppression instructions were given ($M = 6.8$). Interestingly however, when participants were subsequently invited to take a seat in the same row of chairs as where a skinhead was sitting, participants who had previously suppressed stereotypes chose to sit farther away from the skinhead (i.e., 5.3 chairs) than did non-suppressing participants (4.4 chairs). As mentioned before, this finding is not only interesting because it illustrates the inefficiency of suppression attempts, but also because the paradoxical effect manifested itself in an overt behavioral action. In another study, Macrae and colleagues (1994) showed a picture of a male skinhead to 24 undergraduates, and instructed them to write for 5 minutes about how they imagined a typical day in this man's life. Again, half of them were told to suppress stereotyped ideas while carrying out the writing assignment, while the other half received no such additional instruction. Next, all participants underwent a reaction time test in which they had to decide as quickly as possible whether a word shown on a computer screen was an actual word or a non-word. Participants were shown 56 words: 14 words that were stereotypic of skinheads, 14 non-stereotypic words, and 28 non-words. Overall, participants were faster to identify stereotypic words (631 milliseconds) than non-stereotypes (778 milliseconds). As expected, suppressors were even faster (i.e., 571 milliseconds) in their correct classification of stereotypes than were control participants (690 milliseconds).

A few years later, the same research group conducted a series of studies on the suppression of stereotypes in which they took a slightly different angle (Macrae, Bodenhausen, & Milne, 1998). In these studies, the central idea was that individuals are more likely to spontaneously engage in the suppression of stereotyped ideas if they are more self-conscious. Reason for this may be that when confronted with their own appearance, people are less likely to make negative and stereotype judgments about others. In the first experiment by Macrae and colleagues, 28 female undergraduate students were simply asked to rate the appropriateness of judging others based on their social group membership, on a scale from 0 (*completely inappropriate*) to 9 (*completely appropriate*). Higher scores on this item reflect stereotypic thinking. While completing this question, half of the participants' self-focus was increased by being placed in front of a mirror, while the other half completed the item in absence of such a mirror. As expected, participants in the high self-consciousness condition (i.e., in presence of a mirror) judged stereotyping to be less appropriate (i.e., 1.36) than did the other group of participants (2.21). In their second study, 28 female undergraduates were shown a picture of a construction worker. Next, they were instructed to talk about that man for 30 seconds, for example about what his hobbies might be, and about his general lifestyle. While completing this verbalization task, half of the participants stood in front of a mirror, while the other half did not. The verbalizations were coded for two variables. First, the number of self-referent words (e.g., I, me, my) was counted, because self-consciousness is known to increase the frequency of these words. Second, the number of stereotypes was counted. As expected, participants who had completed the task in front of a mirror included more self-referent words (i.e., 2.28) than did controls (0.93). Also, they produced fewer stereotyped descriptions (i.e., 3.71) than did controls (5.85). The third study was a replication of the finding that self-consciousness fuels suppression attempts. In this version, 36 females saw a picture of a male yuppie (i.e., a young urban professional wearing a suit and carrying a briefcase), and had to talk about this man for 30 seconds. Self-consciousness was manipulated through a computer screen on which participants either saw themselves online, or saw a recording of a stranger (control condition). Compared to the mirror intervention in studies 1 and 2, the current induction has the advantage that controls can watch the monitor rather than just seeing nothing due to the absence of a mirror. As in study 2, results suggested that being confronted with one's appearance leads to an increase in self-referent words (i.e., 1.69 compared to 0.56 in the control condition), and a decrease of stereotypes (i.e., 4.13 vs. 6.19). In the fourth study, 32 female students were instructed to talk about a female model for 30 seconds. This time, there was an actual concurrent task. That is, participants had to perform a dot probe reaction task in which they had to press the space bar of a computer keyboard as quickly as possible whenever a series of letters occurred on the screen. However, in fact, half of the participants were subliminally primed, because before every letter sequence, their own surname appeared on screen for no more than 30 milliseconds (i.e., beyond conscious perception threshold). This repeated display of participants' name was hypothesized to increase self-consciousness. In the control condition, participants were subliminally exposed to surnames unfamiliar to them (e.g., Wegner). As expected, participants in the experimental condition uttered more self-references in their narrative (i.e., 1.56 compared to 0.37 in the control condition), but fewer stereotypes about the model (i.e., 3.69 vs. 4.56). In study 5, a new variable was introduced, namely the participants' personal attitudes toward stereotypic thinking. It was hypothesized that individuals who really dislike stereotypes will be more susceptible to the stereotype suppressing effect of self-consciousness than people who have no problem with thinking stereotypically. Based on the questionnaire used in their first study, Macrae and colleagues selected 24 anti-stereotype and 24 pro-stereotype female students, and showed them all a picture of a balding and overweight man who was identified as Sir Peter Mappley, a member of Parliament. As in the other studies, participants were given 30 seconds to utter their opinion about the target. During the verbalization, some participants stood in front of a mirror, while others did not. Just like in the previous studies, the pattern of results in the anti-stereotype group suggested that being self-conscious reduced stereotyped thinking (i.e., 2.93 compared to 3.90 in absence of a mirror). However, in the subgroup of women who had no problem with stereotyping, the opposite pattern occurred. In this group, being in front of a mirror increased the number of stereotypes (i.e., 8.08) compared to the control condition (6.91).

In the studies by Macrae and colleagues (1998) discussed so far, ample evidence was obtained for the notion that self-consciousness fosters spontaneous stereotype suppression. However, the longer-term effects of such suppression attempts were not addressed. This was done in their sixth experiment. The basic set-up of this study was similar to that of the previous ones. Thirty-six female undergraduates expressed their opinion about, this time, a mail hairdresser. Some completed this task while looking at themselves on a television screen, while others saw a stranger on TV. In order to explore a possible rebound effect of the stereotype suppression imposed by self- consciousness, participants underwent the verbalization task twice. This was achieved by telling them, after completion of the first task, that a technical flaw had prevented the appropriate measurements from taking place. Hence, participants were kindly asked to do it over, but this time based on a picture of another male hairdresser. In fact, the repetition of the task enabled the experimenter to vary the participants' self-consciousness. Some saw themselves on screen during both trials, some saw a stranger twice, and in the crucial condition, participants saw themselves during the first trial, and a stranger during the second. In the latter condition, a post suppression rebound was expected, because during trial 2, there was no need to inhibit stereotypes since self-consciousness was reduced. First, the number of self-referent words was analyzed. As can be expected, participants who watched themselves during both trials made more self-references (on average 2.39) than did those who saw a stranger twice (0.83). While these frequencies were stable over the two trials, a differential pattern occurred in the change condition (i.e., first high self-consciousness followed by low self-consciousness). In this condition, self-references decreased from 2.25 to 0.83. As to the number of stereotypes, these occurred less in the continuous high self-consciousness condition (i.e., on average 4.08) than in the continuous low self-consciousness condition (5.63). Again, in both conditions, these frequencies were stable over the two trials. Interestingly, in the change condition, stereotypic descriptions increased from 4.50 in trial 1 to 7.00 in trial 2. Hence, the expected rebound effect of spontaneous stereotype suppression was indeed observed.

Wyer, Sherman, and Stroessner (2000) argued that two processes can prevent the stereotyped ideas activated by suppression attempts from actually being applied. First, the individual who has the stereotypes at the tip of his or her tongue must be motivated not to apply them, and second, he/she must have the cognitive resources (cf. self-regulatory energy) to resist them. The authors conducted two studies, the first of which tested the hypothesis that strong motivation not to apply accessible stereotypes can indeed prevent the application thereof. In this study, 124 undergraduate students were shown a picture of an African American, or an Asian American, and were instructed to imagine a typical day of this individual for 5 minutes. Half of the participants were additionally instructed to avoid stereotypes during this assignment. Next, they were taken to another room in order to strengthen the impression that they would now enrol into another experiment. In this part of the study, participants read a story about a 25-year-old man named Robert. Robert's behavior was described as very diverse. For example, he is sometimes unfriendly, in that he regularly plays his radio so loud that he gets into conflict with his neighbors. On other occasions, he can be very calm and friendly. For example, once he was insulted, but he did not retaliate. Robert can be smart and engage in lively philosophical conversations, but at the same time, he can be bluntly stupid in that it once took him minutes to discover that his television was not broken but simply unplugged. In short, Robert is hard to classify, because of his wide behavioral repertoire. He displays behavior that is considered to be stereotypic of African Americans (e.g., hostility, stupidity), and also behavior stereotypic of Asian Americans (e.g., respectfulness, intelligence). After having read the story, participants rated Robert's behavior on various nine-point scales pertaining to hostility, passivity, aggression, respectfulness, intelligence, and so on. The scales were clustered to form an African American stereotypical cluster and an Asian American stereotypical cluster. Importantly, some participants were told that Robert had the same race as the man of which they had seen a photograph earlier (i.e., the same race condition), while others were given no information about Robert's race. It was hypothesized that participants who had suppressed stereotypes in the first phase of the study, and were given no information about Robert's race, would display a stereotype rebound. This was expected because for these participants, stereotypes were hyperaccessible (due to suppression), and there was no reason to continue suppressing the stereotypes. By contrast, suppressors in the same race condition were not expected to show a stereotype rebound, because they might find it inappropriate to let loose all the previously suppressed and now activated stereotypes on Robert. Data were analyzed for the same race and unspecified race conditions separately. As expected, participants in the same race condition rated Robert's behavior equally stereotypically regardless of whether they had previously suppressed. In the unspecified condition however, former suppressors rated his behavior more stereotypically ($M = 5.17$) than did participants who had not previously suppressed ($M = 4.65$). Hence, these findings suggest that the rebound effect of stereotype suppression can itself be suppressed if one is motivated to refrain from stereotyping.

Wyer and colleagues (2002) go on to argue that motivation is not the only factor that determines the non-application of activated stereotypes. The individual additionally requires sufficient cognitive resources to resist stereotypic thinking. In their second study, the effect of cognitive resource was investigated. As in study 1, a sample of undergraduates were first shown a picture of an African American or Asian American male, and had to talk about this man for 5 minutes. Half of them received additional stereotype suppression instructions. In the second phase, participants read the story about Robert. This time, all participants underwent a same race procedure, that is, for all participants, Robert was described to be of the same race as the person of whom a photograph had previously been shown. Thus, all participants could be expected to feel obliged to omit stereotypic ratings of Robert's behavior. However, for some participants, the cognitive load was raised during the second phase of the study, because they had to remember an eight-digit number while reading the story about Robert. It was expected that participants in this increased cognitive load condition would display a stereotype rebound, while those who had not been given extra load would not. Indeed, when exclusively looking at the condition without additional cognitive load, suppression during the first phase did not affect ratings during the second phase. By contrast, in the high load condition, suppression did result in a stereotype rebound ($M = 5.40$), compared to non-suppression ($M = 4.73$).

Kulik, Perry, and Bourhis (2000) studied the effect of stereotype suppression in the context of the evaluation of job applicants. In organizational psychology, it is customary to work with diversity training programmes. These programmes seek to encourage those who hire employees, to keep an open mind during the selection process. Hence, diversity trainings explicitly encourage managers to fight stereotypic thinking, and to suppress prejudice. In this study, 116 business administration undergraduates were shown a video that is typical of a diversity training, and subsequently had to evaluate three job applicants. Participants saw one of three videos. In the control condition ($n = 40$), the video merely encouraged participants to keep an open mind. Participants in the demography suppression condition ($n = 37$) were shown a video in which it was explicitly stated that managers should actively try to suppress thoughts about applicants' age, gender, race, or ethnicity during the hiring process, because those thoughts might inappropriately influence their decision. In the age suppression condition ($n = 39$), the video contained an explicit instruction to suppress age-related thoughts during the selection process. After having watched the instruction video, all participants rated three female job applicants. These applicants were presented on video. They were preselected so that one of them represented a highly qualified middle-aged (i.e., 35 years old) applicant, one was a low qualified middle-aged applicant, and one was an average qualified "old" applicant (i.e., in her fifties). Cognitive load was increased for some participants by telling them that they would be videotaped at the end of the experiment, and that they had to observe and learn from the three application videos under their review. Thus, some participants not only watched the three videos to evaluate the applicants, but also with the idea of getting inspiration for their own video fragment. Participants then evaluated the applicants on various seven-point rating scales, pertaining to likelihood of hiring, video performance, job qualifications, and background adequacy. These ratings were averaged into one overall evaluation. In general, the highly qualified applicant received the best evaluation (i.e., 6.02), while the low qualified applicant received the worst evaluation ($M = 2.82$), and the old, average candidate received a medium evaluation ($M = 4.24$). When looking exclusively at the scores of the old applicant, six participant groups can be distinguished, based on three instruction videos (control, demography suppression, and age suppression) time two cognitive loads (extra load vs. no extra load) conditions. Interestingly, while five of the six groups evaluated the old applicant with a similar score, only the age suppression with extra load group found her significantly less suitable than average for the job ($M = 3.14$). Thus, suppression of age stereotypes under cognitive load was found to be paradoxically ineffective.

In sum, there is little reason to be optimistic about the human capacity to suppress stereotypes. For one thing, it must be acknowledged that although stereotyping may be bad in some circumstances, it is also an inevitable way of organizing information in the first place. In the words of Monteith, Sherman, and Devine: "There can be little doubt that the human mind is inclined to think with the aid of categories" (1998, p. 63). Furthermore, in some instances where stereotypic thinking is actually bad, strong societal or personal norms against stereotyping are really lacking. Monteith and colleagues argue that this is true for skinhead stereotypes, among others. In other cases, where stereotyping is unwanted, individuals may try to suppress stereotypic ideas. However, from the research discussed previously, it can be concluded that such suppression attempts are generally ineffective. Based on their review of the relevant literature, Monteith and colleagues conclude that "rebound effects seem most likely to occur among high-prejudice persons who lack the requisite internal motivation, tools, and skills to suppress stereotypic thinking" (1998, p. 76).

Another context in which thought suppression may be crucial is the context of legal decision making. Individuals who are required to decide about suspects' guilt need to include certain pieces of evidence in their decision making process, but they also may want to exclude specific pieces of evidence (e.g., because these were obtained in an illegal manner). What if the exclusion of evidence turns out to be as ineffective as might be expected based on thought suppression literature? A first study of interest is that by Kassin and Neumann (1997). These authors were interested in the strong effect that confessions have on the conviction of guilt. Their main aim was to illustrate that once a suspect confesses, he is very likely to be judged guilty, even if he retracts his confession soon afterward, and claims that it was false. In their crucial experiment, Kassin and Neumann instructed 62 undergraduates to play the role of jury member in a fictitious murder case. Participants had to read a 2-page case vignette about a man who was charged with murdering his wife and neighbor, and subsequently had to indicate whether they would convict this suspect or not. Four conditions were included. In the control condition, the case vignette stated that the suspect allegedly found his wife and neighbor at home, and killed them both in a rage of jealousy. He, however, claimed to have found the dead bodies on his arrival. Strangely, he had called his lawyer before calling the police. In addition, he had hired a private investigator to follow his wife. In a second condition, the following additional information was included. Another neighbor claimed to have seen someone running out off the house at the time of the murder. Later, he identified the suspect in a line up as the person who ran out off the house. However, at cross examination, the witness admitted that he had been at least 60 feet away. In the third condition, the extra witness was replaced by a character testimony. That is, another neighbor testified that the suspect had always been ill tempered. However, at cross examination, this witness admitted to not personally knowing the suspect. In the fourth and final condition, the additional evidence comprised that the suspect admitted the murders during a police interrogation. However, he immediately retracted the confession, and the police officer testified that the suspect was very upset and incoherent at the time of the confession. In the control condition, only 13% of the participants convicted the suspect. This percentage rose to 27% in the eyewitness condition, and 25% in the character condition. Most importantly however, as predicted by Kassin and Neumann, no less than 62% convicted the suspect in the confession condition. As mentioned earlier, this study addressed the power of confession evidence. However, the data also illustrate that the suppression of confession (and other) evidence is ineffective, given that the case vignette was written in such a way that participants would be likely to suppress the information about the confession.

In a more direct test of the suppression of evidence, Kassin and Sukel (1997) conducted a similar study ($N = 85$ undergraduates) in which participants read one of five case files. These files were considerably longer (i.e., 22 to 24 pages) compared to those in the Kassin and Neumann (1997) study, but revolved around the same murder case. In the control condition, the suspect, named Wilson, denied the charge. There were four additional conditions, based on two variables. One variable was the amount of interrogational pressure. In the low pressure conditions, the interrogation was fairly relaxed, because the suspect confessed immediately. In the high pressure conditions, however, the interrogator handcuffed Wilson tightly, hurt him in that process, and even waved his gun at him. The second variable was the (in)admissibility ruling of the judge. Upon objection by the defence attorney, the judge can either rule the objection sustained, and thereby term the evidence (i.e., the confession) inadmissible, or alternatively, the objection can be overruled, leaving the confession evidence admissible. If the confession is ruled inadmissible, the jury (cf. the participants in this study) are to disregard the pertinent remarks. Based on this set-up, five conviction rates could be computed. In the control condition, only 6% of the participants reported that they would convict Wilson. In the low pressure, admissible condition, the percentage rose to 29%, while in the low pressure, inadmissible condition, 18% of the participants voted guilty. In the high pressure, admissible condition, 24% ruled guilty. In the crucial, high pressure, inadmissible condition, no less than 29% of the participants voted guilty. Hence, the inadmissible ruling of the judge, which can be construed as a suppression instruction, paradoxically increased the conviction rate, suggesting that suppression was not only ineffective, but also counterproductive, although not statistically significantly.

In a study by Edwards and Bryan (1997), 74 undergraduate students were given a transcript based on an actual case in which the defendant was charged with robbery and murder. In the control condition, the transcript contained eight pieces of (partly circumstantial) evidence. In four additional conditions, there was a crucial piece of extra evidence, namely the documented fact that the defendant had been sentenced previously for assault. The precise information given to participants in these four conditions was based on combinations of two variables: The emotional valence of the information (i.e., neutral wordings such as "assault with a deadly weapon" vs. emotional wordings such as "hacking up a woman"), and the (in)admissibility ruling of the judge. After reading the case vignette, participants rendered a verdict (guilty or not guilty), rated their confidence on a nine-point scale, rated the likelihood that the suspect was indeed guilty, and rated the appropriate severity of the sentence on a nine-point scale. All these items were averaged into one variable that could range from −9 to 9, with higher positive scores indicating that the suspect was considered to be guilty and should receive severe punishment. On average, participants in the control condition scored 2.5, those in the neutral, admissible condition 1.5, those in the neutral, inadmissible condition 2, those in the emotional, admissible condition 2.6, and finally those in the emotional, inadmissible condition 5. Hence, these data suggest that suppression of forbidden information is quite counterproductive, especially if that information is emotionally laden.

In summary, the studies discussed in this section illustrate that the concept of thought suppression has penetrated the social psychology literature. Reviewing the pertinent studies, it seems fair to conclude that stereotype suppression is as difficult as the suppression of any other cognitive contents. Likewise, suppression of inadmissible evidence is ineffective, if not counterproductive.

Conclusion

Looking at the original thought suppression article by Wegner and colleagues (1987), one might get the impression that the paradigm should have its most prominent impact on the area of traumatic memories. However, as discussed previously, thought suppression was originally especially applied to the context of obsession. After a latency of, say, 5 years, publications began to emerge in which the paradigm was applied to various other psychiatric conditions. For example, numerous studies have addressed the effects of suppressing anxious impulses, such as thoughts about spiders or the dentist. It seems that suppression of anxiety-related cognitions may produce a thought rebound similar to that observed in case of obsession. In addition, anxiety seems to further reduce the efficacy of suppression attempts. An anxiety disorder that deserves special attention is GAD, because worries can be construed as both anxious symptom as well as a coping strategy (cf. distraction) similar to suppression. Apart from anxiety, thought suppression has been studied in the light of depression and addiction. As to depression, there is reason to believe that depressed mood deteriorates the efficacy of suppression attempts.

Thought suppression has not only been studied in the context of various psychiatric syndromes, but has also been applied to non-clinical phenomena. For example, the process of keeping a secret is likely to rest on suppression attempts, and is therefore susceptible to all of its flipsides. A particularly interesting idea is that implied in the self-regulation theory and its inherent component of ego depletion. That is, thought suppression may be one of several strategies to regulate one's cognitive states and/or behavioral activities. According to this account, all the different regulatory activities draw from one common energy source. Given that this energy source is limited, repeated regulatory activities are likely to fail. The process of draining the energy source is referred to as ego depletion. This phenomenon is in line with the finding in the thought suppression literature that increasing cognitive load by carrying out concurrent cognitive activities, decreases the efficacy of suppression attempts. One very interesting aspect of this theory is that the suppression of covert behaviors (e.g., thoughts about chocolate) may actually affect subsequent overt behaviors (e.g., not being able to resist the temptation of eating chocolates). Given the effects of thought suppression on various cognitions and even on overt behaviors, it is conceivable that suppression may also have its effect in social interactions. Indeed, at least in two social psychology contexts, thought suppression has been found to have, counterproductive, effects. More specifically, suppression of stereotyped ideas seems to foster distance taking from the stereotyped individuals. Likewise, in the context of legal decision making, the suppression of inadmissible evidence is at least ineffective, and may even be counterproductive.

To summarize, it seems fair to conclude that the applicability of the thought suppression paradigm has gone far beyond the borders of obsession, traumatic memory, anxiety disorders in general, and even clinical psychology. The statement "suppression of any stimulus is likely to fail" may not be that far from the truth, after all.

Chapter 9

Conclusion

Summary

Wegner and colleagues (1987) found that people who try not to think of a white bear for 5 minutes cannot help themselves thinking of a white bear approximately seven times. Furthermore, after the 5 minutes of suppression, deliberate expression of white bear thoughts resulted in 22 target thoughts, while expression without prior suppression yielded only 16]white bear thoughts. These findings suggest that suppression is not only an ineffective control strategy, but also a counterproductive one in the long run (cf. a rebound effect). The conclusion that follows from these findings is that it is unwise to suppress unwanted thoughts. Although the idea behind Wegner and colleagues' study is quite clear, its precise methodology can be, and has been, criticized. Important questions are: Does the paradoxical effect of thought suppression also occur with other targets, especially personally relevant and unwanted thoughts? Is deliberate expression an ecologically valid instruction for the control period? Is it possible to suppress thoughts successfully anyway? And if so, are there individual differences in the extent to which people are able to successfully suppress thoughts? What are the practical implications of the observed paradoxical effect of thought suppression? These and other questions have been addressed in subsequent replications of the original experiment by Wegner and colleagues. This book summarizes the findings of various research lines within the thought suppression field. The chapters can be clustered into three areas. The first two chapters deal with the definition of thought suppression. Chapters 3 through 5 address methodological issues relevant to the suppression research. Finally, Chapters 6 through 8 discuss the applications of the thought suppression paradigm.

In Chapter 1, the original white bear study by Wegner and colleagues (1987) is described. It is also concluded that their findings have been replicated more than once. For example, Clark and colleagues (1991) found results similar to those of Wegner and colleagues, using a green rabbit as target thought. Muris and colleagues (1992) found that suppression of an emotionally valent thought (about a car crash) has similar effects as those of white bear thoughts. As another example, Salkovskis and Campbell (1994) observed suppression inefficiency with a personally relevant thought. In addition, these authors found that the effects were prolonged over at least 4 days. As to the theoretical explanation of the observed inefficiency, two accounts can be given. First, the environmental cueing hypothesis states that suppression attempts generally take the form of distraction seeking. However, external distractors (e.g., a painting on the wall) are likely to become associated with the to-be-suppressed target, and can thus transform into retrieval cues. Due to iteration of this process, the individual will eventually find himself surrounded by cues that remind him of the suppression target. The second account builds on the environmental cueing hypothesis. According to Wegner (1994), distraction seeking is only one of two processes that constitute suppression attempts. The second process is the monitoring of one's thought stream. Indeed, before one engages in suppression attempts, one has to be alerted that the target has intruded consciousness. Unfortunately, there is a mismatch between these two processes. Whereas the operating process (i.e., the search for distraction) is a conscious and effort-demanding endeavor, the monitoring process is unconscious and relatively effortless. Therefore, the operating process drains energy and is thus limited, while the monitoring process is not. In time, the monitoring process will take the upper hand, resulting in a rebound of target thought detection. From Chapter 1, it can be concluded that the white bear study has been replicated many times. In addition, several reviews and even books have been devoted to the study of thought suppression. Hence, it is fair to speak of a thought suppression paradigm.

Chapter 2 deals with the difference between suppression on the one hand, and repression and dissociation on the other. According to some psychologists, repression refers to the old Freudian notion of motivationally forgetting complete autobiographical memories. However, it must be acknowledged that contemporary researchers differ strongly in their ideas about how Freud thought about differences and similarities between repression and suppression. The differences in opinion pertain to the question whether repression is a conscious or unconscious process, and whether Freud differentiated between repression and suppression anyway. Regardless of this scientific (or historical) discussion, repression, in the sense of completely and motivationally doing away with recollections, is somewhat problematic from a strict scientific stance. For one thing, the hypothesis that people can repress recollections is in part unfalsifiable and thus unscientific (cf. Popper, 1968). Although Silverman and colleagues (1978) produced some evidence for this notion with their subliminal psychodynamic activation paradigm, their research has been subject of much criticism (see Weinberger & Hardaway, 1990). Whereas Silverman and colleagues (1978) sought to find experimental evidence for the concept of repression, others fiercely claim the existence of repression by referring to case reports (e.g., Karon & Widener, 1997), thus ignoring contemporary standards of scientific psychology. Notwithstanding the poor scientific status of Freudian repression, lay people, but psychologists as well seem to embrace the concept of repression unconditionally. Crombag and Van Koppen (1994) found that a majority of their participants believed that repression (in the meaning of completely forgetting traumatic events) is possible. These participants even believed that they themselves might have repressed traumatic memories. In contrast with Freudian repression, some researchers have defined repression not as a reaction to trauma, but rather as a chronic coping tendency, in which one is inclined to ignore threatening or otherwise unwanted information (e.g., Gleser & Ihilevich, 1969; Weinberger and colleagues, 1979). This trait-repression is susceptible to self-report measurement, and several studies have yielded results to suggest that individuals indeed differ in their tendency to ignore unwanted information. The concept of dissociation is related to repression and suppression in the sense that it pertains to loss of memory for unpleasant experiences. However, unlike repression and suppression, dissociation is not a postevent coping mechanism, but a peritraumatic strategy. According to the theory, a traumatic event can cause an individual to block information processing, resulting in a reduction of information storage. This reduction in turn causes a fragmented recollection of the pertinent event, which can be referred to as dissociative amnesia. Hence, dissociation simultaneously refers to a coping strategy and a psychiatric complaint. Indeed, dissociation is included in the DSM-IV-TR. However, research findings suggest that nonclinical dissociation is prevalent in the general population to a very large extent. It can even be argued that, as with repression, some manifestations of dissociation tend to possess trait-like qualities. This kind of dissociation is not necessarily rooted in traumatic experiences. DID is a particularly problematic dissociative phenomenon because growing evidence suggests that this condition is not to be construed as a presence of multiple persons in one body, but rather, "merely" as a fragmented self-perception. There is also reason to argue that DID is an iatrogenic disorder (i.e., caused by therapeutic intervention; see Lilienfeld & Lynn, 2003). In sum, while suppression is sometimes mentioned in one breath with repression and dissociation, there are marked differences between these three concepts.

Chapter 3 addresses an important methodological issue, namely the nature of the variables used in thought suppression studies. Most of the time, suppression studies involve self-reports. Therefore, one might argue that the validity of findings can never be guaranteed. Schwarz (1999) summarizes problems that can occur with the use of self-reports. However, in spite of possible problems with validity of self-reports, such measures are important in the thought suppression paradigm, if for no other reason than there is no alternative for the measurement of intrusive thoughts. Although much effort and money are invested in biologic markers of psychological phenomena (cf. Anderson and colleagues, 2004, who claim to have discovered the brain location responsible for the act of suppression with use of functional magnetic resonance imaging), ultimately, self-report is still the only measure of what goes on in one's mind. Or in McNally's words: "Likewise, certain phenomena, such as obsessions, have no outward manifestations other than that revealed in language. Even PET studies of OCD patients require one to confirm that the person is, indeed, obsessing in the scanner" (2001, p. 520). Apart from the fact that nonself-reports are not always available, it remains to be seen whether psychologists should invest time in seeking such alternatives. Benschop and Draaisma (2000) illustrated this point with an analysis of the old Wundtian laboratory development. Eventually, Wundt and his colleagues were so involved in the refinement of their instruments, that these became too fine-grained for the measurement of the to-be-observed behavior. Another reason to confidently rely on self-reports is that the few studies that addressed the validity of self-reports in thought suppression studies yielded no reason to suspect invalidity (Rassin, 2004; Rassin and colleagues, 1999). In addition, although intrusion frequency is the main dependent variable, several thought suppression experiment employed other variables that are not under conscious control, and are thus not susceptible to self-report bias. For example, thought suppression has been documented to increase reaction time (Lane & Wegner, 1995), to increase physiological arousal as measured by skin conductance (Wegner and colleagues, 1990), and even to negatively affect the immune system (Petrie and colleagues, 1998). Hence, the conclusion to be drawn from Chapter 3 is that the findings obtained in thought suppression experiments cannot be attributed to self-report bias.

Chapter 4 continues the search for methodological artefacts. There is reason to believe that the expression instruction ("think of white bears as much as possible") given by Wegner and colleagues (1987) in the control condition limits the validity of study. That is, this instruction may yield more target thoughts than a liberal instruction ("think of anything, including white bears"). For example, expression after suppression may inflate the rebound effect, compared to a liberal instruction. Indeed, several experiments have yielded results suggesting that expression instructions produce more intrusions than liberal ones (Merckelbach et al., 1991; Rassin et al., 2005), although a meta-analysis by Abramowitz and colleagues (2001) suggests that eventually the choice for expression or liberal instructions is futile. Another concern about the instructions given to participants in suppression studies revolves around the phenomenon of spontaneous suppression (Purdon, 1999). Apparently, participants in the control condition, sometimes engage in suppression attempts. This kind of spontaneous suppression is likely to occur if the target thought is particularly unpleasant. Spontaneous suppression can be hazardous to the experiment, in that it eliminates the control condition. That is, if all participants engage in suppression, regardless of the instructions they receive, the control condition resolves. To prevent spontaneous suppression, an "antisuppression" instruction can be included (see Purdon, 1999). Apart from concerns about the internal validity of thought suppression research, the paradigm also suffers from external competition. For example, findings derived from the directed forgetting paradigm are far more optimistic about the human capacity to block information from consciousness (e.g., Myers et al., 1998). Methodological differences between thought suppression and directed forgetting are probably the cause of the differential findings. For example, Whetstone and Cross (1998) demonstrated that the focus on intrusions is a crucial factor determining suppression inefficacy, while such a focus is absent in directed forgetting. Furthermore, while the thought suppression paradigm is essentially a mental control paradigm, directed forgetting pertains to memory performance. Likewise, Anderson and Green (2001) claim to have found solid evidence for successful suppression, but it has to be acknowledged that "suppression" in the study of these authors is a completely different cognitive operation as suppression in a regular thought suppression experiment.

Chapter 5 discusses individual differences in thought suppression. Wegner and Zanakos (1994) argued that suppression is not only a transient activity, but that it can, at the same time, manifest as a chronic tendency, much like repression and dissociation. These authors introduced the WBSI as a measure of suppression proneness. Although several studies have produced support for the validity of this scale, it has been criticized for including a number of items that do not pertain to suppression, but rather to the experience of intrusions. Thus, the WBSI seems to be biased toward failing suppression attempts (Blumberg, 2000; Höping & De Jong-Meyer, 2003; Rassin, 2003). An expanding field of research is that of individual differences in successful suppression. Although thought suppression is generally found to be ineffective, researchers have tried to identify predictors of successful suppression. One such predictor may be fluid intelligence (Brewin & Beaton, 2002). Likewise, practice may add to the capacity to successfully suppress target thoughts (Wegner, 1994). As another example, the precise technique used to suppress a thought may be of influence to the eventual effect. While Wegner and colleagues (1987) assume that distraction is the vehicle behind suppression, and its paradoxical effect, Wells and Davies (1994) argue that distraction can be further differentiated into positive distraction, worrying about personal problems, and self-punishment. Research with the TCQ, a measure specifically designed by these authors to tap these different strategies, suggests that worrying and punishment are particularly ineffective, while positive distraction appears to be somewhat effective after all. In addition, the extent to which a distractor (regardless of emotional valence) really captures one's attention may determine suppression efficacy. Successful suppression and individual differences therein deserve attention in future research.

Chapter 6 addresses the main clinical application of the thought suppression research, that is its hypothesized contribution to the development of obsession. From earlier studies (Rachman & De Silva, 1978; Salkovskis & Harrison, 1984), it is known that the experience of obsessive intrusions is not exclusive to clinical conditions. Approximately 80% of the nonclinical population regularly experience intrusive thoughts. However, in spite of similarity in content, normal intrusions occur less frequently, are less intense and discomforting, and last less long, compared to clinically relevant obsessions. These clinical characteristics – especially the increased frequency – can be explained by the findings of Wegner and colleagues (1987). By this view, those people who suppress their, originally harmless, intrusion, will unknowingly produce a paradoxical increase of intrusion frequency, ultimately resulting in a clinical obsession (Wegner, 1989). Many papers have referred to the development of obsession as a major implication of thought suppression research. Indeed, many research reports have been published in which the association between suppression and obsession was targeted. However, many of these studies relied on cross-sectional set-ups, and on non-clinical samples. Against the background of these numerous analogue studies (Abramowitz et al., 2001), the number of studies employing actual OCD patients is disappointingly small. Furthermore, the handful of experimental studies relying on patients yielded only limited support for the notion that OCD patients engage in failing suppression attempts (Janeck & Calamari, 1999; Tolin et al., 2002). Apart from the limited clinical evidence for the detrimental effects of thought suppression on obsession, there is a strong and still growing alternative explanation for the development of obsessions. In this so-called cognitive theory of obsession (Rachman, 1993; Salkovskis, 1985), it is not necessarily the thought control strategy that is crucial, but rather the original interpretation of an intrusive thought. For instance, an intrusive thought about sex is probably upsetting to people who think that the occurrence of such a thought is a sign of bad character, but not to people who accept an incidental sexual impulse coming out of the blue. There is some neat evidence suggesting that the interpretation of stimuli indeed influences the valence of these stimuli. For example, Ladouceur and colleagues (1995) instructed participants to sort pills by color. Interestingly, participants who were told that the pills were to be shipped to countries in the third world, and that they had to be very precise in their sorting effort, became more stressed and eager to check, compared to those who had not received such additional instruction. Likewise, Rassin and colleagues (1999) connected high schoolers to a bogus computer via electrodes, and succeeded in convincing them that thoughts of apple would result in another person receiving electrical shocks. This instruction evidently made thoughts of the (previously neutral) apple discomforting. According to the cognitive theory, flawed interpretation of intrusions is particularly likely to occur with individuals who exhibit certain cognitive biases. For example, people who believe that their own thoughts predict actual future events, are more likely to become upset if the intrusion ("I hope that I will get cancer") flashes through their mind (Rachman et al., 1996). The example mentioned here probably illustrates that we all display cognitive bias to some extent (except for those who like to think of getting cancer, or to tempt fate). Interestingly, several questionnaires have been introduced to differentiate the extent to which respondents suffer from cognitive bias relevant to the development of obsessive-compulsive disorder (OCD) (Shafran et al., 1996). Although thought suppression is far from essential within the cognitive theory, it does play a role as an accelerant. That is, the discomfort caused by the misinterpretation of intrusions is a likely motive to engage in suppression attempts, with all of its detrimental consequences (Rachman, 1998). In summary, the strength of the clinical evidence for the effect of thought suppression on the development of obsession is somewhat disappointing, because there are only few experimental studies that rely on actual OCD samples. In addition, there is a strong concurrent theory that reduces the theoretical impact of suppression on obsession.

In Chapter 7, a second application of the thought suppression paradigm is discussed, namely traumatic recollections. Like obsessions, traumatic memories can be construed as intrusive thoughts, and can thus become the target of suppression attempts. Indeed, there is evidence to suggest that obsessions and traumatic recollections share several characteristics. For example, unlike lay people may think, recollections of traumatic events, although vivid and impressive, can become distorted and transformed into worst case scenarios to the extent that they resemble obsessive rumination (Bryant & Harvey, 1998). In fact, OCD and posttraumatic stress disorder (PTSD) are not seldom misdiagnosed as each other (Lipinski & Pope, 1994). One difference between obsession and traumatic memory is that the latter is far more elaborate. In spite of this difference, suppression of traumatic memories has been found to be just as ineffective as that of obsessive intrusions. There is even reason to suspect that elaborated thoughts such as traumatic memories are more difficult to suppress than single, discrete thoughts. In the words of Abramowitz and colleagues (2001): "larger rebound effects were found with nondiscrete target thoughts (e.g., a story) than with discrete thoughts (e.g., a white bear)" (p. 700). Given the relative elaborateness of traumatic recollections, suppression may not only affect intrusion frequency, but also the actual content of the suppressed memory. Wegner and colleagues (1996) argue that suppression deteriorates memory, especially sequence memory. The study by these authors has been replicated in a handful of experiments, but the findings so far have been somewhat contradictory, precluding strong conclusions about the effect of thought suppression on memory. Hence, this topic deserves future study.

Chapter 8 addresses a variety of suppression applications. Although obsession and traumatic memory are the two phenomena to which the thought suppression research has been applied most prominently, the effects of suppression on numerous other thoughts have been studied as well. To begin with, anxiety-related cognitions (other than obsession and traumatic memory) can become suppression targets. For example, the relation between anticipation anxiety (Koster et al., 2003), trait anxiety (Muris & Merckelbach, 1994), specific phobia (Muris et al., 1998), and thought suppression has been addressed in various studies. The most parsimonious conclusion to be drawn from this research is that anxiety further reduces the ability to suppress thoughts successfully. Excessive worrying as seen in GAD is a breed apart, because it is not only an intrusive cognition that can be targeted by suppression attempts, but at the same time a suppressive thought control strategy (Borkovec & Inz, 1990; Wells & Davies, 1994). In many studies, thought suppression has been applied to psychiatric symptoms other than those related to anxiety disorders. Suppression of urges to consume cigarettes (Haaga & Allison, 1994), alcohol (Palfai et al., 1997), and food (e.g., Johnston et al., 1999) has been reported to be ineffective. As to the relation between suppression and depressive rumination, the latter may – like anxiety – significantly reduce suppression capability (Wenzlaff et al., 1988). Another example is the suppression of pain sensations, which has, again, been found to be ineffective (Cioffi & Holloway, 1993). Although many researchers are primarily interested in the clinical applications of thought suppression research, suppression also takes place outside the clinical domain. In our daily lives, we all may suppress a thought from time to time. Several studies have focused on thought suppression without making reference to a specific psychiatric syndrome. For example, Bouman (2001), and Lane and Wegner (1995) concluded that suppression may be implicated in secrecy. Thus, it may be the paradoxical effects of thought suppression that make it so hard to keep a secret. Another nonclinical application is the suppression of stereotypes. Several studies have yielded results suggesting that suppression of stereotyped ideas is, in the longer run, ineffective and probably indeed paradoxical (Macrae et al., 1994). Furthermore, the suppression of forbidden information (e.g., inadmissible evidence in court) while preparing a verdict, has been proven to have paradoxical effects (Kassin & Neumann, 1997). This is an important finding, suggesting that judges had better not rule illegal evidence inadmissible. In this chapter, the thought suppression paradigm is discussed against the background of the wider theory of self-control and ego depletion (Baumeister and colleagues, 1998). This theory boils down to the notion that all acts of self-control (whether mental or physical) consume one common energy source that is easily depleted. Therefore, our ability to engage in self-control is very limited. This theory is attractive because it does not distinguish between mental and overt physical behaviors. By contrast, thought suppression research mainly pertains to cognitive contents. One ironical implication of the self-control theory is that trying not to think of eating fattening food consumes so much mental energy, that one is subsequently no longer able to resist the temptation of actually eating precisely that food. Indeed, some preliminary evidence for the idea that we display exactly those behaviors that we try to suppress most strongly, is offered by Wegner and colleagues (1998). The effects of suppressing behavioral impulses seem to be an important topic for future suppression research.

Beyond Frequency: A Cognitive Theory of Suppression?

Although various dependent variables have been employed in thought suppression research (e.g., reaction time, skin conductance, immune system functioning, memory), the number of intrusive thoughts is the most prominent one. The effect of suppression on intrusion frequency is probably the most researched relation within this paradigm. If suppression does not reduce the subsequent number of intrusions, it is claimed to be ineffective. As mentioned previously, in the longer run, suppression may even produce an increased number of intrusions (i.e., the rebound effect). Although it is perfectly legitimate to draw conclusions about suppression efficacy based on intrusion frequency, other variables may be of influence to the eventual clinical relevance of the paradigm. A few years ago, Purdon concluded that suppression may not even have its most important effects on intrusion frequency, "but may have its most important effects on thought appraisal, metacognitive beliefs about thought processes, extent of cognitive preoccupation and mood state" (1999, p. 1047). In a recent review, Purdon (2004), postulates that, in addition to its effect on intrusion frequency, thought suppression seems to make the individual hypervigilant to the target thought, to terminate exposure to the thought, and to enhance negative appraisal of the thought. Imagine someone who wants to suppress a specific thought, but in spite of his suppression attempts, the target thought intrudes consciousness twice within a few minutes. These two intrusions are probably more upsetting to the individual if he believes that complete suppression is an achievable goal, than if he does not expect to be completely intrusion-free. Hence, prior expectations about suppression efficacy may determine the interpretation of suppression failure. Therefore, it is not intrusion frequency per se that determines the eventual discomfort and psychological complaints, because one and the same intrusion frequency can be experienced as either normal or upsetting, depending on the interpretation by the individual.

Recently, researchers have started to study the relation between actual thought suppression and cognitions about suppression. Purdon and Clark (2001) submitted 219 undergraduate students to two 6-minute periods of thought monitoring. Some participants received suppression instructions during the first period, while others merely monitored their thoughts during both periods. The target thought varied across groups: Participants either monitored a neutral thought (white bear), a positive personally relevant, or a negative personally relevant thought. In addition to intrusion frequency, target thought related discomfort and mood state were measured. On average, suppression participants did not report significantly more intrusions than controls during the first (i.e., 7.8 vs. 13.3) or second period (8.6 vs. 8.2). In spite of this absence of an immediate or rebound effect, discomfort ratings after the second interval indicated that participants who had previously suppressed a negative thought, experienced more discomfort than those who had merely monitored their negative thought. In addition, the former participants' mood state after the second interval was significantly worse than that of the latter participants. Thus, these findings suggest that suppression indeed has effects on appraisal of intrusions and on mood, regardless of its effects (or absence thereof) on intrusion frequency.

Purdon, Rowa, and Antony (2005) subjected 50 patients with OCD to two thought monitoring periods of 4 minutes each. As in the Purdon and Clark (2001) study, half of the participants received additional suppression instructions during the first period only. In this case, suppression targets were the most upsetting personally relevant obsessions of participants. Intrusion frequencies during the two periods were 8.2 and 10.7 in the suppression condition, and 20.0 and 18.3 in the control condition. Thus, no immediate or rebound effect of thought suppression emerged. However, additional analyses indicated that the perceived need to control one's own thoughts significantly predicted depressed mood during the second period. Again, this finding suggests that intrusion frequency may not be the most important, and certainly not the only relevant variable in thought suppression research. Future focus on variables other than intrusion frequency is important, because the literature on intrusion frequency is growingly difficult to summarize. In the words of Purdon and colleagues: "Empirical investigations of the actual effects of thought suppression on thought frequency have yielded highly inconsistent findings with some studies finding a 'rebound' effect (greater frequency after suppression), some finding an immediate enhancement effect (greater frequency during suppression) and many finding no effect" (2005, p. 95).

Belloch, Morillo, and Giménez (2004) conducted a comparable study in which 87 undergraduates underwent three thought monitoring periods. Half of them received suppression instructions during the second period. For some participants, the target thought was that of a white bear, while for others, a personally relevant unwanted thought was targeted. Among other variables, the annoyance caused by experiencing the pertinent intrusion was measured. As to intrusion frequency, there was no effect of target thought valence, or of suppression instruction. The only significant effect was a time effect, in that the number of intrusions gradually decreased over the three periods, in all conditions from approximately 2.8 to 2.0. Interestingly, annoyance decreased significantly as well, in all groups except for the group of participants who had suppressed a personally relevant unwanted thought. Apparently, in this case the paradoxical effect of thought suppression did not manifest itself in intrusion frequency, but rather in negative appraisal.

Tolin, Abramowitz, Hamlin, Foa, and Synodi (2002) were interested in how participants in a thought suppression experiment (Tolin et al., 2002) attributed the occurrence of intrusions in spite of suppression attempts. They asked 17 patients with OCD, 11 patients with non-OCD anxiety disorder, and eight nonanxious controls to complete several questionnaires addressing the experience of intrusions, and thus the failure of suppression attempts. One of the questionnaires pertained to the internal (e.g., "I am mentally weak") or external (e.g., "It was a silly thing to do") attribution of suppression failure. As expected by the authors, patients with OCD scored higher than the other two groups on internal attribution. In addition, they were the only group that scored higher on internal than on external attribution. This finding lends support to the notion that it is not suppression inefficacy per se that predicts obsessive complaints, but rather the interpretation of such inefficacy.

Finally, McLaren and Crowe (2003) conducted a questionnaire study in which they used, among others, the WBSI and PADUA. Using median split analyses, these authors found that, in a sample of 269 undergraduate students, obsessive complaints were not only predicted by thought suppression, but specifically by the combination of suppression and perceived lack of control over stressful life events. Interestingly, the authors replicated this finding in a clinical sample of 91 patients with OCD and other anxiety disorders. Even though this study did not pertain to cognitions about suppression per se, it does illustrate that thought suppression alone may not be the best predictor of obsessional complaints.

To summarize, recent studies suggest that intrusion frequency may not be the most important dependent variable in thought suppression experiments. Metacognitions about intrusions and suppression may play a more important role than previously acknowledged. Several biased cognitions can be identified. First, a basic distorted belief is that it is unnatural to experience intrusive thoughts. Research has clearly suggested that most people experience intrusions, from time to time (Brewin, Christodoulides, & Hutchinson, 1996; Rachman & De Silva, 1978). Salkovskis (1999) goes even further and argues that intrusive thoughts are sometimes useful and comparable to creative brainstorm. A second and related biased idea is that intrusions should be suppressed. Even if one believes that intrusions are unnatural, this does not necessarily mean that suppression is the only way to respond to intrusive thoughts. Third, people may have flawed cognitions about suppression itself. Particularly, the beliefs that suppression attempts should be successful, and that one must, at all times, be in complete control of one's thoughts, are dangerous biases. These beliefs may result in a state of hypersensitivity to target thoughts, which in turn leads to an overestimation of intrusion frequency. Furthermore, these ideas may lead to additional distress if thought suppression does not seem to produce the intended effect. The maintenance or even increase of intrusive thoughts may be interpreted as emphasizing the importance of the suppressed thought, or as indicating the loss of mental control (Purdon, 1999).

Clinical Implications

For decades, during the second half of the twentieth century, people who suffered from obsessive or other anxious ruminations were encouraged by their psychotherapists to engage in "thought stopping." This intervention entailed that the patient prevents the target thought from entering consciousness, simply by mentally rehearsing or actually saying the word "stop," whenever the target occurs. The efficacy of the thought stopping procedure has been proven to be disappointing, which is not surprising given the similarity with thought suppression (Tryon, 1979). Indeed, Wegner is clear about the lessons for treatment to be learned from thought suppression studies: "in many cases of unwanted thought, it may be best to stop suppressing" (1989, p. 174). Indeed, by now, thought stopping is no longer a very current intervention, although some authors still recommend it (Nolen-Hoeksema, 2001).

While the "stop stopping" movement may have been partly inspired by the original study by Wegner and colleagues (1987), it must be acknowledged that the recent thought suppression literature invites a slightly more balanced view. For one thing, given the individual differences in suppression capability, this control strategy may be effective for some individuals after all (Abramowitz et al., 2003). In addition, it may well be so that the act of suppression per se is not the most detrimental element in the development of clinically relevant intrusions, but rather flawed cognitions about suppression. There-fore, correcting maladaptive cognitions about thought suppression and intrusions should be an important goal of therapy, perhaps even more important than preventing the act of suppression itself (Purdon & Clark, 2000). This can be achieved by conducting a small behavioral experiment derived from the study by Wegner and colleagues (1987). Patients who tend to yield to suppression can be instructed to not think of a white bear for a few minutes during a therapy session, to see whether suppression is a fruitful reaction (Purdon, 1999; Salkovskis, 1999). Thus, the white bear experiment can be turned into a therapeutic procedure. More broadly speaking, suppression can also be used as a paradoxical intention intervention. For example, a couple complaining about a lack of intimacy in their relationship can be instructed by their therapist to refrain from intimate acts for 1 week. This "prohibition" is then likely to result in "forbidden" intimacy. In this way, intimacy or at least awareness thereof is promoted.

If suppression is, generally, not an appropriate technique to control intrusions, what should be done instead? According to Wegner, thought suppression experiments provide a straightforward rationale for habituation- or exposure-oriented treatments. In clinical literature, some good examples can be found that seem to underline Wegner's position. For example, systematic exposure to obsessive intrusions appears to be a promising treatment strategy. To illustrate, Salkovskis and Westbrook (1989) tape-recorded ob-sessive thoughts of their patients and then instructed these patients to listen to the tapes for several days at selected times. Patients were also taught how to refrain from covert avoidance tendencies (e.g., thought suppression). The combination of exposure and response prevention led to a decrease in obsessive thoughts and this positive outcome was maintained at long-term follow-up. Taped habituation and prevention of thought suppression tendencies may also be fruitfully applied to other types of psychopathology. For example, Vaughan and Tarrier (1992) asked patients with PTSD to describe their traumatic experiences and these descriptions were then audiotaped. Patients were instructed to listen to the audiotaped traumas for 1 hour per day over a 1-week period. They were also taught not to react with thought suppression to these tapes. Most of the patients benefited from treatment and this positive effect was maintained at 6-months follow-up. Likewise, Reynolds and Tarrier (1996) instructed patients with PTSD to monitor their traumatic intrusions by keeping a detailed diary over a 2-month period. This resulted in an overall improvement so that at the end of the study, four of six patients no longer met PTSD criteria. Thus, confrontation with and elaboration of unwanted, negative thoughts seem to be effective elements in the treatment of PTSD. This is further illustrated by studies in which individuals had to write about personally upsetting events over and over again (Pennebaker, 1993; Esterling, L'Abate, Murray, & Pennebaker, 1999). In general, positive outcomes in terms of physical and mental health have been reported in studies that relied on this diary method.

The previous studies concur with Wegner's (1989) suggestion that confronting an unwanted thought is a good starting point for treatment. However, this conclusion needs to be qualified. First, while it has become common wisdom that confronting and expressing painful thoughts and emotions is therapeutically effective, there are several research findings that cast some doubt on the general applicability of this notion. For example, dysphoric individuals who are instructed to ruminate about themselves and their feelings have been found to be more pessimistic and impaired in their problem solving capabilities than are dysphoric individuals who distract their attention from their moods (Lyubomirsky, Caldwell, & Nolen-Hoeksema, 1998). As another example, there are indications that unstructured exposure to trauma reminders might be harmful in the treatment of PTSD (Boudewyns & Hyer, 1990; Johnson, Rosenheck, Fontana, Lubin, Charney, & Southwick, 1996). Commenting on these disappointing findings, Littrell (1998) concluded that confronting painful memories and thoughts will only yield benefit if the treatment also encourages cognitive restructuring of the traumatic experiences. In her words: "Revisiting painful emotion has the potential to improve health and psychological functioning. However, success is not explained by a purging/discharge mechanism or because the opposite of attending to emotion, viz., inhibition is precluded. Mere attention to feelings of distress can enhance distress. To preclude increasing distress as a consequence of revisiting trauma, some new response to the negative-emotion–eliciting stimulus (..) must be found" (Littrell, 1998, p. 96). Recently, Lohr, Hooke, Gist, and Tolin (2003) argued that the efficacy of group debriefings after colossal traumatic events (e.g., plane crashes or disasters) is unsubstantiated. In fact, such a forced debriefing can even have negative effects on psychological well-being (see De Silva, 1999, for a humorous attack on the a contraria reasoning that expression must be good if suppression is proven to be bad). Second, it remains to be determined to what extent abstinence from thought suppression is a mediator of therapeutic success in the treatment of obsessive or traumatic intrusions. In the Reynolds and Tarrier (1996) study, it was found that monitoring of traumatic intrusions had beneficial effects, even when it was accompanied by avoidant control strategies (e.g., thought suppression). The authors suggested that keeping a diary of intrusive recollections increases the amount of patients' perceived control over their thoughts. Perhaps, then, it is an increased sense of being in control rather than abstinence from thought suppression that constitutes the therapeutically active element in the studies referred to previously (McLaren & Crowe, 2003). As another example, Antony, McCabe, Leeuw, Sano, and Swinson (2001) failed to find effects of blunting (i.e., visual avoidance) on exposure therapy outcome. Apparently, the spider phobics in this study who regularly looked away when therapeutically confronted with spiders profited to an equal extent from the intervention as did those who were completely concentrated during the whole therapy.

In summary, the general clinical implication of thought suppression research is that individuals who suffer from intrusions should not engage in suppression, but should seek alternative ways to think about these intrusions, if necessary with help from a therapist. However, it is important to remember that this general conclusion (as does any other) suffers from exceptions.

Unresolved Issues and Future Research

As mentioned previously, thought suppression is a popular field of research. A literature search in Psycinfo with "thought suppression" as target delivers slightly more than 230 hits from 1987 to 2005. Thirty-two of these hits stem from 2004 and 2005, suggesting that the scientific interest in this topic is not decreasing. Unfortunately, this implies that any review is doomed to be incomplete. It also implies that researchers are not short of inspiration to conduct thought suppression studies. Nonetheless, it is important to try to identify fruitful future areas of thought suppression research. Evidently, future research is needed to solve issues that are currently unresolved.

One important issue is that currently, a clear taxonomy of suppression and related control strategies is lacking. To date, there is a large, but scattered literature on the various avoidance and escape oriented strategies that people may resort to when confronted with intrusive cognitions. These strategies have been labeled blunting (Miller, 1992), cognitive avoidance (Foa & Kozak, 1986), retrieval inhibition (Bjork, 1989), distraction (Baum, 1987), self-punishment, and worrying (Wells & Davies, 1994) to name a few examples. To a certain extent, these concepts overlap with thought suppression, due to the fact that they all assume the existence of inhibitory mechanisms that deactivate mental representations. Note, however, that there are also marked differences between these concepts in whether or not a maladaptive (i.e., counterproductive) quality is ascribed to them. For example, Miller (1992) concluded that in medical contexts, people who typically avoid threat-relevant information (i.e., blunters) are often less distressed in response to health threats than are individuals who monitor threat-relevant cues (i.e., monitors). There are even indications that during anticipation of a medical visit, monitors display a higher frequency of intrusive thoughts than do blunters. However, whether blunting is an adaptive strategy depends on an array of conditions (e.g., nature and type of medical intervention, short versus long-term consequences of blunting). Findings such as these demonstrate that this research domain would profit from a refined taxonomy of avoidant strategies. Distraction is a particular important strategy, because Wegner and colleagues (1987) argue that distraction is the vehicle behind the paradoxical effects of thought suppression. However, Wells and Davies (1994) argue that distraction can take various forms (e.g., positive distraction, worrying, or punishment), and that these differential manifestations differ in efficacy.

A second issue that deserves further study, is the relation between thought suppression on the one hand, and various other paradigms (e.g., directed forgetting, repressive coping, and retrieval induced forgetting) on the other. How can the divergent findings of the various paradigms be reconciled? In part, the precise methodology explains the different conclusions. For example, in directed forgetting, the forgetting (preferably permanently) of information is pivotal, while in thought suppression, intrusion frequency is the major dependent variable. Although it is tempting to use the concepts of suppression, repression, and forgetting interchangeably, there are important differences. For example, one can have intrusions about a traumatic event, but at the same time, have forgotten certain details of that event. Likewise, one can be free of intrusive thoughts about an upcoming examination, while remembering all the information necessary to pass the examination.

An issue that has received too little attention so far is the effect of specific methodological choices on the eventual findings in suppression research. For example, expression instead of liberal instructions seems to inflate the rebound effect of thought suppression. Larger rebound effects have also been associated with prolonged suppression attempts relative to short suppression periods (Abramowitz et al., 2001). Another, new, research topic is spontaneous suppression, that is, suppression by participants who have not received suppression instructions (Purdon, 2004). More studies are needed to investigate the effects of specific methodology on suppression outcomes.

While the precise definition of thought suppression is evidently crucial for scientific research, something similar can be said for intrusions, and other dependent variables in suppression studies. Various psychiatric disorders are characterized by the occurrence of unwanted intrusions (Clark, 2005). Although these intrusions are similar to a certain degree, there are also differences. So far, meta-analysis has yielded only one relevant target characteristic, namely elaborateness (Abramowitz et al., 2001). Suppression of elaborate targets (e.g., a story) seems to result in a larger rebound effect than suppression of discrete targets (e.g., white bears). This implies that suppression of intrusive memories may be more difficult than suppression of obsessive thoughts. This observation by Abramowitz and colleagues raises similar questions concerning the effect of other target characteristics. For example, is it more difficult to suppress a visual image than a verbal thought? Is it more difficult to suppress a visual recollection of an actual event than a visual fantasy? Given that various intrusions can become the target of suppression attempts, it would be worthwhile to know which intrusion characteristics influence suppression efficacy.

A fifth possible future research topic pertains to the factors that determine suppression efficacy. Although suppression is generally ineffective, recent studies suggest that under some circumstances, some individuals are quite capable of suppressing unwanted thoughts. Mood (Wenzlaff et al., 1988), expectations (Rassin et al., 2003), practice (Wegner, 1994), intelligence (Brewin & Beaton, 2002), and personality (Myers et al., 1998) are examples of predictors of suppression efficacy. The study of effective suppression certainly deserves further study.

Finally, cognitions about suppression recently emerged as an important factor. For example, irrational cognitions may lead individuals to become upset by the experience of certain intrusions, and may thus underlie the need to engage in suppression in the first place (cf. the cognitive theory of obsession). Furthermore, flawed suppression-related beliefs (e.g., the conviction that completely successful suppression is achievable, or that suppression is a sign of good character) may result in increased discomfort when suppression attempts do not have the desired result. Also, strong beliefs about the efficacy of suppression may lead people to rigidly continue their suppression attempts even if they are in fact not successful. The identification and correction of such beliefs may help individuals to understand that thought suppression is an obvious, but not necessarily a fruitful thought control strategy.

References

Abramowitz, J.S., Tolin, D.F., & Street, G.P. (2001). Paradoxical effects of thought suppression: A meta-analysis of controlled studies. *Clinical Psychology Review, 21*, 683–703.

Abramowitz, J.S., Whiteside, S., Kalsy, S.A., & Tolin, D.F. (2003). Thought control strategies in obsessive-compulsive disorder: A replication and extension. *Behaviour Research and Therapy, 41*, 529–540.

Adler, R. (1999, December 18). Crowded minds. *New Scientist*, 26–31.

American Psychiatric Association (APA) (1987). *Diagnostic and Statistical Manual of Mental Disorders, 3rd edition, revised (DSM-III-R)*. Washington, D.C.: APA.

American Psychiatric Association (APA) (1994). *Diagnostic and Statistical Manual of Mental Disorders, 4th edition (DSM-IV)*. Washington, D.C.: APA.

American Psychiatric Association (APA) (2000). *Diagnostic and Statistical Manual of Mental Disorders, 4th edition, Text Revision (DSM-IV-TR)*. Washington, D.C.: APA.

Amir, N., Cashman, L., & Foa, E.B. (1997). Strategies of thought control in obsessive-compulsive disorder. *Behaviour Research and Therapy, 35*, 775–777.

Amir, M., Kaplan, Z., Efroni, R., Levine, Y., Benjamin, J., & Kotler, M. (1997). Coping styles in post-traumatic stress disorder (PTSD) patients. *Personality and Individual Differences, 23*, 399–405.

Anderson, M.C. & Green, C. (2001). Suppressing unwanted memories by executive control. *Nature, 410*, 366–369.

Anderson, M.C. & Levy, B. (2002). Repression can (and should) be studied empirically. *Trends in Cognitive Sciences, 6*, 502–503.

Anderson, T. & Leitner, L.M. (1991). The relationship between the defense mechanisms inventory and reported symptomatology in college females. *Personality and Individual Differences, 12*, 967–969.

Anderson, M.C., Ochsner, K.N., Kuhl, B., Copper, J., Robertson, E., Gabrieli, S.W., Glover, G.H., & Gabrieli, J.D.E. (2004). Neural systems underlying the suppression of unwanted memories. *Science, 303*, 232–235.

Andrews, G., Singh, M., & Bond, M. (1993). The Defense Style Questionnaire. *Journal of Nervous and Mental Disease, 181*, 246–256.

Ansfield, M.E., Wegner, D.M., Bowser, R. (1996). Ironic effects of sleep urgency. *Behaviour Research and Therapy, 34*, 523–531.

Antony, M.M., Downie, F., & Swinson, R.P. (1998). Diagnostic issues and epidemiology in obsessive-compulsive disorder. In R.P. Swinson, M.M. Martin, S. Rachman, & M.A. Richter (eds.). *Obsessive-compulsive disorder: Theory, research, and treatment* (pp. 3–32). New York: The Guilford Press.

Antony, M.M., McCabe, R.E., Leeuw, I., Sano, N., & Swinson, R.P. (2001). Effect of distraction and coping style on in vivo exposure for specific phobia of spiders. *Behaviour Research and Therapy, 39*, 1137–1150.

Baum, M. (1987). Distraction during flooding (exposure): Concordance between results in animals and man. *Behaviour Research and Therapy, 25,* 227–228.

Baumeister, R.F., Bratslavsky, E., Muraven, M., & Tice, D.M. (1998). Ego depletion: Is the active self a limited resource? *Journal of Personality and Social Psychology, 74,* 1252–1265.

Baumeister, R.F. & Cairns, K.J. (1992). Repression and self-presentation: When audiences interfere with self-deceptive strategies. *Journal of Personality and Social Psychology, 62,* 851–862.

Baumeister, R.F., Muraven, M., & Tice, D.M. (2000). Ego depletion: A resource model of volition, self-regulation, and controlled processing. *Social Cognition, 18,* 130–150.

Baumeister, R.F. & Vohs, K.D. (2004). *Handbook of self-regulation: Research, theory, and applications.* New York: The Guilford Press.

Bebbington, P.E. (1998). Epidemiology of obsessive-compulsive disorder. *British Journal of Psychiatry, 173,* 2–6.

Beck, A.T. (1976). *Cognitive therapy and the emotional disorders.* New York: International University Press.

Beck, A.T., Rush, A.J., Shaw, B.F., & Emery, G. (1979). *Cognitive therapy of depression.* New York: Guilford.

Becker, E.S., Rinck, M., Roth, W.T., & Margraf, J. (1998). Don't worry and beware of white bears: Thought suppression in anxiety patients. *Journal of Anxiety Disorders, 12,* 39–55.

Belloch, A., Morillo, C., & Giménez, A. (2004). Effects of suppressing neutral and obsession-like thoughts in normal subjects: Beyond frequency. *Behaviour Research and Therapy, 42,* 841–857.

Benschop, R., & Draaisma, D. (2000). In pursuit of precision: The callibration of minds and machines in late nineteenth-century psychology. *Annals of Science, 57,* 1–25.

Bernstein, D.P. & Fink, L.A. (1998). *CTQ: Childhood trauma questionnaire: A retrospective self-report.* San Antonio: Psychological Corporation.

Bernstein, E.M. & Putnam, F.W. (1986). Development, reliability and validity of a dissociation scale. *Journal of Nervous and Mental Disease, 174,* 727–735.

Bjork, R.A. (1989). Retrieval inhibition as an adaptive mechanism in human memory. In H.I. Roediger III & F.I.M. Craik (eds.) *Varieties of memory and consciousness: Essays in honour of Endel Tulving* (pp. 309–330). Hillsdale: Lawrence Erlbaum Associates.

Blackman, J.S. (2004). *101 defenses: How the mind shields itself.* New York: Brunner-Routledge.

Blumberg, S.J. (2000). The white bear suppression inventory: Revisiting its factor structure. *Personality and Individual Differences, 29,* 943–950.

Boden, J.M. & Baumeister, R.F. (1997). Repressive coping: Distraction using pleasant thoughts and memories. *Journal of Personality and Social Psychology, 73,* 45–62.

Borkovec, T.D. & Inz, J. (1990). The nature of worry in generalized anxiety disorder: A predominance of thought activity. *Behaviour Research and Therapy, 28,* 153–158.

Boudewyns, P.A. & Hyer, L. (1990). Physiological response to combat memories and preliminary outcome in Vietnam veteran PTSD patients treated with direct therapeutic exposure. *Behavior Therapy, 21,* 63–87.

Bouman, T.K. (2003). Intra- and interpersonal consequences of experimentally induced concealment. *Behaviour Research and Therapy, 41,* 959–968.

Bowers, K.S. & Farvolden, P. (1996). Revisiting a century-old Freudian slip: From suggestion disavowed to the truth repressed. *Psychological Bulletin, 119,* 355–380.

Brewin, C.R. & Andrews, B. (2000). Psychological defence mechanism: The example of repression. *The Psychologist, 13,* 615–617.

Brewin, C.R. & Beaton, A. (2002). Thought suppression, intelligence, and working memory capacity. *Behaviour Research and Therapy, 40,* 923–930.

Brewin, C.R., Christodoulides, J., & Hutchinson, G. (1996). Intrusive thoughts and intrusive memories in a nonclinical sample. *Cognition and Emotion, 10,* 107–112.

Brewin, C.R., Dalgleish, T., & Joseph, S. (1996). A dual representation theory of posttraumatic stress disorder. *Psychological Review, 103,* 670–686.

Bryant, R.A. & Harvey, A.G. (1995). Avoidant coping style and post-traumatic stress following motor vehicle accidents. *Behaviour Research and Therapy, 33,* 631–635.

Bryant, R.A. & Harvey, A.G. (1998). Traumatic memories and pseudomemories in posttraumatic stress disorder. *Applied Cognitive Psychology, 12,* 81–88.

Buhr, K. & Dugas, M.J. (2002). The intolerance of uncertainty scale: Psychometric properties of the English version. *Behaviour Research and Therapy, 40,* 931–945.

Butcher, J.N., Dahlstrom, W.G., Graham, J.R., Tellegen, A., & Kaemmer, B. (1989). *Manual for administration and scoring: MMPI-2.* Minneapolis: University of Minnesota press.

Calamari, J.E., Wiegartz, P.S., & Janeck, A.S. (1999). Obsessive-compulsive disorder subgroups: A symptom-based clustering approach. *Behaviour Research and Therapy, 37,* 113–125.

Cartwright-Hatton, S. & Wells, A. (1997). Beliefs about worry and intrusions: The meta-cognition questionnaire and its correlates. *Journal of Anxiety Disorders, 11,* 279–296.

Chalmers, A.F. (1976). *What is this thing called science?* St. Lucia: University of Queensland Press.

Christanson, S.A. & Bylin, S. (1999). Does simulating amnesia mediate genuine forgetting for a crime event? *Applied Cognitive Psychology, 13,* 495–511.

Cioffi, D. & Holloway, J. (1993). Delayed costs of suppressed pain. *Journal of Personality and Social Psychology, 64,* 274–282.

Clark, D.A. (ed.) (2005). *Intrusive thoughts in clinical disorders: Theory, research, and treatment.* New York: The Guildford Press.

Clark, D.M., Ball, S., & Pape, D. (1991). An experimental investigation of thought suppression. *Behaviour Research and Therapy, 29,* 253–257.

Clark, D.M., Winton, E., & Thynn, L. (1993). A further experimental investigation of thought suppression. *Behaviour Research and Therapy, 31,* 207–210.

Clayton, I.C., Richards, J.C., & Edwards, C.J. (1999). Selective attention in Obsessive-Compulsive Disorder. *Journal of Abnormal Psychology, 108,* 171–175.

Coles, M.E., Mennin, D.S., & Heimberg, R.G. (2001). Distinguishing obsessive features and worries: The role of thought-action fusion. *Behaviour Research and Therapy, 39,* 947–959.

Conway, M. A. (2001). Repression revisited. *Nature, 410,* 319.

Conway, M., Howell, A., & Giannopoulos, C. (1991). Dysphoria and thought suppression. *Cognitive Therapy and Research, 15,* 153–166.

Coons, P.M., Milstein, V., & Marley, C. (1982). EEG studies of two multiple personalities and a control. *Archives of General Psychiatry, 39,* 823–825.

Coxon, P. & Valentine, T. (1997). The effects of the age of eyewitnesses on the accuracy and suggestibility of their testimony. *Applied Cognitive Psychology, 11,* 415–430.

Cramer, P. (2000). Defense mechanisms in psychology today: Further processes for adaptation. *American Psychologist, 55,* 637–646.

Crombag, H. & Van Koppen, P. (1994). Verdringen als sociaal verschijnsel [Repression as a social phenomenon]. *De Psycholoog, 29,* 409–415.

Crowne, D.P. & Marlowe, D.A. (1964). *The approval motive: Studies in evaluative dependence.* New York: Wiley.

Davey, G.C.L. (1993). A comparison of three worry questionnaires. *Behaviour Research and Therapy, 31,* 51–56.

Davies, M.I. & Clark, D.M. (1998). Thought suppression produces a rebound effect with analogue post-traumatic intrusions. *Behaviour Research and Therapy, 36,* 571–582.

De Bruin, G.O., Rassin, E., & Muris, P. (2004). *Correlates of the Thought Control Questionnaire.* Unpublished manuscript.

De Jongh, A., Muris, P., Merckelbach, H., & Schoenmakers, N. (1996). Suppression of dentist-related thoughts. *Behavioural and Cognitive Psychotherapy, 24*, 117–126.

De Silva, P. (1999). Thought-starting: A review of new developments. *Behaviour Research and Therapy, 37*, S175–S180.

De Silva, P. & Marks, M. (1999). The role of traumatic experiences in the genesis of obsessive-compulsive disorder. *Behaviour Research and Therapy, 37*, 941–951.

DePaulo, B.M., Lindsay, J.J., Malone, B.E., Muhlenbruck, L., Charlton, K., & Cooper, H. (2003). Cues to deception. *Psychological Bulletin, 129*, 74–118.

Derakshan, N. & Eysenck, M.W. (1999). Are repressors self-deceivers or other-deceivers? *Cognition and Emotion, 13*, 1–17.

Derogatis, L.R. (1977). *SCL-90. Administration, scoring and procedures manual-I for the revised version.* Baltimore: Johns Hopkins School of Medicine.

Edwards, K. & Bryan, T.S. (1997). Judgmental biases produced by the instructions to disregard: The (paradoxical) case of emotional information. *Personality and Social Psychology Bulletin, 23*, 849–864.

Ehlers, A. & Clark, D.M. (2000). A cognitive model of posttraumatic stress disorder. *Behaviour Research and Therapy, 38*, 319–345.

Emmelkamp, P.M.G. & Aardema, A. (1999). Metacognition, specific obsessive-compulsive beliefs and obsessive-compulsive behaviour. *Clinical Psychology and Psychotherapy, 6*, 139–145.

Erdelyi, M.H. (1993). Repression: The mechanism and the defense. In: D.M. Wegner & J.W. Pennebaker (eds.) *Handbook of mental control* (pp. 126–148). New Jersey: Prentice Hall.

Erdelyi, M.H. (2001). Defense processes can be conscious or unconscious. *American Psychologist, 56*, 761–762.

Esterling, B.A., L'Abate, L., Murray, E.J., & Pennebaker, J.W. (1999). Empirical foundations for writing in prevention and psychotherapy: Mental and physical health outcomes. *Clinical Psychology Review, 19*, 79–96.

Eysenck, H.J., Wilson, G., & Jackson, C. (1996). *Manual of the Eysenck Personality Profiler.* Guilford: Psi-Press.

Faber, R.J. & Vohs, K.D. (2004). To buy or not to buy? Self-control and self-regulatory failure in purchase behavior. In R.F. Baumeister & K.D. Vohs (eds.). *Handbook of self-regulation: Research, theory, and applications* (pp. 509–524). New York: The Guilford Press.

Fincher, D., Palahniuk, C., & Uhls, J. (1999). *Fight club.* USA: Twentieth-century Fox.

Foa, E.B. & Kozak, M.J. (1986). Emotional processing of fear: Exposure to corrective information. *Psychological Bulletin, 99*, 20–35.

Foa, E.B., Kozak, M.J., Salkovskis, P.M., Coles, M.E., & Amir, N. (1998). The validation of a new obsessive compulsive disorder scale: The obsessive compulsive inventory (OCI). *Psychological Assessment, 10*, 206–214.

Formea, G.M. & Burns, G.L. (1995). Relation between the syndromes of bulimia nervosa and obsessive complusive disorder. *Journal of Psychopathology and Behavioral Assessment, 17*, 167–176.

Frederiksen, L.W., Epstein, L.H., Kosevsky, B.P. (1975). Reliability and controlling effects of three procedures for self-monitoring smoking. *Psychological Record, 25*, 255–263.

Freud, A. [1936] 1946. *The ego and the mechanisms of defense.* Translation C. Baines. New York: International Universities Press.

Freud, S. [1909] 1955. Notes upon a case of obsessional neurosis. Translation A. Strachey & J. Strachey. In J. Strachey (ed.) *The standard edition of the complete psychological works of Sigmund Freud,* Vol. 10. London: Hogarth.

Freud, S. [1915] 1963. Repression. Translation C. Baines. In P. Rieff (ed.) *Freud: General psychological theory* (pp. 104–115). New York: Collier.

Freud, S. (1959a). The aetiology of hysteria. In J. Riviere (ed). *Sigmund Freud: Collected papers*, Vol. 1 (pp. 183–219). New York: Basic Books.

Freud, S. (1959b). My views on the part of sexuality in the aetiology of the neurosis. In J, Riviere (ed.). *Sigmund Freud: Collected papers*, Vol. 1 (pp. 272–283). New York: Basic Books.

Friedkin, W. & Blatty, W.P. (1973). *The exorcist*. USA: Warner Brothers.

Frost, R.O. & Steketee, G. (Eds.) (2002) *Cognitive approaches to obsessions and compulsions: Theory, assessment, and treatment*. New York: Pergamon.

Garcia-Montes, J.M., Perez-Alvarez, M., & Fidalgo, A.M. (2003). Influence of the suppression of self-discrepant thoughts on the vividness of perception of auditory illusions. *Behavioural and Cognitive Psychotherapy*, *31*, 33–44.

Gershuny, B.S., Bear, L., Radomsky, A.S., Wilson, K.A., & Jenike, M.A. (2003). Connections among symptoms of obsessive-compulsive disorder and posttraumatic stress disorder: A case series. *Behaviour Research and Therapy*, *41*, 1029–1041.

Gershuny, B.S. & Thayer, J.F. (1999). Relations among psychological trauma, dissociative phenomena, and trauma-related distress: A review and integration. *Clinical Psychology Review*, *19*, 631–657.

Gleser, G.C. & Ihilevich, D. (1969). An objective instrument for measuring defense mechanisms. *Journal of Consulting and Clinical Psychology*, *33*, 51–60.

Golding, J.M., Sego, S.A., Sanchez, R.P., & Hasemann, D. (1995). The believability of repressed memories. *Law and Human Behavior*, *19*, 569–592.

Goldsmith, T., Shapira, N.A., Phillips, K.A., & McElroy, S.L. (1998). Conceptual foundations of obsessive-compulsive spectrum disorders. In R.P. Swinson, M.M. Martin, S. Rachman, & M.A.Richter (eds.). *Obsessive-compulsive disorder: Theory, research, and treatment* (pp. 397–425). New York: The Guilford Press.

Gross, J.J. & Levenson, R.W. (1997). Hiding feelings: The acute effects of inhibiting negative and positive emotions. *Journal of Abnormal Psychology*, *106*, 95–103.

Gudjonsson, G.H. (1984). A new scale of interrogative suggestibility. *Personality and Individual Differences*, *5*, 303–314.

Gudjonsson, G.H. (1997a). Accusations by adults of childhood sexual abuse: A survey of the members of the British False Memory Society (BFMS). *Applied Cognitive Psychology*, *11*, 3–18.

Gudjonsson, G.H. (1997b). *Gudjonsson Suggestibility Scales*. Hove: Psychology Press.

Gudjonsson, G.H. (2003). *The Psychology of interrogations and confessions: A handbook*. New York: John Wiley & Sons.

Guthrie, R. & Bryant, R. (2000). Attempting suppression of traumatic memories over extended periods in acute stress disorder. *Behaviour Research and Therapy*, *38*, 899–907.

Haaga, D.A.F. & Allison, M.L. (1994). Thought suppression and smoking relapse: A secondary analysis of Haaga (1989). *British Journal of Clinical Psychology*, *33*, 327–331.

Harnden, J.L., McNally, R.J., & Jimerson, D.C. (1997). Effects of suppressing thoughts about body weight: A comparison of dieters an nondieters. *International Journal of Eating Disorders*, *22*, 285–290.

Harvey, A.G. (2002). A cognitive model of insomnia. *Behaviour Research and Therapy*, *40*, 869–893.

Harvey, A.G. (2003). The attempted suppression of presleep cognitive activity in insomnia. *Cognitive Therapy and Research*, *27*, 593–602.

Harvey, A.G. & Bryant, R.A. (1998b). The effect of attempted thought suppression in acute stress disorder. *Behaviour Research and Therapy*, *36*, 583–590.

Harvey, A.G. & Bryant, R.A. (1998a). The role of valence in attempted thought suppression. *Behaviour Research and Therapy, 36*, 757–763.

Harvey, A.G. & McGuire, B.E. (2000). Suppressing and attending to pain-related thoughts in chronic pain patients. *Behaviour Research and Therapy, 38*, 1117–1124.

Harvey, A.G. & Payne, S. (2002). The management of unwanted pre-sleep thoughts in insomnia: Distraction with imagery versus general distraction. *Behaviour Research and Therapy, 40*, 267–277.

Hasher, L. & Zacks, R.T. (1984). Automatic processing of fundamental information: The case of frequency of occurrence. *American Psychologist, 39*, 1372–1388.

Hirschi, T. (2004). Self-control and crime. In R.F. Baumeister & K.D. Vohs (eds.). *Handbook of self-regulation: Research, theory, and applications* (pp. 537–552). New York: The Guilford press.

Hodgson, R.J. & Rachman, S. (1977). Obsessional-compulsive complaints. *Behaviour Research and Therapy, 15*, 389–395.

Höping, W. & De Jong-Meyer, R. (2003). Differentiating unwanted intrusive thoughts from thought suppression: What does the white bear suppression inventory measure? *Personality and Individual Differences, 34*, 1049–1055.

Horowitz, M.J., Wilner, N., & Alvarez, W. (1979). Impact of event scale: A measure of subjective stress. *Psychosomatic Medicine, 41*, 209–218.

Huntjens, R. (2003). *Apparent amnesia: Interidentity memory functioning in dissociative identity disorder*. Academic thesis, Utrecht University.

Jacobs, B.L. (1994). Serotonin, motor activity and depression-related disorders. *American Scientist, 82*, 456–463.

Janeck, A.S. & Calamari, J.E. (1999). Thought suppression in Obsessive-Compulsive Disorder. *Cognitive Therapy and Research, 23*, 497–509.

Jensen, L.H. & Kane, C.F. (1996). Cognitive theory applied to the treatment of delusions of schizophrenia. *Archives of Psychiatric Nursing, 10*, 335–341.

Johnson, H.M. (1994). Processes of successful intentional forgetting. *Psychological Bulletin, 116*, 274–292.

Johnson, M.K., Foley, M.A., Suengas, A.G., & Raye, C.L. (1988). Phenomenal characteristics of memories for perceived and imagined autobiographical events. *Journal of Experimental Psychology: General, 117*, 371–376.

Johnson, D.R., Rosenheck, R., Fontana, A., Lubin, H., Charney, D., & Southwick, S. (1996). Outcome of intensive inpatient treatment of combat-related posttraumatic stress disorder. *American Journal of Psychiatry, 153*, 771–777.

Johnston, L., Bulik, C.M., & Anstiss, V. (1999). Suppressing thoughts about chocolate. *International Journal of Eating Disorders, 26*, 21–27.

Johnston, L., Hudson, S.M., & Ward, T. (1997). The suppression of sexual thoughts by child molesters: A preliminary investigation. *Sexual Abuse: A Journal of Research and Treatment, 9*, 303–319.

Jones, M.K. & Menzies, R.G. (1997). The cognitive mediation of obsessive-compulsive hand-washing. *Behaviour Research and Therapy, 35*, 843–850.

Joseph, R. (1999). The neurology of traumatic "dissociative" amnesia: Commentary and literature review. *Child Abuse & Neglect, 23*, 715–727.

Juni, S. (1982). The composite measure of the defense mechanism inventory. *Journal of Research in Personality, 16*, 193–200.

Kamieniecki, G.W., Wade, T., & Tsourtos, G. (1997). Interpretive bias for benign sensations in panic disorder with agoraphobia. *Journal of Anxiety Disorders, 11*, 141–156.

Karon, B.P. & Widener, A.J. (1997). Repressed memories and World War II: Lest we forget! *Professional Psychology: Research and Practice, 28*, 338–340.

Kassin, S.M. & Neumann, K. (1997). On the power of confession evidence: An experimental test of the fundamental difference hypothesis. *Law and Human Behavior, 21*, 469–484.

Kassin, S.M. & Sukel, H. (1997). Coerced confessions and the jury: An experimental test of the "harmless error" rule. *Law and Human Behavior, 21*, 27–46.

Katz, R.J. (1991). Neurobiology of obsessive compulsive disorder: A serotonergic basis of Freudian repression. *Neuroscience & Biobehavioral Reviews, 15*, 375–381.

Kelly, A.E. & Kahn, J.H. (1994). Effects of suppression of personal intrusive thoughts. *Journal of Personality and Social Psychology, 66*, 998–1006.

Kessler, R.C., McGonagle, K.A., Zhao, S., Nelson, C.B., Hughes, M., Eshleman, S., Wittchen, H., & Kendler, K.S. (1994). Lifetime and 12-month prevalence of DSM-III-R psychiatric disorders in the United States. *Archives of General Psychiatry, 51*, 8–19.

Khanna, S., Rajendra, P.N., & Channabasavanna, S.M. (1998). Life events and onset of obsessive compulsive disorder. *The international Journal of Social Psychiatry, 34*, 305–309.

Kihlstrom, J.F. (2002). No need for repression. *Trends in Cognitive Sciences, 6*, 502.

Kihlstrom, J.F., Glisky, M.L., & Angiulo, M.J. (1994). Dissociative tendencies and dissociative disorders. *Journal of Abnormal Psychology, 103*, 117–124.

Kindt, M. & Van den Hout, M. (2003). Dissociation and memory fragmentation: Experimental effects on meta-memory but not on actual memory performance. *Behaviour Research and Therapy, 41*, 167–178.

Kohlenberg, R.J. (1973). Behaviorist approach to multiple personality: A case study. *Behavior Therapy, 4*, 137–140.

Koster, E.H.W., Rassin, E., Crombez, G., & Näring, G.W.B. (2003). The paradoxical effects of suppressing anxious thoughts during imminent threat. *Behaviour Research and Therapy, 41*, 1113–1120.

Kulik, C.T., Perry, E.L., & Bourhis, A.C. (2000). Ironic evaluation processes: Effects of thought suppression on evaluations of older job applicants. *Journal of Organizational Behavior, 21*, 689–711.

Ladouceur, R., Rhéaume, J., Freeston, M.H., Aublet, F., Jean, K., Lachance, S., Langlois, F., & De Pokomandy-Morin, K. (1995). Experimental manipulations of responsibility: An analogue test for models of obsessive-compulsive disorder. *Behaviour Research and Therapy, 33*, 937–946.

Ladouceur, R., Talbot, F., & Dugas, M.J. (1997). Behavioral expressions of intolerance of uncertainty in worry. *Behavior Modification, 21*, 355–271.

Lane, J.D. & Wegner, D.M. (1995). The cognitive consequences of secrecy. *Journal of Personality and Social Psychology, 69*, 237–253.

Lavy, E.H. & Van den Hout, M. (1990). Thought suppression induces intrusions. *Behavioural Psychotherapy, 18*, 251–258.

Lee, H.J. & Kwon, S.M. (2003). Two different types of obsession: autogenous obsessions and reactive obsessions. *Behaviour Research and Therapy, 41*, 11–29.

Liberman, N. & Förster, J. (2000). Expression after suppression: A motivational explanation of postsuppressional rebound. *Journal of Personality and Social Psychology, 79*, 190–203.

Lilienfeld, S.O. & Lynn, S.J. (2003). Dissociative identity disorder: Multiple personalities, multiple controversies. In S.O. Lilienfeld, S.J. Lynn, & J.M. Lohr (eds.). *Science and pseudoscience in clinical psychology* (pp. 109–142). London: The Guilford press.

Lilienfeld, S.O., Lynn, S.J., Kirsch, I., Chaves, J.F., Sarbin, T.R., Ganaway, G.K., & Powell, R.A. (1999). Dissociative identity disorder and the sociocognitive model: Recalling the lessons of the past. *Psychological Bulletin, 125*, 507–523.

Lipinski, J.F. & Pope, H.G. (1994). Do "flashbacks" represent obsessional imagery? *Comprehensive Psychiatry, 35*, 245–247.

Littrell, J. (1998). Is the reexperience of painful emotion therapeutic? *Clinical Psychology Review*, *18*, 71–102.

Loftus, E.F. (1993). The reality of repressed memories. *American Psychologist*, *48*, 518–537.

Loftus, E.F., Joslyn, S., & Polage, D. (1998). Repression: A mistaken impression. *Development and Psychopathology*, *10*, 781–792.

Lohr, J.M., Hooke, W., Gist, R., & Tolin, D.F. (2003). Novel and controversial treatments for trauma-related stress disorders. In S.O. Lilienfeld, S.J. Lynn, & J.M. Lohr (eds.). *Science and pseudoscience in clinical psychology* (pp. 243–272). London: The Guilford press.

Lopatka, C. & Rachman, S. (1995). Perceived responsibility and compulsive checking: An experimental analysis. *Behaviour Research and Therapy*, *33*, 673–684.

Lynn, S.J. & Rhue, J.W. (1988). Fantasy proneness: Hypnosis, developmental antecedents, and psychopathology. *American Psychologist*, *43*, 35–44.

Lyubomirsky S., Caldwell, N.D., & Nolen-Hoeksema, S. (1998). Effects of ruminative and distracting responses to depressed mood on retrieval of autobiographical memories. *Journal of Personality and Social Psychology*, *75*, 166–177.

MacDonald, P.A., Antony, M.M., Macleod, C.M., & Richter, M.A. (1997). Memory and confidence in memory judgments among individuals with obsessive compulsive disorder and non-clinical controls. *Behaviour Research and Therapy*, *35*, 497–505.

Macrae, C.N., Bodenhausen, G.V., & Milne, A.B. (1998). Saying no to unwanted thoughts: Self-focus and the regulation of mental life. *Journal of Personality and Social Psychology*, *74*, 578–589.

Macrae, C.N., Bodenhausen, G.V., Milne, A.B., & Jetten, J. (1994). Out of mind but back in sight: Stereotypes on the rebound. *Journal of Personality and Social Psychology*, *67*, 808–817.

Malik, R., Apel, S., Nelham, C., Rutkowski, C., & Ladd, H. (1997). Failure to uncover the effects of unconscious symbiotic fantasies on heart rate and fine motor performance. *Perceptual and Motor Skills*, *85*, 1231–1241.

Masson, J.M. (1985). *The assault on truth: Freud's suppression of the seduction theory*. New York: Penguin books.

Mathews, A. & Milroy, R. (1994). Effects of priming and suppression of worry. *Behaviour Research and Therapy*, *32*, 843–850.

Mayer, B. & Merckelbach, H. (1999). Unconscious processes, subliminal stimulation, and anxiety. *Clinical Psychology Review*, *19*, 571–590.

McKay, D. & Greisberg, S. (2002). Specificity of measures of thought control. *Journal of Psychology*, *136*, 149–160.

McLaren, S. & Crowe, S.F. (2003). The contribution of perceived control of stressful life events and thought suppression to the symptoms of obsessive-compulsive disorder in both non-clinical and clinical samples. *Journal of Anxiety Disorders*, *17*, 389–403.

McNally, R.J. (2001). On the status of cognitive appraisal models of anxiety disorder. *Behaviour Research and Therapy*, *39*, 513–521.

McNally, R.J. & Kohlbeck, P.A. (1993). Reality monitoring in obsessive-compulsive disorder. *Behaviour Research and Therapy*, *31*, 249–253.

Menzies, R.G., Harris, L.M., Cumming, S.R., & Einstein, D.A. (2000). The relationship between inflated personal responsibility and exaggerated danger expectancies in obsessive-compulsive concerns. *Behaviour Research and Therapy*, *38*, 1029–1037.

Merckelbach, H., Devilly, G.J., & Rassin, E. (2002). Alters in dissociative identity disorder: Metaphors or genuine entities? *Clinical Psychology Review*, *22*, 481–497.

Merckelbach, H., Horselenberg, R., & Muris, P. (2001). The creative experiences questionnaire (CEQ): A brief self-report measure of fantasy proneness. *Personality and Individual Differences*, *31*, 987–995.

Merckelbach, H., Horselenberg, R., & Schmidt, H. (2002). Modeling the connection between self-reported trauma and dissociation in a student sample. *Personality and Individual Differences, 32,* 695–705.

Merckelbach, H. & Muris, P. (2001). The causal link between self-reported trauma and dissociation: A critical review. *Behaviour Research and Therapy, 39,* 245–254.

Merckelbach, H., Muris, P., Van den Hout, M., & De Jong, P. (1991). Rebound effects of thought suppression: Instruction dependent? *Behavioural Psychotherapy, 19,* 225–238.

Merckelbach, H., Muris, P., Wessel, I., & Van Koppen, P.J. (1998). The Gudjonsson Suggestibility Scale (GSS). Further data on its reliability, validity, and metacognition correlates. *Social Behavior and Personality, 26,* 203–210.

Meyer, T.J., Miller,M.L., Metzger,R.L., & Borkovec, T.D. (1990). Development and validation of the Penn State Worry Questionnaire. *Behaviour Research and Therapy, 28,* 487–495.

Miller, S.M. (1992). Monitoring and blunting in the face of threat: Implications for adaptation and health. In L. Montada, S.H. Filipp, & M.J. Lerner (eds.) *Life crises and experiences of loss in adulthood* (pp. 255–273). Englewood Cliffs: Erlbaum.

Mineka, S. & Sutton, S.K. (1992). Cognitive biases and the emotional disorders. *Psychological Science, 3,* 65–69.

Monteith, M.J., Sherman, J.W., & Devine, P.G. (1998). Suppression as a stereotype control strategy. *Personality and Social Psychology Review, 2,* 63–82.

Morrison, A.P. (1998). A cognitive analysis of auditory hallucinations: Are voices to schizophrenia what bodily sensations are to panic? *Behavioural and Cognitive Psychotherapy, 26,* 289–302.

Morrison, A.P. & Baker, C.A. (2000). Intrusive thoughts and auditory hallucinations: A comparative study of intrusions in psychosis. *Behaviour Research and Therapy, 38,* 1097–1106.

Muraven, M., Collins, R.L., & Nienhaus, K. (2002). Self-control and alcohol restraint: An initial application of the self-control strength model. *Psychology of Addictive Behaviors, 16,* 113–120.

Muraven, M., Tice, D.M., & Baumeister, R.F. (1998). Self-control as limited resource: Regulatory depletion patterns. *Journal of Personality and Social Psychology, 74,* 774–789.

Muris, P., De Jongh, A., Merckelbach, H., Postema, S., & Vet, M. (1998). Thought suppression in phobic and non-phobic dental patients. *Anxiety, Stress, and Coping, 11,* 275–287.

Muris, P. & Merckelbach, H. (1994). Defense style, trait anxiety, worry, and bodily symptoms. *Personality and Individual Differences, 16,* 349–351.

Muris, P., Merckelbach, H., & Clavan, M. (1997). Abnormal and normal compulsions. *Behaviour Research and Therapy, 35,* 249–252.

Muris, P., Merckelbach, H., & Horselenberg, R. (1996). Individual differences in thought suppression. The white bear suppression inventory: Factor structure, reliability, validity and correlates. *Behaviour Research and Therapy, 34,* 501–513.

Muris, P. Merckelbach, H., Horselenberg, R., Sijsenaar, M., & Leeuw, I. (1997). Thought suppression in spider phobia. *Behaviour Research and Therapy, 35,* 769–774.

Muris, P., Merckelbach, H., Van den Hout, M., & De Jong, P. (1992). Suppression of emotional and neutral material. *Behaviour Research and Therapy, 30,* 639–642.

Myers, L.B. (1998). Repressive coping, trait anxiety and reported avoidance of negative thoughts. *Personality and Individual Differences, 24,* 299–303.

Myers, L.B., Brewin, C.R., & Power, M.J. (1998). Repressive coping and the directed forgetting of emotional material. *Journal of Abnormal Psychology, 107,* 141–148.

Myers, L.B., Vetere, A., & Derakshan, N. (2004). Are suppression and repressive coping related? *Personality and Individual Differences, 36,* 1009–1013.

Nagtegaal, M.H. & Rassin, E. (2004). The usefulness of the thought suppression paradigm in explaining impulsivity and aggression. *Personality and Individual Differences, 37,* 1233–1244.

Nelson-Gray, R.O., Herbert, D.L., Herbert, J.D., Farmer, R., Badawi, I., & Lin, K.N. (1990). The accuracy of frequency estimation as compared with actual counting in behavioural assessment. *Behavioral Assessment, 12*, 157–178.

Nestadt, G., Samuels, J.F., Romanoski, A.J., Folstein, M.F., & McHugh, P.R. (1994). Obsessions and compulsions in the community. *Acta Psychiatrica Scandinavica, 89*, 219–224.

Newman, L.S., Duff, K.J., & Baumeister, R.F. (1997). A new look at defensive projection: Thought suppression, accessibility, and biased person perception. *Journal of Personality and Social Psychology, 72*, 980–1001.

Newman, L.S. & Hedberg, D.A. (1999). Repressive coping and the inaccessibility of negative autobiographical memories: Converging evidence. *Personality and Individual Differences, 27*, 45–53.

Newth, S. & Rachman, S. (2001). The concealment of obsessions. *Behaviour Research and Therapy, 39*, 457–464.

Nolen-Hoeksema, S. (2001). *Abnormal psychology*. Boston: McGraw-Hill.

Palfai, T.P., Monti, P.M., Colby, S.M., & Rohsenow, D.J. (1997). Effects of suppressing the urge to drink on the accessibility of alcohol outcome expectancies. *Behaviour Research and Therapy, 35*, 59–65.

Peasley-Miklus, C. & Vrana, S.R. (2000). Effect of worrisome and relaxing thinking on fearful emotional processing. *Behaviour Research and Therapy, 38*, 129–144.

Pennebaker, J.W. (1993). Putting stress into words: Health, linguistic and therapeutic implications. *Behaviour Research and Therapy, 31*, 539–548.

Petrie, K.J., Booth, R.J., & Pennebaker, J.W. (1998). The immunological effects of thought suppression. *Journal of Personality and Social Psychology, 75*, 1264–1272.

Pitman, R.K. (1993). Posttraumatic obsessive-compulsive disorder: A case study. *Comprehensive Psychiatry, 34*, 102–107.

Plutchik, R. (1989). Measuring emotions and their derivates. In R. Plutchik & H. Kellerman (eds.). *The measurement of emotions* (pp. 1–35). New York: Academic Press.

Polivy, J. & Herman, C.P. (1985). Dieting and binging: A causal analysis. *American Psychologist, 40*, 193–201.

Pope, H.G., Hudson, J.I., Bodkin, J.A., Oliva, P. (1998). Questionable validity of 'dissociative amnesia' in trauma victims: Evidence from prospective studies. *British Journal of Psychiatry, 172*, 210–215.

Popper, K.R. (1968). *The logic of scientific discovery*. London: Hutchinson.

Purdon, C.L. (1998). *The role of thought suppression and meta-cognitive beliefs in the persistence of obsession-like intrusive thoughts*. Academic thesis, University of New Brunswick.

Purdon, C. (1999). Thought suppression and psychopathology. *Behaviour Research and Therapy, 37*, 1029–1054.

Purdon, C. (2004). Empirical investigations of thought suppression in OCD. *Journal of Behavior Therapy and Experimental Psychiatry, 35*, 121–136.

Purdon, C. & Clark, D.A. (2000). White bears and other elusive intrusions: Assessing the relevance of thought suppression for obsessional phenomena. *Behavior Modification, 24*, 425–453.

Purdon, C. & Clark, D.A. (2001). Suppression of obsession-like thoughts in nonclinical individuals: Impact on thought frequency, appraisal and mood state. *Behaviour Research and Therapy, 39*, 1163–1181.

Purdon, C., Rowa, K., & Antony, M.M. (2005). Thought suppression and its effects on thought frequency, appraisal and mood state in individuals with obsessive-compulsive disorder. *Behaviour Research and Therapy, 43*, 93–108.

Rachman, S. (1993). Obsessions, responsibility and guilt. *Behaviour Research and Therapy, 31*, 149–154.

Rachman, S. (1997). A cognitive theory of obsessions. *Behaviour Research and Therapy*, *35*, 793–802.

Rachman, S. (1998). A cognitive theory of obsessions: Elaborations. *Behaviour Research and Therapy*, *36*, 385–401.

Rachman, S. & De Silva, P. (1978). Abnormal and normal obsessions. *Behaviour Research and Therapy*, *16*, 233–248.

Rachman, S. & Shafran, R. (1999). Cognitive distortions: Thought-action fusion. *Clinical Psychology and Psychotherapy*, *6*, 80–85.

Rachman, S., Shafran, R., Mitchell, D., Trant, J., & Teachman, B. (1996). How to remain neutral: An experimental analysis of neutralization. *Behaviour Research and Therapy*, *34*, 889–898.

Rachman, S., Thordarson, D.S., Shafran, R., & Woody, S.R. (1995). Perceived responsibility: Structure and significance. *Behaviour Research and Therapy*, *33*, 779–784.

Radomsky, A.S., De Silva, P. Todd, G., Treasure, J., & Murphy, T. (2002). Thought-shape fusion in anorexia nervosa: An experimental investigation. *Behaviour Research and Therapy*, *40*, 1169 1177.

Radomsky, A.S. & Rachman, S. (1999). Memory bias in obsessive-compulsive disorder (OCD). *Behaviour Research and Therapy*, *37*, 605–618.

Rasmussen, S.A. & Tsuang, M.T. (1986). Clinical characteristics and family history in DSM-III obsessive-compulsive disorder. *American Journal of Psychiatry*, *143*, 317–322.

Rassin, E. (2000). *Limitations of the thought suppression paradigm as a model of obsessive intrusions and memory loss.* Academic thesis, Maastricht University.

Rassin, E. (2001a). The contribution of thought-action fusion and thought suppression in the development of obsession-like intrusions in normal participants. *Behaviour Research and Therapy*, *39*, 1023–1032.

Rassin, E. (2001b). Thought suppression, memory, and interrogative suggestibility. *Psychology, Crime & Law*, *7*, 45–55.

Rassin, E. (2003). The white bear suppression inventory (WBSI) focuses on failing suppression attempts. *European Journal of Personality*, *17*, 285–298.

Rassin, E. (2004). *Snatching thoughts: The validity of self-reported thought frequency in thought suppression experiments.* Unpublished manuscript.

Rassin, E. & Diepstraten, P. (2003). How to suppress obsessive thoughts. *Behaviour Research and Therapy*, 41, 97–103.

Rassin, E., Diepstraten, P., Merckelbach, H., & Muris, P. (2001). Thought-action fusion and thought suppression in obsessive-compulsive disorder. *Behaviour Research and Therapy*, *39*, 757–764.

Rassin, E. & Koster, E. (2003). The correlation between thought-action fusion and religiosity in a normal sample. *Behaviour Research and Therapy*, *41*, 361–368.

Rassin, E., Merckelbach, H., & Muris, P. (1997). Effects of thought suppression on episodic memory. *Behaviour Research and Therapy*, *35*, 1035–1038.

Rassin, E., Merckelbach, H., Muris, P., & Schmidt, H. (2001). The thought-action fusion scale: Further evidence for its reliability and validity. *Behaviour Research and Therapy*, *39*, 537–544.

Rassin, E., Merckelbach, H., Muris, P., & Spaan, V. (1999). Thought-action fusion as a causal factor in the development of intrusions. *Behaviour Research and Therapy*, *37*, 231–237.

Rassin, E., Merckelbach, H., & Spaan, V. (2001). When dreams become a royal road to confusion: Realistic dreams, dissociation, and fantasy proneness. *Journal of Nervous and Mental Disease*, *189*, 478–481.

Rassin, E., Muris, P., Jong, J., & De Bruin, G. (2005). Summoning white bears or letting them free: The influence of the content of control instructions on target thought frequency. *Journal of Psychopathology and Behavioral Assessment, 27*, 253–258.

Rassin, E., Van Brakel, A., & Diederen, E. (2003). Suppressing unwanted memories: Where there is will, there is a way? *Behaviour Research and Therapy, 41*, 727–736.

Rassin, E. & Van der Heiden, S. (2004). *Swearing voices: A laboratory investigation of the suppression of hostile hallucinations.* Unpublished manuscript.

Rassin, E. & Van Rootselaar, A.F. (in press). From dissociation to trauma? Individual differences in dissociation as predictor of 'trauma' perception. *Journal of Behavior Therapy and Experimental Psychiatry.*

Reinders, A.A.T.S., Nijenhuis, E.R.S., Paans, A.M.J., Korf, J., Willemsen, A.T.M., & den Boer, J.A. (2003). One brain, two selves. *Neuroimage, 20*, 2119–2125.

Reynolds, M. & Tarrier, N. (1996). Monitoring of intrusions in post-traumatic stress disorder: A report of single case studies. *British Journal of Medical Psychology, 69*, 371–379.

Richards, J.M. & Gross, J.J. (2000). Emotion regulation and memory: The cognitive costs of keeping one's cool. *Journal of Personality and Social Psychology, 79*, 410–424.

Ritchie, G. (2000). *Snatch: Stealin' stones and breakin' bones.* United Kingdom: Columbia Pictures.

Roemer, E. & Borkovec, T.D. (1994). Effects of suppressing thoughts about emotional material. *Journal of Abnormal Psychology, 103*, 467–474.

Ross, C.A. (1997). *Dissociative identity disorder: Diagnosis, clinical features, and treatment of multiple personality.* New York: Wiley.

Ross, C. & Currie, S.J.R. (1991). Dissociative experiences in the general population: A factor analysis. *Hospital and Community Psychiatry, 42*, 297–301.

Rutledge, P.C. (1998). Obsessionality and the attempted suppression of unpleasant personal intrusive thoughts. *Behaviour Research and Therapy, 36*, 403–416.

Rutledge, P.C., Hancock, R.A., & Rutledge, J.H. (1996). Predictors of thought rebound. *Behaviour Research and Therapy, 34*, 555–562.

Rutledge, P.C., Hollenberg, D., & Hancock, R.A. (1993). Individual differences in the Wegner rebound effect: Evidence for a moderator variable in thought rebound following thought suppression. *Psychological Reports, 72*, 867–880.

Salkovskis, P.M. (1985). Obsessional-compulsive problems: A cognitive-behavioural analysis. *Behaviour Research and Therapy, 23*, 571–583.

Salkovskis, P.M. (1999). Understanding and treating obsessive-compulsive disorder. *Behaviour Research and Therapy, 37*, S29–S52.

Salkovskis, P.M. & Campbell, P. (1994). Thought suppression induces intrusion in naturally occurring negative intrusive thoughts. *Behaviour Research and Therapy, 32*, 1–8.

Salkovskis, P.M., Forrester, E., & Richards, C. (1998). Cognitive-behavioural approach to understanding obsessional thinking. *British Journal of Psychiatry, 173*, 53–63.

Salkovskis, P.M. & Harrison, J. (1984). Abnormal and normal obsessions: A replication. *Behaviour Research and Therapy, 22*, 549–552.

Salkovskis, P.M. & Reynolds, M. (1994). Thought suppression and smoking cessation. *Behaviour Research and Therapy, 32*, 193–201.

Salkovskis, P., Shafran, R., Rachman, S., & Freeston, M.H. (1999). Multiple pathways to inflated responsibility beliefs in obsessional problems: Possible origins and implications for therapy and research. *Behaviour Research and Therapy, 37*, 1055–1072.

Salkovskis, P.M., Thorpe, S.J., Wahle, K., Wroe, A.L., & Forrester, E. (2003). Neutralizing increases discomfort associated with obsessional thoughts: An experimental study with obsessional patients. *Journal of Abnormal Psychology, 112*, 709–715.

Salkovskis, P.M. & Westbrook, D. (1989). Behaviour therapy and obsessional ruminations: Can failure be turned into success? *Behaviour Research and Therapy, 27*, 149–160.

Salkovskis, P.M., Wroe, A.L., Gledhill, A., Morrison, N., Forrester, E., Richards, C., Reynolds, M., & Thorpe, S. (2000). Responsibility attitudes and interpretations are characteristic of obsessive compulsive disorder. *Behaviour Research and Therapy, 38*, 347–372.

Sanavio, E. (1988). Obsessions and compulsions: The Padua inventory. *Behaviour Research and Therapy, 26*, 169–177.

Sarafino, E.P. (1998). *Health psychololy: Biopsychosocial interactions*. New York: John Wiley & sons.

Schacter, D.L. (1999). The seven sins of memory: Insights from psychology and cognitive neuroscience. *American Psychologist, 54*, 182–203.

Schwarz, N. (1999). Self-reports: How the questions shape the answers. *American Psychologist, 54*, 93–105.

Schwarz, N., Knäuper, B., Hippler, H.J., Noelle-Neuman, E., & Clark, F. (1991). Rating scales: Numeric values may change the meaning of scale labels. *Public Opinion Quaterly, 55*, 570–582.

Schwarz, N., Strack, F., & Mai, H.P. (1991). Assimilation and contrast effects in part-whole question sequences: A conversational logic analysis. *Public Opinion Quaterly, 55*, 3–23.

Scott, M.J. & Stradling, S.G. (1994). Post-traumatic stress disorder without the trauma. *British Journal of Clinical Psychology, 33*, 71–74.

Seligman, M.E.P., Walker, E.F., & Rosenhan, D.L. (2001). *Abnormal psychology*. London: WW Norton & Company.

Shafran, R. & Mansell, W. (2001). Perfectionism and psychopathology: A review of research and treatment. *Clinical Psychology Review, 21*, 879–906.

Shafran, R., Teachman, B.A., Kerry, S., & Rachman, S. (1999). A cognitive distortion associated with eating disorders: Thought-shape fusion. *British Journal of Clinical Psychology, 38*, 167–179.

Shafran, R., Thordarson, D.S., & Rachman, S. (1996). Thought-action fusion in Obsessive Compulsive Disorder. *Journal of Anxiety Disorders, 10*, 379–391.

Shipherd, J.C. & Beck, J.G. (1999). The effects of suppressing trauma-related thoughts on women with rape-related posttraumatic stress disorder. *Behaviour Research and Therapy, 37*, 99–112.

Silverman, L.H., Ross, D.L., Adler, J.M., & Lustig, D.A. (1978). Simple research paradigm for demonstrating subliminal psychodynamic activation: Effects of oedipal stimuli on dart-throwing accuracy in college males. *Journal of Abnormal Psychology, 87*, 341–357.

Singer, J.L. (1990). *Repression and dissociation*. Chicago: University of Chicago Press.

Smári, J., Birgisdóttir, A.B., & Brynjólfsdóttir, B. (1995). Obsessive-compulsive symptoms and suppression of personally relevant unwanted thoughts. *Personality and Individual Differences, 18*, 621–625.

Smári, J., Sigurjónsdóttir, H., & Saemundsdóttir, I. (1994). Thought suppression and obsession-compulsion. *Psychological Reports, 75*, 227–235.

Spielberger, C.D. (1983). *State-Trait Anxiety Inventory*. Palo Alto, California: Consulting Psychologists Press.

Spinhoven, P. & Van der Does, A.J.W. (1999). Thought suppression, dissociation, and psychopathology. *Personality and Individual Differences, 27*, 877–886.

Stöber, J. (1998). Worry, problem elaboration and suppression of imagery: The role of concreteness. *Behaviour Research and Therapy, 36*, 751–756.

Strack, F., Schwarz, N., & Gschneidinger, E. (1985). Happiness and reminiscing: The role of time perspective, mood, and mode of thinking. *Journal of Personality and Social Psychology, 49*, 1460–1469.

Stroop, J.R. (1935). Studies of interference in serial verbal reactions. *Journal of Experimental Psychology, 18,* 643–662.

Summerfeldt, L.J., Richter, M.A., Antony, M.M., & Swinson, R.P. (1999). Symptom structure in obsessive-compulsive disorder: A confirmatory factor-analytic study. *Behaviour Research and Therapy, 37,* 297–311.

Tallis, F. (1997). The neuropsychology of obsessive-compulsive disorder: A review and consideration of clinical implications. *British Journal of Clinical Psychology, 36,* 3–20.

Tallis, F., Pratt, P., & Jamani, N. (1999). Obsessive compulsive disorder, checking, and nonverbal memory: A neuropsychological investigation. *Behaviour Research and Therapy, 37,* 161–166.

Thelen, M.H., Farmer, J., Wonderlich, S., & Smith, M. (1991). A revision of the bulimia test: The BULIT-R. *Psychological Assessment: A Journal of Consulting and Clinical Psychology, 3,* 119–124.

Tolin, D.F., Abramowitz, J.S., Hamlin, C., Foa, E.B., & Synodi, D.S. (2002). Attributions for thought suppression failure in obsessive-compulsive disorder. *Cognitive Therapy and Research, 26,* 505–517.

Tolin, D.F., Abramowitz, J.S., Przeworski, A., & Foa, E.B. (2002). Thought suppression in obsessive-compulsive disorder. *Behaviour Research and Therapy, 40,* 1255–1274.

Tolin, D.F., Hamlin, C., & Foa, E.B. (2002). Directed forgetting in obsessive-compulsive disorder: Replication and extension. *Behaviour Research and Therapy, 40,* 793–803.

Trinder, H. & Salkovskis, P.M. (1994). Personally relevant intrusions outside the laboratory: Long-term suppression increases intrusion. *Behaviour Research and Therapy, 32,* 833–842.

Tryon, G.S. (1979). A review and critique of thought stopping research. *Journal of Behavior Therapy and Experimental Psychiatry, 10,* 189–192.

Tsai, G.E., Condie, D., Wu, M.T., & Cheng, I. (1999). Functional magnetic resonance imaging of personality switches in a woman with dissociative disorders. *Havard Review of Psychiatry, 7,* 119–122.

Tversky, A. & Kahneman, D. (1973). Availability: A heuristic for judging frequency and probability. *Cognitive Science, 5,* 207–232.

Van Balkom, A.J.L.M. & Van Dyck, R. (1998). Combination treatments for obsessive-compulsive disorder. In R.P. Swinson, M.M. Martin, S. Rachman, & M.A. Richter (eds.). *Obsessive-compulsive disorder: Theory, research, and treatment* (pp. 349–367). New York: The Guilford press.

Van den Hout, M. & Kindt, M. (2003b). Phenomenological validity of an OCD-memory model and the remember/know distinction. *Behaviour Research and Therapy, 41,* 369–378.

Van den Hout, M. & Kindt, M. (2003a). Repeated checking causes memory distrust. *Behaviour Research and Therapy, 41,* 301–316.

Van den Hout, M., Merckelbach, H., & Pool, K. (1996). Dissociation, reality monitoring, trauma, and thought suppression. *Behavioural and Cognitive Psychotherapy, 24,* 97–108.

Van den Hout, M., Van Pol, M., & Peters, M. (2001). On becoming neutral: Effects of experimental neutralizing reconsidered. *Behaviour Research and Therapy, 39,* 1439–1448.

Van Koppen, P.J. & Merckelbach, H. (1999). Characteristics of recovered memories: A Dutch replication of Gudjonsson's (1997) British survey. *Applied Cognitive Psychology, 13,* 485–489.

Van Niekerk, J.K., Möller, A.T., & Nortje, C. (1999). Self-schemas in social phobia and panic disorder. *Psychological Reports, 84,* 843–854.

Vaughan, K. & Tarrier, N. (1992). The use of image habituation training with post-traumatic stress disorder. *British Journal of Psychiatry, 161,* 658–664.

Vrij, A. (2000). *Detecting lies and deceit: The psychology of lying and implications for professional practice*. Chichester: John Wiley & Sons.

Wagenaar, W.A. & Groeneweg, J. (1990). The memory of concentration camp survivors. *Applied Cognitive Psychology, 4*, 77–87.

Waldinger, M.D. & Van Strien J.W. (1995). Repression and cerebral laterality: A study of selective hemispheric activations. *Neuropsychiatry, Neuropsychology, and Behavioral Neurology, 1*, 1–5.

Walker, W.R., Vogl, R.J., Thompson, C.P. (1997). Autobiographical memory: Unpleasantness fades faster than pleasantness over time. *Applied Cognitive Psychology, 11*, 399–413.

Warren, R., Zgourides, G., & Jones, A. (1989). Cognitive bias and irrational belief as predictors of avoidance. *Behaviour Research and Therapy, 27*, 181–188.

Watson, M. & Greer, S. (1983). Development of a questionnaire of emotional control. *Journal of Psychosomatic Research, 27*, 299–305.

Wegner, D.M. (1989). *White bears and other unwanted thoughts: Suppression, obsession, and the psychology of mental control*. London: The Guilford press.

Wegner, D.M. (1994). Ironic processes of mental control. *Psychological Review, 101*, 34–52.

Wegner, D.M., Ansfield, M., & Pilloff, D. (1998). The putt and the pendulum: Ironic effects of the mental control of action. *Psychological Science, 9*, 196–199.

Wegner, D.M., Broome, A., & Blumberg, S.J. (1997). Ironic effects of trying to relax under stress. *Behaviour Research and Therapy, 35*, 11–21.

Wegner, D.M. & Erber, R. (1992). The hyperaccessibility of suppressed thoughts. *Journal of Personality and Social Psychology, 63*, 903–912.

Wegner, D.M. & Gold, D.B. (1995). Fanning old flames: Emotional and cognitive effects of suppressing thoughts of a past relationship. *Journal of Personality and Social Psychology, 68*, 782–792.

Wegner, D.M., Quillian, F., & Houston, C. (1996). Memories out of order: Thought suppression and the disassembly of remembered experience. *Journal of Personality and Social Psychology, 71*, 680–691.

Wegner, D.M. & Schneider, D.J. (2003). The white bear story. *Psychological Inquiry, 14*, 326–329.

Wegner, D.M., Schneider, D.J., Carter, S.R., & White, T.L. (1987). Paradoxical effects of thought suppression. *Journal of Personality and Social Psychology, 53*, 5–13.

Wegner, D.M., Schneider, D.J., Knutson, B., & McMahon, S.R. (1991). Polluting the stream of consciousness: The effect of thought suppression on the mind's environment. *Cognitive Therapy and Research, 15*, 141–152.

Wegner, D.M., Shortt, J.W., Blake, A.W., & Page, M.S. (1990). The suppression of exciting thoughts. *Journal of Personality and Social Psychology, 58*, 409–418.

Wegner, D.M. & Wheatley, T. (1999). Apparent mental causation: Sources of the experience of will. *American Psychologist, 54*, 480–492.

Wegner, D.M. & Zanakos, S. (1994). Chronic thought suppression. *Journal of Personality, 62*, 615–640.

Weinberger, D.A. (1990). The construct validity of the repressive coping style. In J.L Springer (ed). *Repression and dissociation: Implications for personality, psychopathology and health* (pp. 337–386). Chicago: University of Chicago Press.

Weinberger, J. & Hardaway, R. (1990). Separating science from myth in subliminal psychodynamic activation. *Clinical psychology Review, 10*, 727–756.

Weinberger, D.A., Schwartz, G.E., & Davidson, R.J. (1979). Low-anxious, high anxious and repressive coping styles: Psychometric patterns and behavioural responses to stress. *Journal of Abnormal Psychology, 88*, 369–380.

Wells, A. & Davies, M.I. (1994). The thought control questionnaire: A measure of individual differences in the control of unwanted thoughts. *Behaviour Research and Therapy, 32*, 871–878.

Wells, A. & Morrison, A.P. (1994). Qualitative dimensions of normal worry and normal obsessions: A comparative study. *Behaviour Research and Therapy, 32*, 867–870.

Wells, A. & Papageorgiou, C. (1995). Worry and the incubation of intrusive images following stress. *Behaviour Research and Therapy, 33*, 579–583.

Wells, A. & Papageorgiou, C. (1998). Relationships between worry, obsessive-compulsive symptoms and meta-cognitive beliefs. *Behaviour Research and Therapy, 36*, 899–913.

Wenzlaff, R.M. & Bates, D.E. (1998). Unmasking a cognitive vulnerability to depression: How lapses in mental control reveal depressive thinking. *Journal of Personality and Social Psychology, 75*, 1559–1571.

Wenzlaff, R.M. & Wegner, D.M. (2000). Thought suppression. *Annual Review of Psychology, 51*, 59–91.

Wenzlaff, R.M., Wegner, D.M., & Roper, D. (1988). Depression and mental control: The resurgence of unwanted negative thoughts. *Journal of Personality and Social Psychology, 55*, 882–892.

Whetstone, T. & Cross, M.D. (1998). Control of conscious content in directed forgetting and thought suppression. *http://psyche.cs.monash.edu.au/v4/psyche-4-16-whetstone.html.*

Wiederman, M. (2004). Self-control and sexual behavior. In R.F. Baumeister & K.D. Vohs (eds.). *Handbook of self-regulation: Research, theory, and applications* (pp. 525–536). New York: The Guilford press.

Wilhelm, S., McNally, R.J., Baer, L., & Florin, I. (1996). Directed forgetting in obsessive-compulsive disorder. *Behaviour Research and Therapy, 34*, 633–641.

Wilhelm, S., McNally, R.J., Baer, L., & Florin, I. (1997). Autobiographical memory in obsessive-compulsive disorder. *British Journal of Clinical Psychology, 36*, 21–31.

Winkielman, P., Schwarz, N., & Belli, R.F. (1998). The role of ease of retrieval and attribution in memory judgments: Judging your memory as worse despite recalling more events. *Psychological Science, 9*, 124–126.

Wright, D.B., Gaskell, G.D., & O'Muircheartaigh, C.A. (1997). The reliability of the subjective reports of memories. *European Journal of Cognitive Psychology, 9*, 313–323.

Wyer, N.A., Sherman, J.W., & Stroessner, S.J. (2000). The role of motivation and ability in controlling the consequences of stereotype suppression. *Personality and Social Psychology Bulletin, 26*, 13–25.

Wyland, C.L., Kelly, W.M., Macrae, C.N., Gordon, H.L., & Heatherton, T.F. (2003). Neural correlates of thought suppression. *Neuropsychologia, 41*, 1863–1867.

Author Index

Subject Index